Regulating Sexuality

Regulating Sexuality: Legal consciousness in lesbian and gay lives explores the impact that recent seismic shifts in the legal landscape have had for lesbians and gay men. The last decade has been a time of extensive change in the legal regulation of lesbian and gay lives in Britain, Canada and the US. Almost every area where the law impacts on sexuality has been reformed or modified. These legal developments combine to create a new, uncharted terrain for lesbians and gay men. And, through an analysis of their attitudes, views and experiences, this book explores the effects of these developments. Drawing on, and developing, the concept of 'legal consciousness', *Regulating Sexuality* focuses on four different 'texts': qualitative responses to a large-scale online survey of lesbians' and gay men's views about the legal recognition of same-sex relationships; published auto/biographical narratives about being and becoming a lesbian or gay parent; semi-structured, in-depth, interviews with lesbians and gay men about relationship recognition, parenting, discrimination and equality; and fictional utopian texts. In this study of the interaction between law and society in social justice movements, Rosie Harding interweaves insights from the new legal pluralism with legal consciousness studies to present a rich and nuanced exploration of the contemporary regulation of sexuality.

Dr Rosie Harding is a lecturer in law at Keele University.

Social Justice

Series editors: Davina Cooper and Kate Bedford
University of Kent at Canterbury, UK

Social Justice is a new, theoretically engaged, interdisciplinary series exploring the changing values, politics and institutional forms through which claims for equality, democracy and liberation are expressed, manifested and fought over in the contemporary world. The series addresses a range of contexts from transnational political fora, to nation-state and regional controversies, to small-scale social experiments. At its heart is a concern, and interdisciplinary engagement with, the present and future politics of power, as constituted through territory, gender, sexuality, ethnicity, economics, ecology and culture. Foregoing struggle, imagined alternatives and the embedding of new norms, *Social Justice* critically explores how change is wrought through law, governance and institutionalism, everyday social and bodily practices, dissident knowledges, and movements for citizenship, belonging, and reinvented community.

Other titles in this series:

Intersectionality and Beyond
Law, power and the politics of location
Emily Grabham, Davina Cooper, Jane Krishnadas and Didi Herman (eds), 2009

Forthcoming:

Rights of Passage
Sidewalks and the regulation of public flow
Nicholas Blomley, 2010

Power, Politics and the Emotions
Impossible governance?
Shona Hunter, 2011

Anarchism and Sexuality
Ethics, relationships and power
Jamie Heckert and Richard Cleminson (eds), 2011

Regulating Sexuality

Legal consciousness in lesbian and gay lives

Rosie Harding

Routledge
Taylor & Francis Group

a GlassHouse book

First published 2011
by Routledge
4 Park Square, Milton Park, Abingdon, Oxon OX14 4RN
605 Third Avenue, New York, NY 10017

A GlassHouse book

Routledge is an imprint of the Taylor & Francis Group, an informa business

First issued in paperback 2011

Typeset in Sabon by Taylor & Francis Books

British Library Cataloguing in Publication Data
A catalogue record for this book is available from the British Library

Library of Congress Cataloguing in Publication Data
Harding, Rosie.
Regulating sexuality : legal consciousness in lesbian and gay lives / Rosie Harding.
p. cm.
Includes bibliographical references.
1. Gays–Legal status, laws, etc.–Great Britain. I. Title.
KD4097.H37 2011
346.4101′3–dc22
2010023486

ISBN: 978-0-415-57438-9 (hbk)
ISBN: 978-0-415-52114-7 (pbk)

For my mother, Joyce Walker Harding (1950–88)

Contents

Acknowledgements

This book has had a rather long and protracted hatching period, and has had the benefit of input from many supportive colleagues at Keele University, the University of Kent and members of and visitors to the Centre for Law, Gender and Sexuality. I want to thank Rosemary Auchmuty, Nicola Barker, Susan Boyd, Dave Cowan, Anisa de Jong, Tony Dugdale, Mary Ewert, Ruth Fletcher, Marie Fox, Emily Grabham, Kathleen Hull, Suhraiya Jivraj, Toni Johnson, Jane Krishnadas, Sarah Lamble, Ambreena Manji, Julie McCandless, Laura-Beth Nielsen, Olga Palevich, Zoe Pearson, Elizabeth Peel, Nicky Priaulx, Sally Sheldon, Miriam Smith, Antu Sorainen, Michael Thomson, Matthew Weait and Claire Young. Many of the chapters have been presented at conferences, workshops and seminars and have benefited greatly from the constructive critical feedback received there. I also want to thank the Social Justice series editors, Kate Bedford and Davina Cooper, for their thoughtful and challenging feedback on drafts. I am also indebted to Holly Davis and Colin Perrin at Routledge, for their interest and assistance. Special thanks must also go to Didi Herman, for her constructive criticism, supportive encouragement and for being a wonderful academic mentor.

My sincere thanks go to all of the participants in both the survey and the interview studies. Their perspectives have made this book possible.

My heartfelt thanks also go to all my friends and family – there's no space to thank you all individually, but I hope you know your support is very much appreciated! Special thanks to Liz for her unswerving support and encouragement and Bramble for making sure I always went out for some fresh air and exercise.

Earlier versions of some of the arguments presented in this book have appeared in the following published form: ' "Dogs are "Registered", People Shouldn't Be": Legal Consciousness and Lesbian and Gay Rights' *Social & Legal Studies* (2006); 'Recognising (and Resisting) Regulation: Attitudes to the Introduction of Civil Partnership' *Sexualities* (2008).

Chapter 1

Introduction

Law, sexuality and everyday life

The last decade has borne witness to an unprecedented level of change in the legal regulation of lesbian and gay lives across the Western world. In the UK in 1999, the age of consent for sex between men was 18; Section 28 of the Local Government Act 1988 prevented local authorities from 'promoting homosexuality'; lesbians and gay men were banned from serving in the military, and were routinely discharged from the armed forces if their sexual orientation was discovered. Alongside these legal restrictions, there was a distinct lack of legal *recognition* of lesbians and gay men and, in particular, of the everyday familial relationships between same-sex couples and their children. In 2010, lesbians and gay men in the UK are no longer subjected to many of these legal detriments. Anti-gay laws have been repealed, and replaced with legal protections from discrimination on the basis of sexual orientation, and legal recognition for lesbian and gay families. The Civil Partnership Act 2004 created a system of recognition for same-sex relationships that is almost identical to marriage, recent reforms to adoption law now allow same-sex couples to adopt children together, and the same-sex partner of a woman who gives birth can now be named on any resulting child's birth certificate and can have the legal status of 'parent'. Yet it would be wrong to surmise that these legislative changes necessarily remove any discrimination from the everyday lives of lesbians and gay men. Elsewhere in the world, some of the gains for lesbians and gay men have been mirrored by increased backlash against same-sex relationships and families. For example, while some US states have granted same-sex couples access to marriage, many more have legislated to remove the possibility of legal recognition for lesbian and gay relationships.

These legal developments combine to create a new, uncharted terrain for lesbians and gay men. This book seeks to explore the effects of this recent seismic shift in the legal landscape for lesbians and gay men and examines the consequences of such dramatic legal change on the everyday lives of lesbians and gay men. The primary focus of this book is to explore lesbians' and gay men's experiences of, attitudes to and views about the interlinked reforms to the legal context of lesbian and gay familial lives. The different approaches to the recognition and regulation of lesbian and gay families in the UK,

Canada and the US provide fertile ground for exploring and understanding how different legal and social contexts impact on the ways lesbians and gay men approach, understand and consider the place of law in their everyday lives. I have three main reasons for foregrounding familial lives in this book: first, lesbian and gay relationship recognition and parenting rights are, to greater or lesser extents, the current focus of lesbian and gay activism within the UK (and in a number of other countries worldwide). Second, parenting and relationships seem more relevant to the everyday lives of lesbians and gay men in the early twenty-first century West than, for example, sexual offences legislation. A third reason for my focus on familial relationships is that it is not necessary to construct lesbians and gay men as 'victims', as may be necessary with an exploration of, for example, discrimination or hate crimes.

This book is concerned, predominantly, with the legal situation of lesbians and gay men. While it has become common to include bisexual and trans people within academic commentary relating to sexual minority rights, I have chosen not to do so in this book for two key reasons. First, the empirical foci of my study (relationship recognition and parenting) give rise to different issues for bisexual people (see e.g. Aviram, 2008; Klesse, 2006) and for transsexual and transgender individuals (see e.g. Coombs, 2001; Whittle, 2002) than they do for lesbians and gay men. While it would have been interesting to be able to compare these perspectives within this research, it is beyond the scope of this book to do justice to the different perspectives that bisexuality and trans issues bring to these areas. Second, as well as being concerned with sexuality, throughout this book I examine places where there are (and are not) gendered differences in attitudes to and perceptions of law and legal process. As such, a focus on the similarities and differences between lesbians' and gay men's views allows these gendered differences to come to the fore.

Regulating lesbian and gay families

The prominence of relationship recognition and same-sex marriage in lesbian and gay struggles for legal equality has led to a wealth of academic commentary and debate, and the place, utility and aims of same-sex marriage remain hotly contested. The details of this debate have been laid out many times, from several different perspectives (see e.g. Cooper, 2004; Goldberg-Hiller, 2002; Peel & Harding, 2004; Sullivan, 1997; Wardle et al., 2003). It has been claimed that same-sex marriage is the ultimate equal rights goal of many lesbians and gay men (Eskridge, 2002), and that it is essential to place same-sex marriage at the heart of lesbian and gay politics because the heterosexism of the 'traditional' family serves to displace lesbians and gay men from both the public and private spheres (Calhoun, 2000). Other commentators argue that same-sex marriage is a 'human right' and therefore should be recognised as such in law (Kitzinger & Wilkinson, 2004a); that same-sex marriage will help to reduce gay male promiscuity and integrate gays into society

(Rauch, 2004; Sullivan, 1996); that civil partnership (or other forms of relationship recognition short of marriage) are simply stepping stones in the direction of same-sex marriage (Eskridge, 2002; Waaldijk, 2001); and that same-sex marriage marks the transition for lesbians and gay men from outsiders to full citizens (Josephson, 2005).[1]

On the other 'side' of the debate, commentators argue against the privileging of marriage in lesbian and gay struggles because, for example: marriage is a site of the continued oppression of women (Jeffreys, 2004); the introduction of same-sex marriage may reduce the possibilities for wider reaching reform of marriage and increase the possibilities of assimilation of same-sex relationships into the heterosexual norm (Auchmuty, 2004); that same-sex marriage (and the legal recognition of same-sex relationships more generally) brings with it increased regulation of and reductions in the welfare and social security benefits of lesbians and gay men in the lowest income brackets (Young & Boyd, 2006); that same-sex marriage continues the privileging of conjugal relationships over other forms of relationship (Barker, 2006; Polikoff, 2003); and that the inclusion of same-sex couples in the institution of marriage serves to strengthen the power of that institution, further marginalising those on the outside (Butler, 2002). This debate is ongoing,[2] even as the legal backdrop to the question of whether the legal recognition of same-sex relationships is an inherently good or bad thing has changed considerably in recent years, as more and more jurisdictions either open up civil marriage to same-sex couples or create other forms of opt-in relationship recognition.

A third dimension to the burgeoning same-sex marriage literature is a growing number of studies exploring the attitudes and experiences of lesbians and gay men to the introduction of legally recognised same-sex relationships. Prior to the widespread availability of forms of legal recognition, studies of lesbian and gay relationships tended to focus on the social meanings of (non-legal) same-sex relationships and commitment ceremonies (e.g. Hull, 2003, 2006; Lewin, 1999; Liddle & Liddle, 2004; Shipman & Smart, 2007; Weeks et al., 2001). More recent studies have, however, begun to focus on the attitudes of lesbians and gay men to legal recognition (e.g. Clarke et al., 2006, 2007; Harding & Peel, 2006; Lannutti, 2005).

Full, legal same-sex marriage is currently available in just a handful of jurisdictions around the world: Belgium (2003), Canada (2005),[3] the Netherlands (2001), Norway (2009), South Africa (2006), Spain (2005), Sweden (2009) and the US states of Connecticut (2008), Iowa (2009)[4] and Massachusetts (2004). Several other jurisdictions are also in the process of introducing same-sex marriage legislation or considering doing so.[5] A large (and exponentially increasing) number of other jurisdictions have introduced some sort of opt-in framework for the legal recognition of same-sex relationships – variously called registered partnership, domestic partnership, civil union or civil partnership (among others).[6] In a minority of jurisdictions, these legal frameworks are open to different-sex as well as same-sex couples (e.g. France, the Netherlands, New Zealand). One of the most interesting aspects to the creation of these 'new' forms of relationship recognition for same-sex couples, aside from myriad names given to them, is the differences between the rights and responsibilities included within them. Whereas some (such as the UK civil partnership provisions) closely mirror marriage law, others are radically different. An example of a very distinct legal framework for recognising same-sex relationships is that available in Tasmania, which also allows for the recognition of other, non-conjugal, caring and dependent relationships (Wong, 2004). A third form of legal recognition of same-sex relationships comes through *de facto* status or cohabitation rules.

In many jurisdictions, including the UK, while there are often very few legal differences there are some important points of contrast between civil partnership and civil marriage. In the UK, the differences between civil marriage and civil partnership were consistently played down by the Government during the passage of the Civil Partnership Act 2004 (CPA). Instead of noting that there are differences between the two, the Government repeatedly claimed that civil partnership was an 'equality' measure, seeking to ensure that same-sex couples entering into a civil partnership were treated in the same way as different-sex couples entering into a civil marriage:

> It is the Government's intention that those people who enter into a civil partnership will receive the same rights and take on the same responsibilities as those that we expect of those who enter into civil marriage.
>
> (Jacqui Smith MP, House of Commons *Hansard*, 12 October 2004: Col. 177)

There are, however, a small number of substantive legal differences between civil partnership and civil marriage, and it is important to be aware of these. First, there are a number of technical differences in the way a civil partnership is constituted from the way that a marriage is formed. Perhaps the most important of these technical differences is that a civil partnership cannot be created in religious premises[7] neither can any religious service be used while the registrar is officiating at a civil partnership.[8] While these provisions were designed (in part) to circumvent claims that the CPA was creating same-sex marriage, they were objected to by the Lord Bishop of Oxford during the course of the CPA through the House of Lords for both infringing the freedom of religious authorities to control the use of their premises and for denying same-sex couples who see civil partnership as a commitment with a religious dimension the opportunity to have a blessing at the same time (or near to) their civil partnership registration.[9]

Second, there is no sex in the CPA. There is no requirement for consummation of the civil partnership and there is no equivalent to adultery as a ground of dissolution. This difference between marriage and civil partnership can be read as both a retrenchment of the 'continuing centrality of penetrative intercourse in the way in which the law *constitutes* heterosexual relationships' (Stychin, 2006: 83) and as a 'negative gap in the CPA, a place where lesbian and gay sexuality is left unspoken' (Barker, 2006: 251). Contrariwise, the absence of a legal requirement for consummation and the absence of 'adultery' as a ground for dissolution could be read as an exercise in creating a legal framework more suited to the realities of same-sex relationships, giving legal 'support' to the differences between same- and difference-sex relationships and recognising that monogamy can be less salient in same-sex relationships.

Finally, when initially introduced, there were a number of important differences in the ways that the parent/child relationship was treated in civil partnership as opposed to marriage. In essence, parenting was all but left out of the civil partnership legislation. The CPA placed civil partners in an analogous position to step-parents in heterosexual marriage, providing that children of civil partners would be considered 'a child of the family', and allowing civil partners access to Parental Responsibility Agreements and the step-parent adoption process. More recently, the Human Fertilisation and Embryology Act 2008 (HFEA 2008) amended the situation so that the civil partner of a woman who conceives through donor insemination (anywhere in the world) will automatically be considered that child's other legal parent. Accessing legal status as a parent is also now possible for same-sex couples not in a civil partnership, provided that the chid was conceived through treatment at a licensed clinic, and the relevant consents have been given.[10] In terms of the legal recognition of lesbian and gay families, these reforms can be thought of as providing the final piece in the puzzle of legal recognition of lesbian and gay families. But in certain respects, lesbian and gay parenting remains on the periphery of legal protections for lesbians and gay men, and understandings of the realities of family life for lesbian and gay parents are much less entrenched than considerations of same-sex relationships. While this may be the case, it is important to note that lesbian and gay parenting is very much a reality in the UK, in spite of the seeming unintelligibility of lesbian and gay parenting to the courts.[11] There are, of course, many lesbian and gay parents in the UK, although (as with all statistics relating to lesbians and gay men) it is nearly impossible to say how many, as these data do not exist in any reliable form.[12]

The regulation of lesbian and gay parenting is, in many ways, more complex than the regulation of same-sex relationships. In contrast to the wealth of academic commentary and debate that exists on same-sex marriage, the position of lesbian and gay parents is one which seems to have been relatively neglected by law, gender and sexuality scholarship in the UK. Nancy Polikoff (2000a) argued that lesbian and gay family law has developed in two separate ways on either side of the Atlantic: in the US, lesbian and gay parents have been legally recognised to the detriment of recognition of same-sex partnerships, and in Europe, same-sex relationships have been granted legal recognition while lesbian and gay parents have been denied such recognition. This binary approach to lesbian and gay family law may account for the relative dearth of UK legal scholarship focusing on the regulation of lesbian and gay families. This is not to say, of course, that there is a dearth of scholarship on lesbian and gay parenting, rather that much of the academic literature on lesbian and gay families hails from outside law, from the social sciences, particularly psychology and sociology.

In psychological literature concerning lesbian and gay parenting, much research into lesbian mothers[13] has cohered around two specific areas. First, whether lesbians who choose to become mothers are as happy and well adjusted as heterosexual mothers, whether non-biological lesbian mothers are more or less active in childcare than heterosexual fathers and whether childcare was shared equally between the parents (e.g. Chan et al., 1998; Flaks et al., 1995; Patterson, 1995). Second, researchers have been concerned with the social and psychological development of children from lesbian (and gay) families (e.g. Patterson, 1992, 1994; Tasker & Golombok, 1997). In the UK, Susan Golombok and Fiona Tasker's research on the development of children of lesbian mothers has perhaps been the most influential (Golombok & Tasker, 1994; Tasker & Golombok, 1991, 1997, 1998). Their research findings suggest that growing up in a lesbian family does not have any major impact on the psycho-social development of children, and that children of lesbian families grow up to be just as well adjusted as children from heterosexual families (Tasker & Golombok, 1997).

The general consensus within lesbian and gay psychological research into the effects on children of being raised in a lesbian family is that 'there is no empirical support for the proposition that the children of lesbian and gay parents are different from other children' (Flaks et al., 1995: 106) and therefore that lesbian and gay families and parents are much the same as heterosexual families (Allen & Burrell, 1996). This type of psychological research evidence has certainly been influential in family law cases regarding custody and residence for children with lesbian mothers (Clarke, 2005), but the aims of this type of 'sameness' research in lesbian and gay parenting have also been subject to critique on the grounds that this research is structured on the basis of (hetero)normative assumptions about the nature of 'the family' (Clarke, 2002; Riggs, 2004).

A second theme within academic literature around lesbian and gay families is a focus on the radical potential of lesbian and gay families to challenge existing gender orders, through a celebration of the differences inherent in lesbian and gay families. A minority of this literature is academic research, predominantly social scientific (e.g. Dunne, 2000; Sullivan, 2004; Weeks et al., 2001; Weston, 1991). This type of (sociological or anthropological) research seeks to show that lesbian (and gay) families 'provide a model of intimate connection that rigorously opposes the violence that is done both within and in the name of the patriarchal family' (Sullivan, 2004: 230). A larger proportion of the literature in this area is, however, drawn from experiential and personal narratives from lesbian and gay parents themselves (e.g. Abbot &

Farmer, 1995; Hicks & McDermott, 1999; Pollack & Vaughn, 1987; Strah & Margolis, 2003). A function of these personal and experiential accounts has been to highlight the invisibility of lesbian and gay parenting within wider struggles for lesbian and gay legal equality (Clarke, 2005).

Legal and socio-legal scholarship on lesbian and gay parenting has taken a slightly different approach to these issues than the social science research outlined above. Much of the literature on lesbian (and gay) parenting in law, gender and sexuality scholarship has cohered around two issues: custody battles (e.g. Arnup & Boyd, 1995; Kelly, 2004; Reece, 1996) and access to assisted conception services (e.g. Douglas, 1993; Jackson, 2002; Langdridge & Blyth, 2001; Millns, 2002; Murphy, 2001; Robinson, 1997). It is probable that legal and socio-legal literature has focused on these two areas because they have, historically, marked the extent of regulation of lesbian and gay parenting. Academic analysis of custody battles has been important because, for many years, a mother's lesbianism would be a reason for denying her custody of her children on the breakdown of a heterosexual marriage. Equally, access to assisted conception services has historically been one of the main methods of restricting lesbians and gay men from creating their families of choice, through donor insemination, IVF or surrogacy.

Key themes and arguments

Regulating sexuality

The key themes and arguments in this book cohere around questions of the work that law does in the everyday lives of lesbians and gay men, understandings of law and legal process and the possibilities and limitations of 'equality' in lesbian and gay struggles. My focus on 'the work that law does' in the lives of lesbians and gay men has two components: first, I am interested in the impacts and effects of new legal developments on the everyday lives of lesbians and gay men; second, the ways in which lesbians and gay men respond to these effects. The impact and effects of law and legal regulation are an essential part of (critical) socio-legal research. Rather than taking the content of law or measuring the 'effectiveness' of law through 'objective' analysis of how people use law (e.g. Genn, 1999), my concern is with the specificities of individual lesbians and gay men's experiences of law. In particular, I am interested in how lesbians and gay men describe their perspectives on recent tectonic shifts in the legal regulation of sexuality from criminalisation, persecution and legal discrimination to the legal protection of lesbian and gay relationships, families and working and social lives.

Where I focus on lesbians and gay men's understandings of law and legal process, I explore how these understandings can be explained. My aim is not to isolate sexuality from the other aspects of people's self-identity, but rather to examine where and how sexuality intersects with other aspects of lesbian and gay lives and identities to impact on the ways that people experience, understand and contextualise the place of law in their everyday lives. My primary focus in this regard is the place of gender in lesbians' and gay men's accounts of law. I focus on gender for two key reasons: first, because political activism and legal reform in relation to sexuality often seem to assume that the issues facing lesbians are the same as the issues facing gay men; and second, that it is often assumed that sexuality and gender are divisible facets of identity. In previous research, I found that, in contrast to some lesbian feminist assumptions that it was only gay men who wanted to get married (e.g. Auchmuty, 2004), there were few differences between lesbians and gay men's views about the legal recognition of same-sex relationships (Harding & Peel, 2006). Taking gender as a primary problematic in this book allows a more detailed analysis of the way(s) that lesbians and gay men's views differ in relation to the place of law in same-sex relationships and lesbian and gay parenting.

A final key problematic in this book is an exploration of how individual lesbians and gay men's everyday experiences can throw light on the ways power and resistance work in everyday life, and on the possibilities and limitations of 'equality' in lesbian and gay struggles. I examine the ways that lesbians and gay men draw on the concept of 'equality' in arguing for legal protection, and the strategies that are deployed to argue for legal equality in lesbian and gay struggles. Another facet of this is the ways in which discrimination and inequality impact on the lives of lesbians and gay men. In considering this, I highlight the ways that lesbians and gay men respond to and deal with encountering discrimination and inequality in their everyday lives, and their reasons for responding in the ways that they do.

Everyday life, legal consciousness and resistance

Charting the presence of 'law in everyday life' has been a part of the (North American) law and society movement for the last two decades (Macaulay, 1987; Sarat & Kearns, 1993a). Broadly speaking, law and society research that examines the place of law in everyday life can be divided into two 'camps': instrumental perspectives and constitutive perspectives (Sarat & Kearns, 1993b). Instrumental perspectives on the place of law in everyday life are predominantly concerned with law as a tool for sustaining or changing aspects of social life, and take the 'effectiveness' of law as the primary subject of inquiry. Instrumentalist accounts of the effect of law in society are perhaps most notable for the conception that law is somehow separate from and distinct from 'society' and that it is possible to measure the impact that law has on society.

Constitutive perspectives, by way of contrast, envisage law as a part of society, such that society (and that part of society which is known as everyday life) creates effects on law as much as law creates effects on society.

A constitutive approach to the study of law in society focuses more on the wider (not necessarily legal) effects and impacts of law and legal change. At the same time, it attempts to map the impact of the ways that individuals approach, use and think about law in their everyday lives on law and legality (Ewick & Silbey, 1998). A major branch of this 'constitutive' approach to law and society research has been the development of the field of 'legal consciousness studies'. 'Legal consciousness' has been examined in socio-legal scholarship since the 1970s, but whereas earlier legal consciousness studies focused on people's awareness of and experience of using law, courts and alternative dispute resolution processes (e.g. Bumiller, 1988; Engel, 1984; Merry, 1990; Sarat 1977), gradually the focus of legal consciousness studies shifted to an expressly constitutive approach to socio-legal scholarship through de-centring law (Ewick & Silbey, 1998; Nielsen, 2004). These more recent legal consciousness studies take 'ordinary' people's accounts of their everyday experiences as the starting point for thinking about law in everyday life, and the way that law works in society. One of the main foundations for these constitutive studies of law and everyday life is that 'everyday life constitutes law and is constituted by it' (Engel, 1993: 126) – a statement that highlights the ways in which 'law' and 'everyday life' are not separate spheres that act independently, rather they are interlinked in such a way so as to suggest that to understand one it is necessary to also examine and understand the other.

As well as using and applying this framework of 'legal consciousness studies', my aim is to develop and extend the theoretical and methodological reach of legal consciousness as a way of exploring the place of law in everyday life. In so doing, I demonstrate that the interlinked concepts of power and resistance are crucial to understanding the place of law in the everyday lives of lesbians and gay men. In discourse around rights struggles, the 'power' of the state, sovereign, government or other seemingly 'powerful' institutions or groups are rarely questioned, and the lesbian and gay social movement itself is easily conceptualised as 'resistant'. Throughout this book I seek to expose the contingency and instability of approaching power and resistance in this way, and to show that resistance is complex, varied and worthy of deeper analysis. Through the theoretical approaches to power and resistance that I draw on, I complicate this picture of a powerful/powerless dyadic relationship between 'the state' and 'lesbians and gay men'. To gain a deeper insight into how relations of power and resistance operate in lesbian and gay legal consciousness, I draw on Foucault's (1979, 1980, 1998, 2002) analytics of power as a creative, technical and productive force, and feminist engagements (e.g. Bell, 1993; Cooper, 1995a; Smart, 1989) with this approach to power. In my consideration of power and resistance I also draw on governmentality theory (e.g. Cowan & McDermont, 2006; Dean, 1999; Foucault, 1991a; Rose, 1999) as a way of interrogating the ways that 'micro' experiences of relations of power and resistance in the everyday lives of lesbians and gay men are informed by and inform broader structural forces.

Another literature that I draw on in developing the field of legal consciousness studies as this relates to lesbians and gay men is new legal pluralism. Legal pluralism is a concept which claims that state law is not the only form of law; rather, a variety of different legal or normative systems exist, all of which can be described as law. Originally, legal pluralism developed in the early twentieth-century law and anthropology movement, as a way of describing the situation where more than one legal system coexists in the same social field (Merry, 1988). The concept of legal pluralism has, however, in more recent times expanded to include 'relations between dominant groups and subordinate groups, such as religious, ethnic or cultural minorities, immigrant groups, and unofficial forms of ordering located in social networks or institutions' (Merry, 1988: 872–73). Tamanaha (2000) put forward a 'new' version of legal pluralism, relying on a non-essentialist definition of law: 'law is whatever people identify and treat through their social practices as "law"' (Tamanaha, 2000: 313). Legal pluralism, therefore, according to Tamanaha, can include any relationship between people that is thought of by them as legal. Martha-Marie Kleinhans and Roderick Macdonald (1997) also offer a more intriguing definition of legal pluralism, one which they describe as 'a *critical* legal pluralism'. Kleinhans and Macdonald's version of legal pluralism seeks to turn analyses of law and society inside out: 'rather than beginning with the premise that society and subjects are real entities that law can treat, it investigates how narrating subjects treat law' (Kleinhans & Macdonald, 1997: 46). These two conceptions of legal pluralism combine to create a form of legal analysis which identifies much more than 'official' law as 'law'. I return to a detailed exposition of how I use the concept of legal pluralism with legal consciousness studies in Chapter 2.

Theory and method

This book is theoretically driven and empirically grounded. All too often in social science and legal research, artificial divides are erected between the 'theoretical' and the 'empirical', humanities and social sciences, texts and data. In this exploration of legal consciousness in lesbian and gay lives, I seek to place both of these research elements on an equal plane. I use four different 'texts' to examine lesbian and gay legal consciousness. I also attempt to move legal consciousness studies away from being a purely descriptive form of law and society research to a more involved theoretical and methodological approach through my analysis of the texts. The texts I utilise are: 1) qualitative responses to a large-scale online survey of lesbians' and gay men's views about the legal recognition of same-sex relationships (Chapter 4); 2) published personal narratives about being and becoming a lesbian or gay parent (Chapter 5); 3) semi-structured, in-depth interviews with lesbians and gay men about relationship recognition, parenting, discrimination and equality (Chapter 6); and 4) fictional utopian texts (Chapter 7).

My use of these different types of text brings a novel approach to the study of legal consciousness. Although one of the texts I draw on – transcripts of in-depth interviews – is the normative approach to legal consciousness studies, the other three present legal consciousness studies with new methods of accessing discourse about the place of law in everyday life. One of the most interesting facets of using a number of texts to examine the key themes outlined above is uncovering the ways that ideas are expressed either in similar or different ways within the texts themselves. In some respects this multi-method approach could be described as a form of triangulation; using different methods to access similar questions. All of the methodological approaches I use are 'qualitative' – thus my focus is on the ways in which people account for their attitudes to and perspectives of law, rather than what they think about specific laws, or how much they 'know' about the legal regulation of sexuality.

I also use a number of different approaches to analysing these texts. Broadly speaking, I take a discursive approach to all the texts, and I am interested in how language and narrative not only reflect the social world, but also the ways in which what people say or write are, in part, constitutive of or embedded in the fabric of the social world. I take, therefore, an applied theoretical approach to empirical socio-legal studies. I explore people's narratives, their stories of how law exists in their everyday lives, because stories 'do not float around abstractly but are grounded in historically evolving communities of memory, structured through age, class, race, gender and sexual preference' (Plummer, 1995). In the course of this book I draw on approaches to the analysis of texts from both social science and humanities research. I utilise variations of thematic analysis (Braun & Clarke, 2006) and Foucauldian discourse analysis (e.g. Rose, 1999) in Chapters 4 and 6, narrative analysis (e.g. Plummer, 1995; Roof, 1996) in Chapter 5, and utopia as method (Levitas, 1990) in Chapter 7.

A key problematic in (empirical) sexualities research has long been the difficulty of accessing research participants, and the associated problems of representativeness and generalisability in research findings. In social science research generally, and in legal consciousness studies in particular, great pains are often taken to obtain a 'representative' sample of participants in the research project, so that the research findings can be generalised to entire populations. By populations, I do not necessarily mean the entire population of a state or jurisdiction, but examples include: the residents of a particular geographical area (Ewick & Silbey, 1998); 'working class Americans' (Merry, 1990); or people who have experienced discrimination (Bumiller, 1988). As this study is concerned with lesbians and gay men, a conventional social-scientific approach would be to identify the entire population of lesbians and gay men, then select at random participants to be contacted to participate in survey research and in-depth interviews.

It is, however, generally recognised in sexualities research that attempting to obtain a representative sample is a near-impossibility, because non-heterosexual people make up an undefined and difficult to represent population

(Fish, 1999; Herek & Berrill, 1992). As it is impossible to manufacture a 'representative' sample of lesbians and gay men, the findings from the portions of this book which rely on empirical data I have collected cannot be 'generalized' to the entire population. This is not, however, as intractable a problem as may initially be thought. My aim in this study is to examine the effect of sexuality on legal consciousness, and the experience of the place of law in the everyday lives of lesbians and gay men, not to come up with grand theories about how people experience law, or how 'law' is experienced by 'society' (see Ewick & Silbey, 1998). As I will demonstrate in later chapters, the 'lack' of generalisability of my 'findings' is less problematic than it may first seem, as the discourse around same-sex relationship recognition and lesbian and gay parenting accessed through different texts is relatively similar, and broad themes around how lesbians and gay men experience and talk about ideas such as regulation, power and resistance infuse different texts in similar ways.

Overview of the book

Chapter 2 explores the related theoretical fields of legal consciousness studies and new legal pluralism. I argue that legal consciousness is a useful framework for studying the place of law in everyday life, but the model of legal consciousness studies that has been developed in previous legal consciousness research requires expansion both theoretically and methodologically. In relation to the theoretical limitations of previous legal consciousness research, I argue that many legal consciousness studies have been overly descriptive and have focused on the views and/or attitudes of 'ordinary' people about law as the end point of the research project. I contend that legal consciousness studies needs to expand theoretically to take people's views of the place of law in everyday life as a starting point to examine the utility of legal systems. I argue that one way of developing legal consciousness studies is to draw it together with the insights that new legal pluralism can provide in considering everyday ideas about what constitutes law.

In Chapter 3, I expand on my development of the theoretical basis of legal consciousness studies through an exploration of the interlinked concepts of power and resistance. I argue that whereas 'power' has been well theorised, resistance is a much less well developed concept in academic scholarship. I also suggest that Foucauldian approaches to power and resistance are useful in understanding the place of law in everyday life, as this approach allows for an awareness of the micro-scale relations of power and resistance that characterise the everyday. In considering the relative under-theorisation of resistance, I propose a tripartite understanding of different types of resistance: stabilising resistance, moderating resistance and fracturing resistance. I define 'stabilising resistance' as the constant counterbalance to power relations, resistance that is a necessary part of disciplinary power. I offer 'moderating resistance', as a term to highlight those forms of public protest that actively seek to change the ways in which power is exercised. Fracturing resistance, by way of contrast, I use to describe those resistant acts which cause breaks in the 'flow' of power, or which stop or reverse the flow of power. I argue that while these 'fracturing' or revolutionary forms of resistance are the most commonly thought of in relation to resistance, they are, in fact the least common way of resisting the exercise of power. I contend that this tripartite schema of resistance allows more detailed consideration of everyday forms of resistance in legal consciousness studies.

In Chapter 4, I begin the empirical analysis that forms the backbone of this book. Through analysis of the qualitative comments from a large-scale online survey (n = 1538) of attitudes to the legal recognition of same-sex relationships, I argue that in discourse around the introduction of same-sex marriage and civil partnership, formal equality is prioritised and reified by lesbians and gay men. Further, I contend that lesbians and gay men have complex perspectives on the relationship between law and social change. Finally, I argue that rights discourse and citizenship claims are common in lesbian and gay attitudes to the legal recognition of their relationships. I demonstrate that the 'right to marry' is seen by many as an important indicator of lesbian and gay human rights. I further argue that citizenship claims both facilitate the normalisation and assimilation of lesbians and gay men into heteronormative society and simultaneously draw attention to legalised forms of discrimination. Throughout this analysis, I weave the theoretical approaches outlined in previous chapters into the empirical analysis. I argue that working my three types of resistance (stabilising resistance, moderating resistance and fracturing resistance) into the 'against the law' category helps legal consciousness studies to be sensitive to the issues raised by a specific consideration of sexuality. I demonstrate, through my analysis of the data presented in Chapter 4, that stabilising and moderating forms of resistance are drawn on by lesbians and gay men in their attitudes to, and engagement with, issues around the legal recognition of relationships.

In Chapter 5, I build on the analysis in Chapter 4 by approaching the topic of lesbian and gay parenting from the perspective of legal consciousness. In this chapter, I explore published personal narratives from lesbian and gay parents. I argue that narrative not only produces a window on the experiences of the storyteller, but also reflects and refracts society. I contend that resistance stories transcend the individual experiences of the power of law in the everyday lives of lesbian and gay parents and allow for more sustained forms of resistance to law's power to legitimate lesbian and gay parents. Three themes emerge from lesbian and gay parents' published personal narratives: first, that the complexities of parenting 'outside the law' compound the invisibility of lesbian and gay parents and erase the differences between lesbian/gay and heterosexual families. Second, I argue that there is a divide between 'real' and 'illegitimate' lesbian and gay parents. I demonstrate that the lack of legal recognition for non-biological or non-adoptive parents puts them and their children in a difficult position in their everyday lives: they are quite literally 'up against' the law. Third, I show that, as with discourse on the legal recognition of same-sex relationships, issues relating to citizenship arise for lesbian and gay parents – some parents feel that they are treated as second-class parents to second-class children, especially when they become parents through state-run fostering and adoption systems. Throughout my analysis in Chapter 5, I highlight the ways that legal consciousness, power and resistance operate in lesbian and gay families, and show that, like in the survey data from Chapter 4, examples of both stabilising and moderating forms of resistance are present in these published accounts of being and becoming a parent.

In Chapter 6, I return to social scientific methodology and present my analysis of in-depth 'legal consciousness' interviews with ten lesbians and gay men. Several themes arise in participants' views about both civil partnership and lesbian and gay parenting. Civil partnership is seen by some interview participants as problematic because it goes against entrenched understandings of the meaning of equality – the creation of civil partnership is therefore seen as a discriminatory, rather than equalising, measure. For other participants, however, legal recognition (in whatever form) is seen to be beneficial for lesbians and particularly for gay men. The financial and pragmatic benefits of entering into a civil partnership are described by these participants as an incentive to lesbians and gay men to think about getting 'hitched'. I demonstrate that there are, however, interesting gendered differences in attitudes to civil partnership that infuse these interview accounts more strongly than in other forms of text presented in this book.

As with the experiences of lesbian and gay parents discussed in Chapter 5, for the interviewees whose stories are analysed in Chapter 6, being and becoming a lesbian (or gay) parent is very much typified by experiences of resistance to the power of law. The participants who are parents describe how they feel it is necessary to emphasise the sameness of lesbian and gay families when in contact with governmental actors in order to make lesbian and gay families understandable to the state. The issue of appropriate role models for children is also an interesting point arising from these interviews. These participants felt that whereas male role models are 'policed' by society and regulation surrounding parenthood, the need for appropriate female role models is not seen as important. The parents interviewed for this study also spoke of the practical difficulties associated with being and becoming a parent as a lesbian/gay man, whether through the hurdles presented by licensed clinics, such as counselling, or the intrusive forms of state regulation that are an inevitable part of becoming a parent through adoption or fostering.

In Chapter 7, the last of my empirical chapters, I again examine perceptions of how law should regulate lesbian and gay parents and relationships, but from a somewhat different angle – through 'utopian' fiction. I shift my focus from lesbians' and gay men's attitudes to and experiences of law in everyday life to considering alternative ways of both thinking about equality, and operationalising it in society. I do this by comparing the different versions of equality in two fictional utopian texts: Marge Piercy's (1987) explicitly feminist novel *Woman on the Edge of Time* and Thomas Bezucha's (2000) film, *Big Eden*. I argue that utopia is useful in exploring alternative visions of society because fictional utopia can be read as examples of legal consciousness and that lesbian/gay and feminist utopias are exemplars of resistance to normative visions of society. I suggest that these utopian texts can offer alternatives to current ways of thinking about and organising the regulation of gender and sexuality. I examine the alternatives to contemporary practices of constraining sexuality through the concretisation and crystallisation of sexual identities and how increased legal regulation contributes to containing and limiting the meanings and possibilities of sexuality in society. I argue that looking to utopia allows different, and possibly better, ways of understanding the place of legal regulation in family life to be brought to the fore. I demonstrate that such utopian vision mirrors some of the attitudes to law, power and resistance expressed by lesbians and gay men in Chapters 4, 5 and 6 and that utopia is typified by the absence of legal frameworks regulating the family. I argue that this 'lack of law' in lesbian/gay/feminist utopian fiction highlights a desire for less regulation of the family, in stark contrast to the 'equal rights' calls in lesbian and gay scholarship and activism for *more* regulation of the familial and relational lives of lesbians and gay men.

Notes

1 See Stychin (2001) for a more critical take on this point.

2 The same-sex marriage debate is also historical, and draws on much of the feminist critique of marriage literature (see e.g. Cott, 1977; Fineman, 1995; Okin, 1989; Pateman, 1988; Polikoff, 1993).

3 Same-sex marriage became fully recognised at a federal level across all Canadian provinces in 2005, although same-sex marriage was legal in Ontario and British Columbia from 2003.

4 Same-sex marriage in US states only covers the state-wide legal aspects of marriage; same-sex marriage is not recognised at a federal level in the US, which means that US same-sex marriages are not recognised for the purposes of federal taxes, among other things.

5 These include Argentina, Iceland, Luxembourg, Nepal, Portugal, Slovenia, Uruguay, Venezuela, and the US states of Maine, New Hampshire and Vermont.

6 As 'civil partnership' is the name used in the UK, throughout this book I will refer to these forms of relationship as civil partnership, unless I am referring to the specific legal framework in another jurisdiction.

7 Civil Partnership Act 2004 s. 6(1)(b), 6(2). See Chapter 6 for a more detailed discussion of this issue. This is in direct contrast to marriage, where couples have the choice to have either a religious marriage, with a religious ceremony (in a religious building), or a register office ceremony, officiated at by a registrar (see the Marriage Act 1949 Part II, for regulations relating to Church of England Marriage, Part III for regulations concerning marriage by a registrar and by the customs of other religions).

8 Civil Partnership Act 2004 s. 2(5). This is the same as for civil marriages conducted in a register office (Marriage Act 1949 s. 45); the difference therefore lies in the denial of choice to same-sex couples about whether to have a civil or religious ceremony.
9 House of Lords *Hansard*, 22 April 2004, col. 399–400.
10 Human Fertilisation and Embryology Act 2008, ss 42–47.
11 See, in particular, the majority House of Lord's reasoning in *M v Secretary of State for Work and Pensions* [2006] 2 AC 27 and the decision of Sir Mark Potter in *Wilkinson v Kitzinger* [2006] EWHC (Fam) 2022.
12 Government estimates suggest that around 6% of the UK population are lesbian or gay (around 3.6 million people), and a research project by Beyond Barriers found that 1 in 5 lesbians and gay men in their sample is a parent. If these two figures are combined, this would put an estimated number of lesbian and gay parents in the UK at somewhere in the region of 720,000.
13 There has, historically, been significantly more research into lesbian mothers than into gay fathers, although recently more academic studies of gay fathers are being undertaken (see e.g. Barret & Robinson, 2000; Mallon, 2004).

Chapter 2

Legal consciousness in lesbian and gay lives

Legal consciousness studies have developed since the 1970s as a form of socio-legal scholarship that traces the place of law in everyday life. Studies of legal consciousness have been predominantly US based (Engel, 1984; Ewick & Silbey, 1998; Merry, 1990), although this theoretical framework is becoming increasingly popular in European socio-legal research (Cooper, 1995a; Cowan, 2004; Gies, 2003; Harding, 2006, 2008; Hertogh, 2004, 2009). The history of legal consciousness studies has been presented a number of times (see e.g. Engel, 1998; Sarat & Kearns, 1993a; Silbey, 2005), but it is worth re-telling its story here, as I wish to highlight aspects, limitations and potentials of 'legal consciousness' which have particular salience for lesbians and gay men. In this chapter, I therefore turn to an exploration of 'legal consciousness studies' as they relate to lesbian and gay lives. I begin with a brief sketch of the development of legal consciousness as a theoretical approach and analytic frame for considering the place of law in everyday life. I then provide an overview of the few legal consciousness studies that have hitherto explored lesbian and gay perspectives (Connolly, 2002; Hull, 2006; Nicol & Smith, 2008; Richman, 2006). In the third part of this chapter, I set out some of the more critical viewpoints on legal consciousness, and suggest that combining legal consciousness with a plural understanding of law will provide a more nuanced understanding of the place of law, regulation and resistance in lesbian and gay lives.

Legal consciousness studies: understanding the place of law in everyday life

In very general terms, legal consciousness studies aim to understand the ways that 'ordinary' people[1] approach, use and think about law in everyday life. The beginnings of legal consciousness research can be mapped back to Roscoe Pound's (1910) identification of the 'gap' between 'law in books' and 'law in action', and the attempts by law and society scholars (see further, Sarat, 1985) to understand this 'gap':

> Legal consciousness as a theoretical concept and topic of empirical research developed within law and society in the 1980s and 1990s to

> address issues of legal hegemony, particularly how the law sustains its institutional power despite a persistent gap between the law on the books and the law in action.
>
> (Silbey, 2005: 323)

To characterise all legal consciousness studies as 'gap studies' however belies the vast differences between legal consciousness projects. Different definitions of what, exactly, legal consciousness 'is' have been propounded by different researchers, and the emphasis of legal consciousness studies has changed over time. Early studies in the 1970s focused on levels of public knowledge of, understandings of and opinion(s) about law (Sarat, 1977). These studies used large-scale quantitative survey data to examine levels of awareness about law and compared these to the content of legal provisions (Hertogh, 2004). In effect these early studies of legal consciousness took an 'instrumentalist' perspective to law and society research, conceiving law as an independent, external body, and examined the effects of 'law' on 'society', which was considered another independent phenomenon (Sarat & Kearns, 1993a). These studies have been described as 'knowledge of law' research, as their primary aim was to identify gaps in legal provision and to offer remedies for such gaps through analysis of individuals' knowledge and experience of particular legal provisions (Hertogh, 2004).

Other more recent studies of legal consciousness have moved away from this instrumentalist approach to law and society research towards a constitutive approach to socio-legal studies (Fleurry-Steiner & Nielsen, 2006). The constitutive approach shifts the focus 'from tracking the causal and instrumental relationship between law and society toward tracing the presence of law *in* society' (Ewick & Silbey, 1998: 35, original emphasis). In so doing, the study of legal consciousness has become more concerned with legal culture and the way(s) in which law interacts with everyday life. The development of legal consciousness studies can be broadly traced through the changing definitions of legal consciousness in different studies. Sally Merry (1990), for example, defined legal consciousness as '[t]he ways people understand and use law' (Merry, 1990: 5), and Kristin Bumiller (1988) approached the 'study of legal consciousness ... to explore the influence of ideology on individual consciousness' (Bumiller, 1988: 33). In their highly influential legal consciousness study, however, Patricia Ewick and Susan Silbey (1998) approached legal consciousness as being based in cultural practice, allowing analysis that 'integrates human action and social constraint' (Ewick & Silbey, 1998: 38). By moving away from a focus on the institutional structures of law to an examination of stories or narratives of 'legality', Ewick and Silbey (1998) endeavoured to facilitate understandings of the variations in legal consciousness both within and between individuals. They define 'legality' as 'an emergent structure of social life that manifests itself in diverse places, including but not limited to formal institutional settings' and claim that: 'legality operates ... as both an interpretive framework and a set of resources with which and through which the social world (including that part known as law) is constituted' (Ewick & Silbey, 1998: 23).

It is important to note that these three slightly differing approaches to the study of legal consciousness have much in common: they all look to the ways in which individuals or 'ordinary' people conceptualise and use law within everyday life. The empirical, socio-legal focus of legal consciousness research therefore has meant that the methodological approach of much recent legal consciousness research has been broadly similar. The most common way to conduct research into legal consciousness has been to use in-depth interviews with members of the public about such topics as: their experience of courts and mediation processes (Conley & O'Barr, 1990; Merry, 1990); their reasons for suing (or not) in personal injury cases (Engel, 1984); lesbian and gay men's views about same-sex marriage (Hull, 2003); homeless people's views about housing decisions (Cowan, 2004); the reasons that 'victims' of discrimination give for engaging (or not) in legal disputes (Bumiller, 1988); the regulation of street harassment (Nielsen, 2000; 2004); and community, neighbourhood, work and family issues (Ewick & Silbey, 1998; Merry, 1990). A number of research projects into legal consciousness have also used transcripts of court or mediation sessions as a data source (Conley & O'Barr, 1990; Engel, 1984; Merry, 1990).

Ewick and Silbey's approach to legal consciousness, which has become the dominant framework, examines the ways in which ordinary people's understandings, awareness and conceptions of what constitutes 'law' or 'legality' affect and create 'legality' (see Ewick & Silbey, 1992, 1998; Silbey & Ewick, 2000). In other words, the ways in which legality is socially constructed. They contend that legal consciousness operates to construct and change law gradually over time (Ewick & Silbey, 1998: 44). From their in-depth interview data with US citizens, they describe three types of legal consciousness, which they call 'conformity *before* the law, engagement *with* the law, and resistance *against* the law' (Ewick & Silbey, 1998: 45, original emphasis). They describe these categories as cultural 'schemas', which are:

> Part of a reciprocal process in which the meanings given by individuals to their world become patterned, stabilized and objectified. These meanings, once institutionalized, become part of the material and discursive systems that limit and constrain future meaning making.
>
> (Ewick & Silbey, 1998: 39)

In essence, then, Ewick and Silbey's version of legal consciousness focuses on consciousness as part of the systems of meaning making that undergird the social world.

According to Ewick and Silbey, legal consciousness that falls into the category of 'before the law' depicts law as a separate sphere from society – objective, distinct, formally ordered and rational. People who conceptualise law in this way 'tell the law's own story of its own awesome grandeur', but sometimes 'people express frustration ... about what they perceive as their own powerlessness' (Ewick & Silbey, 1998: 47). In essence, I see this formulation of a 'before the law' legal consciousness as predominantly concerned with understandings of juridical power, where 'power is taken to be a right, which one is able to possess like a commodity' (Foucault, 1980: 88). By conceptualising 'the law' as a unitary body, this juridical power is emphasised in a number of ways. First, if power is a right, then by going to 'law' to seek a solution to a problem, an individual loses control over the outcome of the situation, as they transfer the 'power' to determine the appropriate solution to their problem to 'the law'. Second, as Carol Smart (1989: 4) pointed out, 'usage of the term "law" operates as a claim to power in that it embodies a claim to a superior and unified field of knowledge'. People who hold a 'before the law' legal consciousness accept that it is the legal actors who hold and exercise power when they turn to law to solve their problems. Their perception of powerlessness is therefore compounded by a reification of law's ability to 'know' what the correct solution should be.

'With the law' legal consciousness, by the same token, considers the 'power of law' in a different way. Here, law is described as a game, where 'the pursuit of self-interest is expected and the skilful and resourceful can make strategic gains', rendering law a process that is not entirely distinct from everyday life, but is 'played' on its own terms (Ewick & Silbey, 1998: 48). This conception of law as a terrain of contest is interesting, as it emphasises the potential for power to be used by individuals in order to elaborate their own conception of 'truth'. By conceptualising 'law' as a 'game', a 'with the law' legal consciousness recognises, to some extent, that 'we cannot exercise power except through the production of truth' (Foucault, 1980: 93). Also, in this form of legal consciousness 'law' is understood in a very specific way; law is manifest in the adversarial nature of lawyers, judges, and courtrooms, rather than in terms of 'the state' or as being an instrument for the political regulation of the populous.

The third type of legal consciousness, 'against the law', works in a slightly different way from the first two models. Here, legality is seen as 'something to be avoided' and 'dangerous to invoke' (Ewick & Silbey 1998: 192). Rather than bowing to law's authority or playing law's game, those who conceptualise legality in the 'against the law' category resist the law by 'pilfering, violence or threats of violence, tricks, institutional disruptions, foot dragging, humor, storytelling and gossip' (Ewick & Silbey, 2003: 1336). The centrality of resistance to Ewick and Silbey's 'against the law' schema is noteworthy, and requires closer analysis. 'Against the law' legal consciousness includes numerous methods of resisting legal power: resistance to both law's power and law's terrain, as well as resistance to law's scope. As such, it is clear that 'against the law' legal consciousness also includes resistance to the disciplinary power of law. Here, rather than juridical power being the only conceptualisation of power, the potential for power to be exercised, utilised and subverted by those who would otherwise be 'powerless' is acknowledged. This has echoes of Foucault's 'new' conceptualisation of power: that rather than power being purely negative, it is 'creative and technical ... the mechanisms of power create resistances and local struggles which operate to bring about new forms of knowledge and resistance' (Smart, 1989: 7). 'Against the law' legal consciousness therefore seems to be of primary importance in any consideration of how lesbians and gay men experience, understand and engage with law in everyday life.

It is important to note that while these three schemas are conceptually distinct, Ewick and Silbey are clear that they are not mutually exclusive, and people can conceptualise all three within one story of law or legal processes: 'legal consciousness is neither fixed nor necessarily consistent; rather it is plural and variable across contexts, and it often expresses and contains contradiction' (Ewick & Silbey, 1998: 50). This inherent contradiction in legal consciousness is not framed by Ewick and Silbey as problematic, but rather that because consciousness entails both 'thinking and doing', the complexities and contradictions within legal consciousness are what make 'legality' a type of social practice and therefore a producer of social structures (Ewick & Silbey, 1998: 224–25).

In summary, legal consciousness studies are concerned with understanding how law impacts on the everyday lives of 'ordinary' people. Ewick and Silbey's seminal study highlighted three overarching schemas, which, they argue, can be used to explain the ways in which individuals conceptualise law. It would be erroneous, however, to suggest that there is one particular approach, or a specific aim of studying 'legal consciousness'. Early law and society research in the legal consciousness field was predominantly concerned with levels of awareness and understanding of law. Legal consciousness studies then blossomed into three distinct approaches to legal consciousness: consciousness as attitude (e.g. Merry, 1990); consciousness as ideology (Bumiller, 1988; Sarat, 1990); and consciousness as a producer of 'legality' (Ewick & Silbey, 1998). In certain respects, it is disingenuous to separate legal consciousness studies into these three distinct 'camps', as there are a number of fundamental premises on which each of these approaches are built. First, all these approaches contend that law is an important part of everyday life. Second, all legal consciousness studies attempt (albeit, perhaps, with differing levels of success) to evaluate the place of law in society (or the relationship between law and society) from a 'bottom up', rather than 'top down' perspective. Legal consciousness studies are, therefore, concerned with the place of law in everyday life, rather than the place of everyday lived experience in law. Finally, most (if not all) legal consciousness studies are explorations of experiences of and attitudes to power/domination and resistance in ordinary people's experience of law. I will return to this final point later, as the interaction of power and resistance and legal consciousness is a central theme throughout this book.

Lesbian and gay legal consciousness

Until recently, very little (of the now voluminous) legal consciousness literature had specifically engaged with the legal situation of lesbians and gay men and the struggle for lesbian and gay rights. Four recent studies do, however, explicitly deal with the issues of same-sex relationships (Hull, 2006; Nicol & Smith, 2008) and lesbian and gay parenting (Connolly, 2002; Richman, 2006). This increasing use of legal consciousness approaches to understand lesbian and gay experiences of law and legal change highlights the importance and flexibility of a constitutive approach to explaining the place of law in 'everyday' lesbian and gay lives.

Catherine Connolly (2002) interviewed 20 lesbian and gay parents who successfully petitioned the US courts for second-parent adoption. Connolly argued that:

> The 'legal consciousness' of these petitioners reflected each of the typologies illustrated by Ewick and Silbey (1998). The petitioners understood that the law, and only the law, could give them status (Before the Law); they manipulated the legal process to their benefit (With the Law); and they resisted offensive procedures and people (After [sic] the Law).
>
> (Connolly, 2002: 344)

Kimberly Richman's (2006) study of lesbian, gay, bisexual and transgender (LGBT)[2] parents in the US explores the differences both between LGBT parents' experiences and the heterosexist and sometimes homophobic legal system, and conflicts within LGBT communities. Richman argues for 'nuanced, constitutive analyses of gay family rights, and a return to the feminist jurisprudence concept of the "dilemma of difference"' (Richman, 2006: 78). The data presented from her research are particularly interesting as they highlight the need for an explicit awareness that understandings of 'gay rights' are not homogenous. The legal consciousness approach she uses demonstrates that legal claims that could be thought of as solutions for one 'category' of LGBT parent (e.g. non-biological or non-adoptive *de facto* parents) can be detrimental for other 'categories' (such as biological parents). An example of this is where recognition of *de facto* parents can lead to claims from others from outside their conception of family (such as grandparents) for custody or visitation. Richman's analysis demonstrates that 'perhaps there is no one LGBT legal consciousness in regard to family – [which] is an important caveat in the constitutive study of gay family rights' (Richman, 2006: 96).

Kathleen Hull (2003) used the framework of legal consciousness to argue that lesbian and gay commitment ceremonies are attempts to enact legality in the absence of 'official' law. In her analysis of interview data where same-sex couples talk about their views concerning the legal recognition of same-sex relationships, she found that lesbians and gay men were not likely to characterise their relationship with law as being 'against the law', which is the category of legal consciousness that Ewick and Silbey (1998) argue that socially marginalised people will be most likely to engage with. Instead, Hull argues that lesbians and gay men fight for legal recognition of their relationships and other rights (i.e. embrace the law and acknowledge its power) while concurrently being situated against the law in their opposition to restrictive legal provision for lesbians and gay men. Same-sex commitment ceremonies, in the absence of legal recognition, are described by Hull as both 'cultural practice and legal ambition' (Hull, 2003: 630).

Similarly, Nancy Nicol and Miriam Smith (2008) used a legal consciousness theoretical frame in their recent analysis of same-sex marriage movements in the US and Canada. They argue that 'the insights of the legal consciousness approach can be readily applied to the exploration of social movement activism in the courts' (Nicol & Smith, 2008: 669). Their analysis of the different paths taken by lesbian and gay social movements and judicial and governmental law-makers to the issue of same-sex marriage in the US and Canada demonstrates that the ways that lesbians and gay men (and their allies) engage with law has an impact on the ways that law develops over time. They argue that 'the engagement of same-sex couples ... contributed to producing new sets of meanings around the concept of legal marriage ... The same-sex marriage movement uses the power and legitimacy of law to engage in political resistance and civil disobedience' (Nicol & Smith, 2008: 684).

The findings from these research projects raise interesting questions about when and whether lesbian and gay legal consciousness could be described as either 'before the law' or 'with the law', and also how the race and class implications of an 'against the law' legal consciousness relate to the position(s) of lesbians and gay men. Hull's (2003) research also raises questions of whether the general theory of legal consciousness as propounded by Ewick and Silbey (1998) can be effectively applied to and translated into research about lesbian and gay rights claims. For example, believing that the legal recognition of same-sex relationships would normalise the presence of same-sex couples in society and 'produce deeper, transformative effects in our society as a whole' (Hull, 2003: 639) seems to be a 'before the law' perspective as it acknowledges the power of legality to affect society. This is not, however the conventional 'before the law' perspective as described by Ewick and Silbey, as legality in this version is 'relatively fixed and impervious to individual action' (Silbey & Ewick, 2003: 507). The conventional 'before the law' perspective does not, therefore, lie comfortably next to the rights seeking and legal change promoting activities of lesbian and gay activism.

Similarly, a 'with the law' legal consciousness conceptualises law as a game, which is played with 'less concern about the legitimacy of legal procedures than about their effectiveness for achieving desires' (Ewick & Silbey, 1998: 48). Hull (2003: 655), however, describes lesbian and gay legal consciousness as being 'with the law' in terms of talking about law 'in strategic, political terms, as a terrain of contest'. This results in another re-conceptualisation of this category, as it is not purely the game of law in the courtroom which is played, but rather the amendment of existing law and the construction of 'new' law, which also necessarily includes political manoeuvring, governance and the state.

The utility of legal consciousness studies in understanding the place of law in lesbian and gay lives is fundamentally that it allows a nuanced exploration of how law is experienced by lesbians and gay men. In the empirical chapters of this book, I provide my own insights into 'lesbian and gay legal consciousness'. I argue that legal consciousness studies is a helpful framework when considering the place of law in the everyday lives of lesbians and gay men, but that Ewick and Silbey's (1998) three schemas of legal consciousness ('before the law', 'with the law' and 'against the law') are not sufficient to explain lesbians and gay men's attitudes to law and legal change. I will demonstrate that while there is evidence of 'before the law' and 'with the law' legal consciousness in lesbians and gay men's accounts of the law, the 'against the law' schema requires development with more nuanced understandings of power and resistance before it can be useful in understanding the impact and effects of legal change on the everyday lives of lesbians and gay men.

Legal consciousness: limitations and possibilities

There have been a number of critiques of legal consciousness as both a theoretical and methodological framework for socio-legal research. The criticisms of legal consciousness broadly fall into four categories: questioning the salience of law in everyday life; the implications of studying 'consciousness'; the drawbacks of ignoring structural constraints; and the descriptive nature of empirical legal research.

Does law really have a place in everyday life?

The first, and most thoroughgoing, critique of legal consciousness as an object of study questions whether it is appropriate to examine law in everyday life. This is an interesting criticism as it highlights the lack of engagement with specifically legal phenomena in 'ordinary' life (Mezey, 2001), and questions the salience of law for 'ordinary' and 'marginalised' people. Levine and Mellema (2001), in their study of legal consciousness and women in the 'street level drug economy' note that the presumption that law is salient in everyday life contributes to interpretive bias, and can result in a devaluation or overshadowing of the role of other structural forces in everyday life (e.g. race, gender, class, poverty). Ewick and Silbey (1998) make extensive assumptions about the salience of law in everyday life, in particular with their (re)conception of legality as including all aspects of power, and impinging on all types of interaction.

It is important to consider here what is meant by 'law' in legal consciousness studies, and consequently to ask how 'law' should be defined for the purposes of legal consciousness. Is it, for example, necessary to define 'law' in a particular way to make it relevant to everyday life? For Ewick and Silbey, 'law' exists in everyday life in material forms such as 'courthouses; parking meters; marriage, birth, death and mortgage certificates; ... and the signs that warn us against trespassing, loitering, right turns, or smoking' (Ewick & Silbey, 1998: 16). They also note that 'law' is present in everyday life through representations in popular media and culture, including books, films and television series. As noted above, however, Ewick and Silbey's (1998) study of legal consciousness focuses on 'legality' rather than 'law', and, as a result, explicitly defines the 'legal' part of legal consciousness in a very open and expansive way, as including 'the meanings, sources of authority, and cultural practices that are commonly recognized as legal, regardless of who employs them or for what ends' (Ewick & Silbey, 1998: 22). Through this expansive definition, the place of law in everyday life seems secure, although it is by no means a solution to the question of whether law actually *is* important in the everyday lives of 'ordinary' people. The other side of this equation would be that law only becomes salient to 'ordinary' people when they experience a particular event or incident that brings them into contact with official legal actors, such as lawyers, courts or the police.

Legal consciousness studies have attempted to address this concern in a number of ways. One way of addressing the question of the salience of law in everyday life has been to conduct legal consciousness research without making the 'legal' focus explicit in interviews (e.g. Ewick & Silbey, 1998; Hull, 2003; Nielsen, 2000) in order to allow conceptions of law (or legality) to arise organically. This approach does not completely circumvent the potential problems of interpretive bias, as the data are undoubtedly then analysed with the aim of finding references to 'law' or 'legality'. But this technique may be appropriate for examining the presence of law in everyday life, as it allows people's own legal narratives to be ascendant, rather than be constrained or shaped by responses to particular questions about experiences of 'justiciable problems' or using 'the law' (e.g. Genn, 1999). Also, studies of particular communities (e.g. Engel, 1984), specific 'groups' (e.g. Hull, 2003), specific legal issues (e.g. Nielsen, 2000) or significantly marginalised people (e.g. Levine & Mellema, 2001) allow insights into the different ways in which non-legal actors engage with and respond to law and legality, and suggest that the law does indeed have at least some salience in everyday life. I would argue that perhaps a more useful solution to this question about the salience of 'law' in everyday life is to consider the definition of 'law' for the purposes of legal consciousness as incorporating ideas of legal pluralism, rather than legal centralism.

By reconfiguring 'law' to include normative frameworks other than state law, the everyday relevance of the 'legal' in ordinary life could become much clearer. I return to the issue of legal pluralism in more detail later.

The problems of defining 'consciousness'

A second major critique of legal consciousness relates to the use of the term 'consciousness' and the meanings ascribed to this word. Certainly 'consciousness' has not had a fixed and immutable meaning throughout all legal consciousness studies. The most common use of the term is a short-hand version of 'the way(s) people think about' (i.e. perceptions or images), but the term is also used to mean aptitude, competence or awareness, is related to ideology, and occasionally is deemed to include all of these meanings (Engel, 1998). As outlined above, the three varieties of legal consciousness studies (consciousness as attitude, consciousness as ideology and consciousness as cultural practice) each give different meanings to 'consciousness'. That different researchers take diverse approaches to the definition of 'consciousness' (and by association of 'legal consciousness') is not, in itself as problematic as some may suggest.

Susan Silbey (2005), for example, argues that the purpose or aim of legal consciousness studies should be to 're-capture the critical sociological project of explaining the durability and ideological power of law' (Silbey, 2005: 358). While this is undoubtedly an important facet of legal consciousness studies, and the focus of Ewick and Silbey's (1998) project, it does not therefore logically follow that all studies of legal consciousness should have the same aim. Instead, legal consciousness studies, as this field has been developed, allows for differing aims across studies, to explore and explain the way particular groups, communities or even individuals think about, talk about, engage and do not engage with law. The richness and potential of legal consciousness as a field of study is intrinsically linked to the diversity of perspectives on law, legality and regulation that can be accessed through different subjects and objects of study.

There are, however, other problems related to the use of the word 'consciousness'. A major problematic is that in ordinary usage, the term 'consciousness' does not simply refer to the state of being conscious and able to experience thoughts, feelings and awareness of the everyday world but also implicitly includes subconsciousness – the unformed, unexpressed and unintended thought processes that feed into our conscious expressions of attitudes or ideas. Thus, research into legal consciousness should ideally focus as much on the subconscious engagement with law by 'ordinary' people as it does on conscious engagement with law. Some studies have attempted to ameliorate these concerns by defining 'consciousness' so as to include elements of subconscious engagement with law. This has been done by explicitly looking for situations in which individuals do not talk about law, or do not use law (in the sense that they do not conceptualise a particular type of problem in a legalistic way) even when this may have been an option for them (Bumiller, 1988; Ewick & Silbey, 1998; Levine & Mellema, 2001; Merry, 1990). However, substantive engagement with legal subconsciousness has been limited to an exploration of the unexpected results of utilising law. For example, the ways in which people who turn to law to increase their power in solving a personal problem find themselves, by contrast, becoming more powerless (Cowan, 2004; Merry, 1990).

Ewick and Silbey's (1998) cultural schemas approach to legal consciousness offers some explanation of legal subconsciousness, as they use the schemas of 'before the law', 'with the law' and 'against the law' to explain why individuals think about law in the ways they do. The problem, however, with attempting to include an analysis of subconscious engagement with law is that it is impossible to know exactly which cultural resources are being drawn on by individuals at any given time, because of the difficulties of understanding the complex subjective experience of individuals. To attempt to study legal subconsciousness may therefore be practically impossible, especially given the lack of reliable methodological techniques for mind reading! As such it should be noted as a caveat that what people say about, do with and do not do with law may not necessarily give a full account of their attitudes to and perceptions of law, or the reasons why they hold such views or act in particular ways. As such, legal consciousness is most accurately considered to be a theoretical and methodological framework for interpreting people's experience of law in their everyday lives, rather than a means providing an epistemologically realist understanding of law.

Accounting for structural constraints

A third problem inherent in the concept of legal consciousness is that the term 'consciousness' implies a somewhat individualistic and reductionist approach. By conceptualising legal consciousness as a product of the individual, and, in particular, a product of an individual's *mind*, it has the potential to ignore structural and social constraints on individual action. For example, in much legal consciousness research, there has been a lack of engagement with the effect(s) of social characteristics (e.g. class, race, gender, education level) that could have an impact on individual legal consciousness (Hirsch, 1993). As a result, the *production* of legal consciousness is sidelined, and therefore where an individual's legal consciousness 'comes from' remains unclear. Ewick and Silbey attempt to address this problem by re-conceptualising consciousness as 'participation in the production of structures' (Ewick & Silbey, 1998: 224). I would argue, however, this does not provide sufficient engagement with structural constraints, as the results of social marginalisation or stigmatisation are that all individuals do not necessarily have the same ability to participate in the 'construction of social structures', particularly those whose primary engagement with law is in the 'against the law' vein of legal consciousness.

One study has engaged more fully with intersectionality and legal consciousness. In her research exploring the problems associated with the legal regulation of hate speech, Nielsen (2000; 2004) used legal consciousness to explore the variations in individuals' attitudes to the regulation of 'hate speech' as a result of their race, gender and class. By focusing more strongly on intersectionality and the production of consciousness, Nielsen's findings highlighted that although most respondents did not favour the legal regulation of hate speech, the reasons given for this varied considerably depending on the race, class and gender of the respondent (Nielsen, 2000: 1085–86). This research suggests that legal consciousness, when it is sensitive to the structural constraints affecting people's attitudes to law, can probe more deeply into the reasons why individuals hold particular views about law and, as such, reach places that other methods of socio-legal enquiry cannot.

Is empirical legal research necessarily descriptive?

The final major critique of legal consciousness I wish to discuss here relates more generally to the consequences of the methodological framework of legal consciousness, and that the reliance on empirical data leads to a neglect of theoretical substance (Garcia-Villegas, 2003). In effect, this critique explores the extent to which an analysis of the stories or narratives that 'ordinary' people use about law can do anything other than describe the ways in which people talk about law. Indeed, the creation of three broad categories ('before the law', 'with the law' and 'against the law') to describe variations in legal consciousness (Ewick & Silbey, 1998) seems to be a predominantly descriptive result of this empirical research. I would agree that, thus far, legal consciousness studies seem to have conceptualised describing legal consciousness as the 'end point' or conclusion of the research, rather than using legal consciousness as the basis for a critique of law and legal processes, or for drawing out relationships of power and resistance in everyday stories of law. Ewick and Silbey, for example, contend that legal consciousness and the ways in which people construct 'legality' serve to construct and change 'legality' over time and give the example of whale song[3] to illustrate their point (1998: 44). This formulation of 'legality' seeks to show that legal consciousness research is more than purely descriptive, by drawing attention to the social construction of law (Litowitz, 2000). However, the contention that 'law' is so malleable that it allows for any and all conceptions of what law is or should be to actually change 'law' seems too simplistic.

In order to respond to these critiques, the framework of legal consciousness needs to expand to allow for the problematisation of theoretical concepts uncovered through legal consciousness research, and this is a primary approach that I take in my exploration of legal consciousness in lesbian and gay lives. The implications of the different conceptions of power and resistance inherent in different forms of legal consciousness need to be unpacked and theorised, and the effects of differential social statuses (e.g. class, gender, race, and sexuality) should be considered as salient factors in the production and effects of legal consciousness. In addition, considering more carefully the meaning of 'law' or 'legal' in legal consciousness research may assist in understanding more clearly the place of law in society.

New legal pluralism: a fruitful new avenue for legal consciousness studies?

One way to clarify what is meant by 'law' in legal consciousness studies is to make the pluralist connotations inherent in Ewick and Silbey's (1998) reformulation of 'law' to 'legality' explicit. Legal pluralism is a concept that challenges the idea that state law is the only form of law; rather, a plural approach to law highlights that a variety of different legal or normative systems exist, all of which can be described as law. In many respects, the literature on legal pluralism highlights that it is very much a contested perspective (von Benda-Beckmann, 2002). My aim in this section is not therefore to give a comprehensive overview of the development of legal pluralism as a concept (for which see Griffiths, 1986; Melissaris, 2004; Merry, 1988) or the many challenges to it from legal positivist and legal centralist positions (e.g. Roberts, 1998; Tamanaha, 1993; Woodman, 1998) but rather to explore the possibilities of legal pluralism as a way of addressing some of the more intractable critiques of legal consciousness studies. What follows is, therefore, a partial and selective account of the complex and contested field of legal pluralism.

Originally, legal pluralism developed through early twentieth-century legal anthropology research, and was used as a descriptive account of societies where more than one legal system coexisted (Merry, 1988). Often legal pluralism was used to describe legal systems where more than one form of law existed, for example in Tanzania in the 1960s, where local legislation, Islamic, Hindu, and 'customary' law existed alongside residual English common law (Twining, 2000). This anthropological concept of legal pluralism has, in more recent times, expanded to include 'relations between dominant groups and subordinate groups, such as religious, ethnic or cultural minorities, immigrant groups, and unofficial forms of ordering located in social networks or institutions' (Merry, 1988: 872–73). John Griffiths (1986), for example, introduced a 'new' form of legal pluralism, which he used to describe a social field with more than one legal order (as distinct from legal pluralism as a colonial and post-colonial term to describe the coexistence of 'official law' and 'customary law'). Griffiths (1986) argued that the (post-)colonial vision of legal pluralism, far from being inconsistent with a statist, monist or centralist version of legal ideology is entirely consistent with the privileging of state law over any other regulatory form, as the customary or indigenous laws were generally granted recognition by and through state law (see also Davies, 2005).

The basic tenet of 'new' legal pluralism literature has been that 'not all the phenomena related to law and not all that are law-like have their source in government' (Moore, 1986). Legal pluralism, as I use the term, posits that there are many normative orders of various descriptions that are not attached to the state, but which nevertheless are 'legal'. This attention to the operation of normative orders is at once the primary source of the potential of legal pluralism (both in conjunction with legal consciousness, and as an independent field of enquiry) and, at the same time, the root of much critique of plural approaches to and understandings of law. Legal pluralism has been subjected to a number of critiques, first, that because legal pluralists are unable to answer the question 'what is law?' adequately, the underlying basis of legal pluralism is on shaky foundations (Tamanaha, 2000). Second, a common critique of legal pluralism is that if 'law' is not that which is written in books or spoken by judges, but rather is anything that can be described as a 'normative order', then it is very difficult to distinguish 'law' from social life. As Sally Merry (1988: 870) asks: 'where do we stop speaking of law and find ourselves simply describing social life?'

Perhaps the most thorough recent consideration of legal pluralism is the 'post-modern' version put forward by Boaventura de Sousa Santos (1995). In this complex treatise, he defines law as:

> A body of regularized procedures and normative standards, considered justiciable in any given group, which contributes to the creation and prevention of disputes, and to their settlement through an argumentative discourse, coupled with the threat of force.
>
> (Santos, 1995: 428–29)

This definition of law is then applied to 'six structural clusters of social relations in capitalist societies' which he defines as: domestic law, production law, exchange law, community law, territorial or state law, and systemic law (Santos, 1995: 429–36). There are a number of problems with this exposition of legal pluralism, not least that the six 'types' of law often overlap and are somewhat indistinguishable from one another, and state law tends to impinge on all the other 'types'. Tamanaha (2000) forcefully critiqued Santos's account of legal pluralism as being too essentialist to offer a satisfactory definition of either law or legal pluralism, because his definition would include almost every social action and relationship.

An alternative approach to legal pluralism is Guther Teubner's (1992) autopoietic version. Teubner argued that 'any communication that observes action under the legal code constitutes an integral part of the legal discourse, including communication among lay people who invoke claims against one another' (Teubner, 1992: 1459). The legal code that Teubner (1992) refers to is his contention that any communication which those involved define in terms of the binary 'legal/illegal' is law. While this perspective is interesting and quite persuasive, it is perhaps too embedded within a functional definition of law. Another alternative is Tamanaha's (2000) approach to legal pluralism, which he described as a 'non-essentialist' version of legal pluralism, relying on a non-essentialist definition of law: 'law is whatever people identify and treat through their social practices as "law"' (Tamanaha, 2000: 313). Legal pluralism, therefore, according to Tamanaha, can include any relationship between people that is thought of by them as legal. This approach seems to circumvent some of the issues of other definitions, as it allows for any relationship that is considered to be legal to be described as law. Martha-Marie Kleinhans and Roderick Macdonald's (1997) version of legal pluralism, which they describe as 'a *critical* legal pluralism', also offers a more interesting approach. Kleinhans and Macdonald's version of legal pluralism seeks to turn analyses of law and society inside out: 'rather than beginning with the premise that society and subjects are real entities that law can treat, it investigates how narrating subjects treat law' (Kleinhans & Macdonald, 1997: 46). These two conceptions of legal pluralism combine to create a form of legal analysis that identifies much more than 'official' law as 'law'.

The potential of legal pluralism in understanding marginalised individuals' experiences of law has been explored by a number of feminist and critical legal scholars. Ambreena Manji (1999) argued that legal pluralism is necessary to understand African women's 'legal world', through a careful analysis of the problematic of legal centralism in gaining an understanding of the way in which women experience law. She argued that a legal centralist approach is 'phallocentric' – and as such, provides a vision of the legal that is clouded by a patriarchal lens. In order to escape this patriarchal understanding of law, legal pluralism is necessary as it allows for 'the articulation of a feminine view of the (legal) world' (Manji, 1999: 450). Similarly, Margaret Davies (2005) suggests that a legal monist or centralist approach, which depends on a singular vision of law, is 'obstructive to the kinds of social change demanded by a plural society' (Davies, 2005: 90). Therefore, it has been argued that the true potential of legal pluralism is the ability for the study of it to be a radical re-thinking of the way we perceive the legal (Melissaris, 2004).

This rich literature, which is sensitive to the complex interplay between law and society has much to offer legal consciousness studies, and I would argue can assist in addressing some of the more trenchant critiques of legal consciousness outlined above. The problematic of whether or not 'law' is actually salient in everyday life becomes a moot point if 'law' is anything that people, in their social practices, treat as law. On this understanding of legal pluralism, if a person describes something as concerned with law or regulation, then it is and must be in some way legal, whether or not it is considered to be part of 'official' law. Understandings of normative orders, systems of rules or alternative legal frameworks can, therefore, be considered as part of an exploration of legal consciousness. In addition, conceptualising 'law' in this way for the purposes of legal consciousness avoids the reification of 'law' or the claims to a singular 'truth' that can be problematic in legal centralist approaches, and allows for the de-centring of official or state law in critique of law and legal process.

A primary motivation in considering legal pluralism alongside legal consciousness in this book is the problematic raised by the operation of heteronormativity in society. Liberal lesbian and gay equality struggles have thus far failed to take sufficient notice of the heteronormativity of the frameworks into which they argue for inclusion (such as marriage, or 'the family'). The problems of assimilation and the recognition of difference in lesbian and gay lives are therefore marginalised. A plural understanding of law allows for the recognition of (and consequent labelling of) normative structures (such as heteronormativity) as not simply moral or cultural norms, but as 'legal'. The benefit of using a claim to law in this way is threefold: first, it exposes the contingency and plurality of law, undermining legal positivist and natural law claims that law is the way it is because either it has always been that way, or because it must be singular and separate from moral claims (e.g. Hart, 1958). Second, a legal pluralist approach allows for greater understanding of the place of law in everyday life as it is attentive to both the 'official' state law and those other normative systems (perhaps outside of, perhaps interior to state law) of rule that are experienced by people as coercive, including such ideas as heteronormativity. Third, such an understanding of heteronormativity and, by extension, other normative systems or structures, such as institutionalised sexism, racism or class privilege, as part of a 'legal order', allows these organising principles of society to be exposed as such. Recognising normative structures as 'legal' therefore also de-centres official law (Smart, 1989) and allows the effects they have on social life to be explored and addressed.

In summary, a plural approach to legal consciousness studies can help to address some of the limitations of previous legal consciousness research. By explicitly recognising that the 'legal' part of legal consciousness can include structural or normative pressures, as well as 'official' law, a plural legal consciousness framework has the potential to be more sensitive to the position of marginalised individuals in society. The focus of this book is understanding the place of law in lesbian and gay lives, and therefore my approach to legal consciousness can help to interrogate and unpack the multiple sources of regulation in lesbian and gay lives. In coupling legal consciousness studies with a plural understanding of law, the potential of constitutive approaches to socio-legal study of lesbian and gay lives becomes clear. I argue, building on Hull's (2003) and Richman's (2006) research, that lesbian and gay parenting and relationships provide fertile ground for understanding not only lesbian and gay men's understandings of and attitudes to 'official' law, but also the more nuanced, less formal systems of regulation, and the effects of power and resistance in lesbian and gay lives.

Developing legal consciousness studies

In this chapter, I have provided an overview of the field of legal consciousness studies: a burgeoning area of socio-legal inquiry in both North America and Europe. I have argued that legal consciousness studies needs to be developed in order to address some of the more intractable critiques that have been put forward. I suggested that in order for the field of legal consciousness studies to be responsive to these critiques it is necessary to unpack and theorise the different conceptions of power and resistance inherent in different forms of legal consciousness, that the effects of differential social statuses (e.g. class, gender, 'race' or ethnicity, sexuality) should be considered as salient factors in the production and effects of legal consciousness, and the plural approach to law that is implicit in ideas of legal consciousness should be made explicit.

I now conclude this chapter with an outline of my approach to legal consciousness studies, to give an overview of how I develop legal consciousness in response to these critiques. While all the critiques of legal consciousness outlined above are important, the question of whether law is salient in everyday life (see Levine & Mellema, 2001; Mezey, 2001) can be dealt with relatively easily in the context of this project. Whether 'law' is, or is not, relevant in the everyday lives of lesbians and gay men is one of the questions at the heart of this book. The sheer scale and quantity of recent legal change (in particular in the areas of relationship recognition/regulation and lesbian and gay parenting) suggests that 'law' certainly has the potential to be salient in the everyday lives of lesbians and gay men at this point in time. As I will demonstrate in Chapters 4 and 6, the introduction of legal recognition for same-sex relationships is an area where 'law' and 'legality' are of major importance in the everyday lives of lesbians and gay men. The other empirical 'lens' I use to access legal consciousness, lesbian and gay parenting, seems, by way of contrast, to offer a more complex account of the place of law in the everyday lives of lesbians and gay men. As I demonstrate in Chapter 5 and Chapter 6, issues around a lack of (appropriate) legal provision for lesbian and gay parents can give rise to interesting solutions such as the creation of informal rules to regulate alternative families.

The other three critiques outlined above (the problems of studying 'consciousness', the need for awareness of structural forces and constraints, and the potential for empirical research to be overly descriptive) are very much linked as a primary problematic in legal consciousness studies. I argued above that approaching legal consciousness with an awareness of intersectionality and the interlocking nature of systems of subordination may help to expose structural constraints and their effects on legal consciousness. In contrast, Susan Silbey (2005) has argued that studies that have utilised the tools of legal consciousness to examine specific legal phenomenon or specific groups (e.g. Hull, 2003; Levine & Mellema, 2001; Marshall, 2003; Nielsen, 2004) have shifted the 'object of analysis ... from law and legality to some other phenomena: sexual harassment, the meanings of marriage ... [etc.] ... thus, the research often ends up tracing not consciousness of law but of something else, e.g., race, gender, class, sexuality ... ' (Silbey, 2005: 355). While this argument has some force, approaching legal consciousness from a plural perspective allows the structural aspects of sexuality, gender, race and class to be explicitly interrogated alongside law.

My primary motivation in this book is to consider the impacts and effects of new legal developments on lesbian and gay lives, and the understandings of law that surface in individuals' narratives around the issues of relationship recognition and the regulation of lesbian and gay parenting. In order to ensure that structural constraints remain relevant when considering individual legal consciousness and to ensure that the empirical nature of legal consciousness does not lead to a purely descriptive analysis, I combine legal consciousness with two key theoretical concepts: power and resistance. In the next chapter, I discuss how I amalgamate legal consciousness with these concepts, and the theoretical underpinnings of my understandings of power and resistance. In many respects, it is the place of resistance (especially in legal consciousness that Ewick and Silbey [1998] called 'against the law') that is my focus in this book. The possibility of legal consciousness research to highlight points of resistance is, for me, a key component of the potential that legal consciousness studies offer for socio-legal research.

Notes

1 The term "'ordinary' people" is used extensively in legal consciousness research, but is somewhat problematic. In some studies, 'ordinary' is used to signify people who have not had legal education or training (e.g. Ewick & Silbey, 1998). I am uncomfortable with this designation as there are no studies that systematically compare the 'legal consciousness' of 'lawyers' and 'non-lawyers'.

2 In her work, Richman (2006) talks of 'LGBT' parents, but does not offer any substantive analysis of the different experiences of bisexual and/or trans parents. Where discussing her work, I therefore use the LGBT acronym, but, in many respects, this work is most representative of lesbian and gay parents.

3 Ewick and Silbey describe the ways in which whale song changes gradually and almost imperceptibly over time, but that if a reasonable amount of time passes, the later song is markedly different from the earlier song (Ewick & Silbey, 1998: 44).

Chapter 3

Reconsidering resistance

In the previous chapter, I argued that in order to make legal consciousness a more useful conceptual frame for understanding the place of law in lesbian and gay lives, it is necessary to develop a more nuanced understanding of the key concepts of power and resistance and to include engagement with a plural understanding of law. I now turn to consider how a more finely grained consideration of power and resistance can be brought to bear on legal consciousness studies. In previous legal consciousness studies, the 'power' of the state, sovereign, government or other seemingly 'powerful' institutions or groups have rarely been questioned (e.g. Ewick & Silbey, 1998; Merry, 1990), and the actions of disadvantaged people, and oppressed groups (such as lesbians and gay men) are easily conceptualised as 'resistant'. When explaining their 'against the law' type of legal consciousness, for example, Ewick and Silbey describe the 'oppositional practices that are employed by subordinate persons against the powerful institutions or organizations in which they find themselves living and working' (Ewick & Silbey, 1998: 181). Throughout this book I seek to expose the contingency and instability of approaching power and resistance in this way, and to show that resistance (in particular) is complex, varied and worthy of deeper analysis. Through the theoretical approaches to power and resistance that I use, I therefore complicate this picture of a powerful/powerless dyadic relationship between 'powerful institutions' and 'subordinate persons'.

I begin with a brief sketch of how I understand 'power', drawing on Foucault, feminist engagements with Foucault's analytics of power and the ways in which governmentality studies have developed understandings of power relations. I do not provide a detailed overview of Foucault's approach to power, as this has been well addressed in a range of contexts,[1] rather, I focus in this section on how I bring a Foucauldian approach together with legal consciousness, and what this means for my proposed 'plural' conception of legal consciousness. I do this through a consideration of heteronormativity, and what it would mean to think of heteronormativity as 'legal', or as a mode of governmentality. In the second section of the chapter, I move on to posit a new lexicon of resistance that draws on Foucauldian approaches to power relations to argue that creative and technical forms of power allow space for similarly creative and technical forms of resistance. I conclude this chapter with an exploration of how my approach to power and resistance helps to provide a more nuanced and helpful understanding of both the 'power of law' and resistance to that power in legal consciousness studies, through a same-sex marriage case study.

Power

Power is a much theorised concept in social and political theory, with many writers going to great lengths to determine both what, exactly, 'power' is and how it is manifest. Rather than replay all of these debates and interventions here (which would divert attention too far away from my central questions about power), I wish to focus on Michel Foucault's (1979, 1980, 1998, 2002) approach to the concept of power, as well as the ways his analytics of power have been developed by feminist scholars (e.g. Bell, 1993; Butler, 1990; Sawicki, 1991, 2004; Smart, 1989; Taylor & Vintges, 2004). How power works and is manifest was a central question in Foucault's work and his (re)conceptualisation of power has been highly influential in feminist and sexualities scholarship. It is, of course, true to say that Foucault's analytics of power have not been wholeheartedly embraced by feminist scholars, and a variety of trenchant critiques have been put forward (see e.g. Hartsock, 1990, 1996; Fraser, 1981, 1985).[2] My concern here, however, is not to consider 'power' as an entirely abstract concept, but rather to address specific questions about how power is and should be approached in legal consciousness studies.

In many respects, power in legal consciousness has been predominantly concerned with legal power – questioning how and why the institutional power of law and legal hegemony is sustained despite the 'gap' between written law and law in action (Silbey, 2005). In my approach to legal consciousness I wish to move beyond these 'gap studies' and take as my focus the operation of power in society (including through legal means) rather than the power of legal institutions *per se*.[3] My reasons for this will become clear throughout my analysis in the following empirical chapters, but in brief, as well as looking to 'official law' which recognises and regulates sexuality, I am concerned with considering how non-legal normative frameworks can be contested, challenged and resisted by lesbians and gay men. As such, Foucault's analytics of power provide a useful way to considering how power works to restrain, normalise and discipline bodies.

In his essay *The Subject and Power*, Foucault (2002) noted that his reasons for thinking about power relations were due to a lack of tools for the study:

> We had recourse only to ways of thinking about power based on legal models, that is: What legitimates power? Or we had recourse to ways of

> thinking about power based on institutional models, that is: What is the state?
>
> (Foucault, 2002: 327)

The 1970s in France heralded a move away from thinking of power as almost wholly domination towards the need to examine power in the context of 'global problems of the regulation and ordering of society' (Pasquino, 1993: 79). Foucault (1980) highlighted two heterogeneous forms of power as domination or repression – juridical power, and power as a field of force relations, as in war, between struggle and submission. In the juridical conception of power, 'power is taken to be a right, which one is able to possess like a commodity, and which one can in consequence transfer or alienate' (Foucault, 1980: 88). In this form of thinking, power is something that is held (either by an individual or, more commonly, by the sovereign or government) and used against subordinates. It is a form of power that is almost wholly dominating and repressive and can only operate in negative ways, through prohibition (Foucault, 1998: 83–84). This juridical power is the way in which the 'power of law' is often conceptualised: 'if we speak of the power of laws, institutions, and ideologies, if we speak of the structures or mechanisms of power, it is only insofar as we suppose that certain persons exercise power over others' (Foucault, 2002: 337). In his second schema of power as repression, he takes 'war' as his example and, drawing on Nietzsche, looks to the ways in which 'the relationship of power lies in the hostile engagement of forces' (Foucault, 1980: 91).

Both of these approaches to power were considered by Foucault to be waning, in favour of a 'new' form: power as normalisation. Rather than thinking of power as domination, within the schemas of juridical power or as a field of hostile force relations, in this 'new' conception of power the disciplinary nature of power becomes the schema for thinking about power, through examples such as psychiatric power or the control of sexuality (Foucault, 1980: 92). Through this focus on the disciplinary mechanisms of power – power as normalisation – Foucault identified power as technical, creative and productive (Foucault, 1979). In identifying this 'new' analytics of power, Foucault implored that:

> We should direct our researches on the nature of power ... towards domination and the material operators of power, towards forms of subjection and the inflections and utilisations of the localized systems, and towards strategic apparatuses ... base our analysis of power on the study of the techniques and tactics of domination.
>
> (Foucault, 1980: 102)

Therefore, we must analyse law from the standpoint of power relations, not power from the standpoint of law (Foucault, 2002: 343); take a bottom up, rather than top down focus. Power, in Foucault's terms, is about shaping the behaviour of another through a particular means – so state power (and hence the power of law) arises from the disciplinary mechanisms brought into play by governance of people. His focus was on laws and regimes that shape the behaviour of individuals; the shaping of the actions of others through action. Foucault argued that disciplinary power would replace power as domination and that it is therefore important to examine power at 'the extreme points of its exercise, where it is always less legal in character' (Foucault, 1980: 97).

In relation to the study of legal consciousness and the place of law in the everyday lives of lesbians and gay men, this idea of disciplinary power is appealing, as while the 'old' forms of juridical power continue to be salient in the lives of lesbians and gay men, thinking about the place of law in everyday life inevitably highlights the ways power is exercised in order to ensure conformity. Normalisation, the marking of ways of being as acceptable or unacceptable behaviour, is a key point in Foucault's discussion of the disciplinary mechanisms of power: 'conformity to the norm is desired and non-conformities are marked and punished with a view to correcting the deviation' (Bell, 1993: 66).

Moving away from thinking about power as wholly concerned with domination also led to Foucault's thinking about the history of 'governmentality', a neologism created to examine 'governmental rationalities', or ways or systems of thinking about the nature of the practice of government (Gordon, 1991). In his lecture of the same name, Foucault (1991a) outlined what he called 'governmentality' – a way or system of thinking about the nature of the practice of government – in particular, the ways that (in the modern western practice of government) the aim is both the individualisation and totalisation of the population. Whereas sovereign power was concerned with territory and disciplinary power with individuals, governmentality takes population as its focus. For Foucault, governmentality is concerned with the regulation of '*omnes et singulatum*' – each and all – and the ways in which the exercise of power over the population controls the actions of the population (Foucault, 1991a). Foucault described governmentality as:

> The ensemble formed by the institutions, procedures, analyses, and reflection, the calculations and tactics that allow the exercise of this … form of power, which has as its target population.
>
> (Foucault, 1991a: 102)

At the heart of governmentality, therefore, is the ways in which government and governmental apparatus overtook sovereign exercises of power, and the methods through which the 'state of justice … transformed into the administrative state' (Foucault, 1991a: 103). Foucault's essay on governmentality has given rise to a 'rethinking of the notion of government' (Dean, 1999: 1), which takes the 'particular mentalities, arts and regimes of government and administration' as its focus (Dean, 1999: 2). Governmentality can therefore be distinguished from 'government' in that its focus rests on the 'how' of governing, rather than the simple act of doing so. Thus, governmentality looks to the half-way ground between power as domination and power as creative, technical and productive.

The utility of a governmentality perspective is that it opens up a space for reflection of individual narratives or stories of law within the context of broader structural concerns. Studies of governmentality aim to unpack why we are governed in the ways we are, and what it means to be governed in these particular ways (Rose, 1999). A governmentality perspective attempts to understand the problems to which the ways of governing become solutions and to expose the contingency of particular modes of being and how governmental aims impact on the everyday lives of individuals (the ways in which governance conducts conduct) and the technologies of the self that are a part of our subjectification and subjectivity. As such, a governmentality perspective is useful in thinking about power in legal consciousness studies as it helps to draw links between the ways that individuals express their views of law and the ways in which governmental rationality attempts to control the population. It is important to remember, however, that utilising a governmentality perspective does not represent a move away from considering everyday, situated experiences of power, whether experienced as disciplinary, or through juridical power. Rather, governmentality 'provides the balance required to intersect micro- and macro-level analyses' (Macleod & Durrheim, 2002: 44), or in Foucault's own terms:

> There is not a sort of break between the level of micro-power and the level of macro-power and that talking about one [does not] exclude talking about the other. In actual fact, an analysis in terms of micro-powers comes back without any difficulty to the analysis of problems like those of government and the state.
>
> (Foucault, 2009: 358)

There have, inevitably, been critiques posed concerning governmentality, the most persuasive perhaps is that of Nancy Fraser (2003), who argued that globalisation and the move towards transnationalism has undermined Foucault's focus on the nationally bounded, socially concentrated, self-regulating operation of power relations. It is, of course, important to consider the recognition and regulation of familial intimacies from a globalised and transnational perspective (e.g. Bedford, 2005). But the other side of this equation, the everyday power relations which are experienced by and through lesbian and gay families, also remain important considerations. The constitution, recognition and regulation of lesbian and gay family forms vary so dramatically across national boundaries[4] that Foucauldian approaches to power relations, including governmentality, still afford fruitful avenues for exploring the place of law in lesbian and gay lives. Governmentality provides a method for thinking about the interaction and intersection of everyday experience and power relations, with macro-strategies of governance and regulation. Foucauldian scholarship on power relations highlights that through disciplinary mechanisms of power, everyone is pushed towards particular, normative, modes of being – not necessarily through the operation of law, perhaps through modes of governance exterior to law. In relation to sexuality, the norm towards which everyone is pushed is that of heterosexuality – or rather, heteronormativity.

Governing heteronormativity

In Chapter 2, I argued that legal consciousness studies would be enriched by drawing on a critical approach to legal pluralism, and by including normative frameworks other than 'official law' within the remit of legal consciousness. One such normative framework is heteronormativity, which has been defined as 'the power of heterosexuality when it operates as a norm' (Chambers, 2007). It is probable that the concept of heteronormativity has a genealogy related to that of compulsory heterosexuality (Rich, 1980). Michael Warner (1993) appears to be the first to use the term heteronormativity, but, unfortunately, he did not simultaneously provide an explicit definition. It is perhaps most easily considered a simple contraction of heterosexual normativity – the idea that society assumes heterosexual identity, practices and behaviour to be normative, and thus law and social structures are organised as if this were the case. Heteronormativity should be thought of as a regulatory practice, rather than a manifestation of discrimination, because:

> The concept of heteronormativity reveals institutional, cultural and legal norms that reify and entrench the normativity of heterosexuality. In other words, 'heteronormativity' tells us that heterosexual desire and identity are not merely assumed, they are expected.
>
> (Chambers, 2007: 664–65)

Disciplinary mechanisms of power have, arguably, pushed lesbians and gay men towards heteronormative ways of living, in order to move beyond criminalisation. By this I mean that when same-sex sexual desire was criminalised, the ways of shaping sexual behaviour relied more on discipline than normalisation. Since decriminalisation, the operation of power on sexuality has been more concerned with normalisation and assimilation; pushing lesbians and gay men towards heteronormative lifestyles. The sorts of normalising forces I am referring to can be seen through the extension of marriage (or quasi-marriage) rights to same-sex couples and the removal of restrictions on lesbian and gay parenting.[5] Rather than completely embracing non-heterosexual lifestyles, and allowing for the growth of non-heteronormative ways of living and being, the recognition of lesbian and gay families in both law and society has limited lesbian and gay rights claims to parts of life which are understandable within the framework of heteronormativity, while still, in many cases, marking lesbians and gay men as different. As such, the problem of heteronormativity does not disappear; the boundaries of it are merely moved.

An example of the shifting boundaries of heteronormativity is the creation of civil partnership, instead of responding to calls for wide reaching reform of marriage (e.g. Polikoff, 2003). This allows same-sex couples to be known and knowable to the state, and therefore governable, while concurrently setting same-sex relationships apart from and marking them as different to the norm. This marking of same-sex couples as 'different' through the creation of a 'new' form of relationship recognition is obviously challenged by the jurisdictions that have extended full marriage rights to same-sex couples. But issues of normalisation, and particularly the privatisation of economic responsibility for caring and dependency (Young & Boyd, 2006), are not erased by the extension of marriage and arguably 'equal marriage' complicates, rather than simplifies analysis of power relations.[6] Another example of the way governmentality operates in lesbian and gay lives can be seen in the context of lesbian and gay adoption. As Stephen Hicks (2005) has argued, UK parliamentary discourse during the passage of the Adoption and Children Act 2002 continued to uphold the hierarchy of parenting, which places heterosexually married couples at the top, then unmarried heterosexual couples, single people and then same-sex couples (whether or not they are civil partners) at the bottom of the pile of potential parents. Of course, this hierarchy only covers those who are included within the sphere of adoption legislation – there is only very limited recognition of more diverse family forms, such as the relationship between known donors and non-birth mothers in planned lesbian families, or co-parenting of children by any number of different adults (Harding, 2005).

Another important aspect of heteronormativity is the way in which, alongside the normalisation of sexual orientation, assumptions of gender, race and class intersect with the imagined, idealised nuclear family. Heteronormativity not only operates to exclude lesbians and gay men from the respectability of the family, but also others whose lives do not fit with this imaginary ideal. As Priya Kandaswamy has argued in the US context, 'representations of black women as sexually deviant have worked to constitute black women (and … welfare recipients more generally) as an "other" against which the successful heteronormative citizen subject has been defined' (Kandaswamy, 2008: 721). Kandaswamy further argues that activists in same-sex marriage movements, in their desire to expand access to marriage 'reproduce this racial structure of heteronormativity' (2008: 721). It is essential, therefore, to consider the heteronormative effects of rights claims, and be sensitive to the 'macro' impact of the 'micro' relations of power and resistance in everyday life. What would it mean, then, to consider heteronormativity as interior to the 'legal' domain in the context of legal pluralism and legal consciousness? My intention in suggesting that it is possible to do so is not through an attempt to raise the status of heteronormativity by somehow considering it to be a part of official 'law', but rather to open it up to more sustained critique by holding it (as an entrenched normative framework) up to the same level of scrutiny that is afforded to those norms that are unproblematically inscribed in law.

In some respects, the 'disciplining' of lesbians, gay men and others into heteronormative ways of living highlights the methods by which power continues to be exercised as domination, and that disciplinary mechanisms of power have not completely colonised or dislodged juridical power. Carol Smart (1989) drew on Foucault's theory of power to argue that juridical power continues to be relevant, through an examination of the problematic nature of legal knowledge and the ways in which legal knowledge excludes other forms of knowledge. One way that law continues to exercise power in a juridical fashion, she argued, is through the 'transformation of power conflicts into the language of rights' (Smart, 1989: 20), and thus the colonisation by law of new forms of knowledge (such as those produced through psychology, psychiatry and psychoanalysis). Another way of conceiving of the continued power of law is through the authority that is placed in law to resolve conflicts, whether over small criminal acts, the ethics of end of life decision-making, or genetic engineering: 'part of the power that law can exercise resides in the authority we give it' (Smart, 1989: 25). Similarly, part of the power that heteronormativity retains is in the implicit authority given to it.

Continuing to assign 'law' the 'power' to describe what does and does not constitute a family maintains and sustains juridical power. Smart (1989) argued that in order to deconstruct the power that law has, and therefore to limit the ability of law to prioritise legal knowledge, it is essential to de-centre law, rather than to preserve 'law's place in the hierarchy of discourses which maintains that law has access to truth and justice' (Smart, 1989: 89). In relation to lesbian and gay struggles, the framing up of claims in relation to legal rights and the resultant reification of formal equality creates problematic comparisons with normative heterosexual family forms, as well as continuing to allow 'law' to decide what constitutes a family. In addition to allowing for the continued exercise of juridical power, rights claims also oversimplify power relations – the creation of a right to a legally recognised same-sex relationship (for example) does not, and cannot, automatically dismantle the power disparities between heteronormative 'society' and sexual or racial minorities. Arguably, this retains the heteronormativity of marriage, and continues to exclude lesbians and gay men from the norm, therefore continuing to subject lesbians and gay men to disciplinary power. Perhaps even legally recognised same-sex relationships are not quite normative enough to be considered as interior to the idealised sphere of the heteronormative family.

It is important to note that in recent years, a number of writers (following Duggan, 2003) have posited a new term 'homonormativity', which they use to describe lesbian and gay activism 'that does not challenge heterosexist institutions and values but rather upholds, sustains and seeks inclusion within them' (Duggan, 2003: 50). I am wary of this turn to considering rights claims for inclusion in basic social norms as inherently anti-progressive, and would agree with Berlant and Warner (2000) that:

> Heteronormativity is ... a concept distinct from heterosexuality. One of the most conspicuous differences is that it has no parallel, unlike heterosexuality, which organizes homosexuality as its opposite. Because homosexuality can never have the invisible, tacit, society-founding rightness that heterosexuality has, it would not be possible to speak of 'homonormativity' in the same sense.
>
> (Berlant & Warner, 2000: 312)

Arguing for lesbian, gay, bisexual and trans access to marriage may not be entirely 'radical' or 'transgressive', nor fundamentally compatible with many feminist and queer critiques of marriage (Barker, 2008) or coupled relationships (Klesse, 2007), but neither can it be considered entirely assimilationist or normative. The heteronormative image of 'the family' (with all its concomitant gender/race/class implications) remains dominant and entrenched in the social imagination; a social category that excludes many alternative family forms, not only same-sex relationships and families. Same-sex marriage, I would argue, as well as harbouring the dangers of assimilation also retains the potential to challenge heteronormativity and for wider transformation of marriage (Harding, 2007).

In summary, I would argue that in order to understand the way in which law works in the everyday lives of lesbians and gay men, it is important to expand our understanding of the power of law to include normative frames, such as heteronormativity. Foucault's analytics of power allows for power relations to be considered from the places where they are less legal and more normative. In drawing this into legal consciousness studies, exploring the ways in which people experience and understand the place of law in their everyday lives can create space for considering how and when people respond to norms in the same or similar ways that they respond to law. My plural approach to legal consciousness, therefore, draws on Foucauldian notions of disciplinary power and governmentality in order to allow analysis of those times when lesbians and gay men are constrained, not by anti-gay laws but by heteronormative pressures, which are experienced as 'legal'. In the next section, I develop my understandings of the place of power in legal consciousness studies by exploring the interlinked concept of resistance.

Resistance

Foucauldian approaches to power do not only create scope for the examination of governmentality and the effects of power on the lives of lesbians and gay men. Thinking about power as a relational system also opens up much more space for considering resistance than thinking of power in terms of domination or juridical power. As Foucault made clear, it is through the relational nature of power that points of resistance are made possible: 'where there is power, there is resistance ... resistance is never in a position of exteriority in relation to power' (Foucault, 1998: 95). In contrast to power, however, resistance is an under-theorised concept. I would not want to suggest that the word 'resistance' is not used regularly in feminist or lesbian and gay studies, but more that it is a concept that has not been the subject of anywhere near the level of critical scrutiny at a theoretical level that 'power' has. Rather, the term 'resistance' is often used either (as an unqualified good) to mean anything that is transgressive, subversive and/or counter-hegemonic or, conversely, as a way of describing negative forces that prevent the achievement of positive social change. In this book, and particularly through this chapter, I wish to clarify what I mean by 'resistance' and offer a new lexicon of resistance, which can help to unpack the different forms of resistance utilised and experienced by lesbians and gay men, and highlighted through legal consciousness studies. As such, the following discussion of resistance is necessarily somewhat conceptual, but I go on to refine, and develop my approach to resistance through the empirical analysis in subsequent chapters.

Some feminist scholars have taken Foucault's (1998) conceptualisation of resistance as being a part of power and argued that resistance is therefore the antithesis of power – in these accounts of power and resistance, 'resistance functions as an antagonistic response to a dominant form of power' (Cooper, 1995b: 126), rather than resistance being one aspect of the relational nature of power. Wendy Brown (1995: 49), for example, argues that 'as Foucault makes clear, resistance is an effect of and reaction to power, not an arrogation of it'. Although I would agree that Foucault does not conceptualise resistance as an arrogation of power, this is perhaps more because in his work on power he refuted the 'old' conceptualisation of power as a right that can be seized, than because he explicitly conceptualised resistance as distinct from power. Rather, he consistently positioned resistance as being interior to, and therefore a part of power.

Following Foucault, instead of conceptualising resistance as the antithesis or corollary of power, I find it more useful to conceptualise resistance as *the same as* power. Just as power is relational, so too is resistance; just as power can be used to discipline and shape, so too can resistance. To define resistance as something separate, apart, or distinct from power is to reify power and the 'powerful' at the expense of those who, from some perspectives, are 'powerless'. In order to elucidate what I mean by this framing of resistance as power, I want to spend a moment considering a very different use of the words 'power' and 'resistance'. If we look at the way in which resistance operates in an electronic circuit[7] it is clear that resistance is as much about the production of effects as power is.

A 'resistor' is used in an electronic circuit in order to regulate the flow of electrons (electric power). The amount of 'resistance' in the resistor determines the scale of the effect that it has on the flow of power through the circuit. In some cases, the resistance can be so great that it blocks the flow of power completely, causing a break, a fracture; in other cases, the purpose of the resistor is to reduce the amount of power within the rest of the circuit, or simply to ensure that the flow of power in the rest of the circuit is even and balanced. So, in this example, resistance stabilises the course and effects of power, has the capacity to moderate power, and even to completely interrupt the flow of power. As a result, resistance has 'power' over power. So, one could argue that resistance *is* power, or at the very least is a form of power and, conversely power is resistance – they are two ways of describing the same thing. Obviously, this metaphor has a number of limitations – first, electronic circuits are planned, controlled and have a constant supply of electric power. I would not want to suggest that power works in this way in society. Second, the effects of resistance in a circuit are calculable, calculated and known in advance, which again cannot be generalised beyond the specific context of electromagnetism. Finally, power relations are much less predictable, much more diffuse and unlikely to be either visible or measurable at any given moment.

My aim in providing this illustration is to bring into focus that by conceptualising power and resistance as dependent on and related to one another, as two sides of the same thing, Foucault's analytics of power as productive and relational becomes clearer. To illustrate this metaphor of the different ways resistance works into lesbian/gay or feminist politics, we need some more obviously related examples of each of the three forms of resistance outlined above: resistance as stabilising the course and effects of power, resistance moderating power, and resistance causing fractures in power relations. I am reluctant to create a hierarchy of these types of resistance, as I see each variety as important in the network of power relations, so although I will illustrate each of them, I do not want to emphasise one of them as being either the most or least important. Each type, I would argue, has the potential to create different effects on power, and each of these effects are as important as the others in understanding the operation of power relations.

Stabilising resistance

The first way of conceptualising resistance, then, where resistance stabilises the course and effects of power is concerned with regulation and normalisation through power relations. The type of effects that this form of resistance generates on power is, therefore, always present wherever power relations exist. It highlights the sort of resistant practices that work within and alongside normalising relations of disciplinary power, without directly challenging the laws or norms being enforced through power relations. One example could be the existence, even within the private sphere, of alternative modes of being outside that which is considered normative. Whenever a particular form of behaviour is normative, other forms of behaviour always exist outside the norm – those forms of behaviour which are subjected to the normalising disciplinary mechanisms of power. If there is nothing outside the norm, there would be no power relations, and therefore no point of resistance. The simple existence of lesbians and gay men, for example, is outside the norm of compulsory heterosexuality (Rich, 1980). Being lesbian and gay parents, being 'out' at work, not conforming to gender norms or roles, or being visibly queer are all examples of resistance to heteronormativity.

I imagine stabilising resistance as the constant antithesis to disciplinary power relations – the behaviours and ways of being that the imposition and enforcement of laws and norms seek to eradicate. Other examples could include driving the 'wrong' way up a one-way road, smoking, 'binge drinking', or eating an unhealthy diet. These could all be thought of as a form of stabilising resistance, especially in the face of disciplinary mechanisms through which science or medicine 'prove' that these behaviours are damaging to health, or even pathological, in that they show a disregard for the normative convention of individualised responsibility for health – that we should be responsible for and looking after our own bodies.

These examples are all working against a governmentalised, disciplinary power – even when there is no real potential for these minor resistant practices to 'change' anything in any tangible or real sense. They are moments that people seize from multi-layered forms of governance; and moments where a person steps, however briefly, over normative boundaries and therefore into doing 'resistance'. If these forms of resistance did not exist, then power would not be relational – as there would be no need for the disciplinary mechanisms that draw people towards the norm. An example of this kind of resistance can be found in the ways in which women resist gendered expressions of medical power, by changing their healthcare providers after experiencing attempts to ignore or overrule their embodied experience (Lorentzen, 2008). In her study, Jeanne M. Lorentzen (2008) explored the 'passive resistance' women describe in relation to medicalised expressions of their bodies as normatively gendered, prioritising their capacity for childbearing in refusing elective hysterectomy surgery. By changing healthcare providers and refusing to submit to 'objective' medicalised versions of their bodies, the individual women in Lorentzen's (2008) study engaged in what I would call stabilising resistance by refusing to accept their doctor's imposition of appropriately gendered embodiment. Stabilising resistance therefore works to stabilise the course and effects of power relations, acting as a constant counterbalance to power, moving outside the norms created through power relations.

Moderating resistance

The second type of resistance is that of resistance as 'moderating' power. By this I mean resistance moderating in the sense of reducing power's exercise, so the exercise of power becomes less violent or intense or rigorous. It is a form of resistance that attempts to tame power – to remove and reduce the more extreme moments of the exercise of power. Examples of this form of resistance would be more public than those associated with stabilising resistance: so marches, public protests, or any public expressions of resistance could fall within this type. These are acts of resistance which seek to place non-normative ideals in the public domain. The anti-war demonstrations across the UK in 2003 before the US–UK-led invasion of Iraq, for example – which were the largest public protests in UK history – were a public expression of dissatisfaction with the government's decisions in relation to starting a war. Although the protest did not prevent the state from exercising its power, arguably the display of resistance to this exercise of power shaped discourse around the Iraq war, and ensured that the government had to continually engage with public resistance to the invasion and subsequent occupation.

Annual gay pride marches could be another example of this form of resistance, as they are public displays of non-normative sexuality.[8] Other examples could include calling civil partnership 'marriage', therefore undermining the distinction that was created by the state between same and different sex legally recognised relationships; or prison riots, where prisoners use the only means available to them to resist the disciplinary power of the state (see Carrabine, 2004). Or moderating resistance could include individuals, pressure groups or charities challenging the decisions of public bodies – for example the Alzheimer's society campaign against the decision by the National Institute for Clinical Excellence (NICE) that £2.50 a day was too much to spend on a drug that can help people in the early to moderate stages of dementia; or the campaign by women with early-stage breast cancer to get the NHS to fund Herceptin, an expensive new drug that could have potentially life-saving effects, at a point when the drug was not licensed (by the state) for that stage of the disease.

As these examples illustrate, modifying forms of resistance do not necessarily have immediate transformative effects on power relations, and they do not prevent the exercise of power. They also do not necessarily have the effect of ending relations of subordination, but they do highlight public antipathy to the decisions of governmental actors, and therefore must have some impact on the effects of power relations in a democratic society. Unlike stabilising forms of resistance, moderating resistance may not exist in all power relations, but when it does, it can be potentially (even if only in minor ways, or over an extended period of time) transformative of power relations.

Fracturing resistance

The third form of resistance I have identified is where the flow of power is fractured or broken completely. My use of the word fracture here is important as, like a broken bone, power relations could 'heal' completely after a fracture, with no lasting effect, or they could be changed in unpredictable and unexpected ways. This is perhaps the least common example of resistance, while concurrently being the form of resistance most often associated with the word – in that resistance is most often described as such when it has revolutionary aims. The sorts of resistance that cause fracture could most easily be exemplified through violence or riots,[9] although any form of resistance that is explicitly concerned with rebellious acts could be described as 'fracturing resistance'. So, any action requiring (fairly immediate) engagement with the resistors' actions by government or other state actors could potentially be captured by this type of resistance. Examples of resistance causing fracture would include the violent protests against the publication of cartoons depicting the prophet Mohammed as a terrorist by Muslim demonstrators around the world in early 2006, or the riots in Paris in October and November 2005.

An important facet of fracturing resistance, as I conceptualise it, is that it requires substantive and fairly immediate engagement by the state with the resistor's actions. Continuing with the example of the Paris riots in 2005, a surge of violence (sparked by a combination of insults directed at the residents of particular suburbs and the death of two teenagers) resulted in a number of different forms of engagement by the state. The first response was that of the police – through a politically motivated 'zero tolerance' approach – leading to an escalation of violence on both sides. After a few days, the state authorised a number of emergency powers, including curfews and bans on public meetings, in an attempt to bring the violence to an end. Eventually, the violence died down, whether as a result of the emergency powers or as the natural end to the protests, and the President pledged to create opportunities for young people as a way to prevent further violence (BBC News, 2005). Initially, it would seem that the violent protests did nothing other than engage the state in a form of 'war' – with citizens battling against police. Next, the state resorted to exercising juridical or sovereign power, by enacting new laws in order to attempt to contain the violence, to which resistance was more difficult, as the consequences to individuals would have been more severe. In the end, however, the type of power that was used was disciplinary power, as a pledge to create opportunities for young people from deprived areas was the ultimate outcome. The resistance therefore 'fractured' power relations, in that a change to government policy in favour of the resistors was the way that this crisis ended. Whether the announced policy changes would actually produce any real effects on social exclusion is another question, of course, and it remains to be seen whether this fracture will heal with no lasting consequence, or whether the resistance movement has achieved a radical change in the exercise of power.

A very different example of fracturing resistance could be the San Francisco same-sex marriages of February 2004. In this example, there was no violence associated with the resistance; it was a purely peaceful form of 'civil disobedience'. Around 4,000 lesbian and gay couples were married between

12 February and 11 March 2004, after the city's mayor decided to test California law by issuing marriage licences to same-sex couples.[10] These couples, and the mayor himself can be considered as resisting the hetero-normative definition of marriage (Nicol & Smith, 2008). Later that year, all these marriages were annulled, after the California Supreme Court ruled that the mayor had acted out with his powers in issuing the marriage licences. I use this as a second example of resistance causing fracture as it is important to show that it is not only violence that can cause the state to become immediately engaged with the resistant action. In this example, again, the state resorted to judicial power in order to curb the resistance. The city was forced to stop issuing marriage licences on 12 March 2004 by a court injunction, and then all the marriages that had been performed were annulled in August 2004. Although this resistance was not effective in changing the laws relating to marriage in California, it is still an example of fracturing resistance because engagement with the resistance was needed in order to reinstate the (sovereign) power of the state.[11] This example also highlights again the ways in which juridical power is much less open to resistance than disciplinary mechanisms of power – as it was courts, and law, that ended this episode of resistance, while it was disciplinary mechanisms of power which allowed the resistance to occur; the mayor of San Francisco used an individual act of resistance to precipitate the whole series of events.

It is important to note that I do not conceptualise these three 'types' of resistance as distinct, mutually exclusive forms of the exercise of resistant power, and I acknowledge that it may be difficult to categorise different resistant acts as particular 'types' of resistance. The boundaries are not concrete, and there will always be actions that could be described as any of the different types, or where contextualising 'resistance' in space and time blurs the boundaries. My aim in creating this tripartite typography of resistance, therefore, is to highlight the interlinked nature of the concepts of power and resistance, to provide a method for differentiating between resistant actions, and to move away from understandings of (counter-hegemonic) resistance that are solely concerned with transgression and/or revolutionary change.

One way of conceptualising the interaction of different forms of resistance, legal consciousness and lesbian and gay struggles, is to take a historical look at the ways lesbians and gay men challenged the disciplinary power of the state in relation to the criminalisation of homosexuality.[12] Criminalisation of same-sex sexual activity does not, and has never actually prevented it from taking place (just as the defining of other behaviours as criminal rarely, if ever, prevents people from doing them). Rather, where homosexual sexual activity is criminalised, the practice of it becomes barely visible, secretive and 'underground'. Specific examples of this can be found in the history of lesbians and gay men in Britain prior to the decriminalisation of (male) homosexual acts in 1967.[13] According to historical accounts of early lesbian and gay communities in the UK, there was a thriving underground nightlife in Britain's cities

(Jivani, 1997), where lesbians and gay men congregated in clubs, socialised, danced and generally lived within their own social norms, for example, the requirement that lesbians be either butch or femme, or the development of Polari.[14] In many respects, the everyday experience of this 'underground' scene fits with the 'against the law' schema of legal consciousness. This 'underground' scene overall can be described as resistant, in that it existed despite the criminal sanctions that could potentially be used against those who were members of this community. I would describe this as a form of 'stabilising resistance' because the lesbian and gay scene existed within and alongside, but largely separate from, wider heterosexual society.

The underground nature of the lesbian and gay scene prior to decriminalisation did not mean, however, that it was not subject to the disciplinary power of the state. Police raids were common, and even though people in lesbian and gay clubs were seldom arrested, they were subjected to regular harassment by the police (Jivani, 1997). The continuing existence of the scene in the face of police harassment, and the fact that people who had been bullied, harassed or held overnight in police cells returned to the bars seems to be more like 'moderating' than 'stabilising' resistance. By moderating resistance in this context, I mean that the commonplace nature of police harassment of lesbian and gay nightclubs and the repetitive and predictable nature of raids (so the clientele knew that they were unlikely to be prosecuted) worked to moderate the effects of the exercise of power by the police. This therefore reduced the overall effect of police power, taming the ferocity of the police actions and paving the way for more acts of resistance.

The most famous example of the results of this sort of police harassment of lesbians and gay men leads us into my third 'type' of resistance, fracturing resistance. The Stonewall Riots of 1969 in Greenwich Village, New York, are commonly seen as the birthplace of the gay liberation movement.[15] Eventually police harassment of the clientele of the Stonewall Inn became too much for its regulars, and they fought back (resisted). Jivani (1997) describes the events through the words of an eye witness to the Stonewall Riots:

> What had happened was that gay men and lesbians suddenly discovered that they didn't have to put up with the harassment ... some hundred people were being chased ... by two cops, someone in the crowd suddenly realized the unequal odds and started yelling 'There are only two of 'em! Catch em!'
>
> (Jivani, 1997: 160)

The sudden switch to violence (fighting back) against police harassment therefore created a fracture in the relations of power. Within a month of the riots, the original Gay Liberation Front was set up, and was followed by similar organisations in the UK. It is widely held that this moment of resistance, or 'fracture' paved the way for a more open and less underground lesbian and gay scene, as well as the more rights-orientated contemporary lesbian and gay social movements.

Theorising resistance: some caveats

My use of this example of the history of the lesbian and gay scene prior to the decriminalisation of homosexuality seems to show these three types of resistance in a linear progression, from stabilising through moderating to fracturing forms of resistance. I would not want to suggest, however, that this is necessarily the way resistance operates. Instead, my aim in using this example is to highlight the interlinked nature of resistance and power. Rather than being something external to and different from power, I see resistance as a way of describing a different exercise of power – where those generally conceptualised as 'powerless' seek to produce effects on those conceptualised as 'powerful' in order to change existing power relations. So, the Stonewall Riots can be viewed from the perspective of a shift from two 'powerful' police officers chasing 100 'powerless' lesbians and gay men to 100 'powerful' lesbians and gay men chasing two 'powerless' police officers. Lesbian and gay resistance to police harassment, therefore, became an exercise of power. This example also highlights another important point about the relationship between power and resistance. Although 'resistance' is most often conceptualised as a counter-hegemonic practice, it need not be thought of solely in those terms. There is no real reason to suppose that the 'powerful' in seeking to discipline the 'powerless' are doing anything other than resisting the exercise of power by the 'powerless'. Examples of this sort of resistance can also be found in the 'backlash' against feminism and positive legal change for women, lesbians and gay men (see e.g. Oakley & Mitchell, 1997).

Susan Heath, for example, writing about living as a lesbian during the 'backlash' against feminism in the US, argues that 'it is the prospect of women, lesbian or not, becoming powerful that has produced the backlash against us' (Heath, 1997: 103). Perhaps more interestingly, from the perspective of current lesbian and gay struggles, the 'backlash' against spousal recognition for same-sex couples that took place in Canada (during the period of change eventually resulting in equal access to legal marriage for same- and different-sex couples) highlights the interlinked nature of power/resistance. During the period leading up to the introduction of same-sex marriage in Canada, conservative groups and individuals launched a two-pronged form of resistance to same-sex marriage (Boyd & Young, 2003). First they (ultimately unsuccessfully) sought to insulate marriage from same-sex couples through 'defence of marriage' legislative acts defining marriage as a purely heterosexual institution. This form of 'resistance' seems to be one that can only be an exercise of power; surely only the powerful have the ability to amend existing and introduce new legislation for their own ends. The second prong of conservative resistance, however, which argued that all economically interdependent relationships should have access to domestic partnership benefits, was a more complex technique of resistance (Boyd & Young, 2003: 768–69).[16] This example brings into focus one of the difficulties of considering 'backlash' as a unidirectional attack from the powerful on the powerless: that it disguises the fluidity and contradictions inherent in conflict between social movements (Herman, 1997). Reading the movement towards same-sex marriage in Canada, it is very difficult to point to one 'group' and label them as powerful and then point to another as powerless; or even to say this group are exercising their power, while this group are exercising resistance because all involved seemed to be engaging in both 'power' and 'resistance'.

It is clear, therefore, that resistance may be better conceptualised as a form of power exercised against the normative framework of an oppositional[17] group (or individual) than as an activity separate and distinct from power. By 'oppositional' I mean in the sense of the group or individual taking a different view from the group or individual who is taken as the focus of attention, rather than 'power' always being conceptualised as the domain of the dominant/majority/powerful group, and resistance as the domain of the oppressed/minority/powerless group. My aim, therefore, in this theoretical approach to power and resistance is threefold: first, to avoid the reification of resistance as always a 'good thing' within oppositional struggle (see Abu-Lughod, 1990); second, to bring into clearer focus the relational nature of power, without sidelining the primacy of inequality and relationships of domination and subjection; and third, to provide a lexicon for differentiating between, describing and understanding different positions within contested power relations. Conceptualising power and resistance in this way also prevents us from seeing only the 'power' side of the equation, so that individuals become docile bodies who are acted on, without any possibility for agency; and also assuming that resistance, *qua* resistance, has one static and specific aim (e.g. counter-hegemony).

A final caveat in my consideration of power/resistance is that I must stress that I do not believe that all forms of power are able to be read as resistance, and that there are, therefore, limitations to this approach. This interlocking web of power and resistance within power relations is limited to those forms of power that Foucault described as the 'new' forms of power. Thus, juridical power and other 'old' conceptions of power as domination (e.g. sovereign power or war) remain outside this theory of power and resistance. As Smart (1989) argued, law 'is able to make … claims to truth … and in so doing exercises a power that is not under threat' (Smart, 1989: 14). Indeed, the continuing existence of these 'old' forms of power complicates the picture somewhat. If we look back to the San Francisco marriages of 2004 (a series of events that I used as an example of 'fracturing' resistance) we see that this exercise of resistant power, and the associated effects this produced on society, were brought to a close by the legal system. The issue of marriage licences to same-sex couples was stopped by a court injunction, and the marriages were all annulled by the state Supreme Court through the exercise of juridical power. By excluding juridical or sovereign power from my tripartite exploration of resistance, I do not want to suggest that law is omnipotent or unable to be resisted. Rather, I simply want to note that more conventional ways of thinking about challenging legal decisions (judicial review, appeal cases, parliamentary lobbying, citizen ballot initiatives, etc.) are perhaps more effective methods of challenging the official law produced by courts and legislature.

Power, resistance and legal consciousness

I conclude this chapter by offering an overview of how my approach to power and resistance takes forward understandings of power and resistance in legal consciousness studies, through an exploration of the issues raised by same-sex marriage. I argued in Chapter 2 that legal consciousness studies would benefit in general from incorporating a more developed understanding of power relations, and in particular, the resistant focus of Ewick and Silbey's (1998) 'against the law' schema would benefit from developing an explicitly more nuanced understanding of the way people experience power and resistance in their everyday lives.

If we think, for example, about same-sex marriage and the various arguments that have been put forward both in support of the legal recognition of lesbian and gay relationships and against the normalising, assimilationist aspects of marriage/civil partnership, then the way Foucault's analysis of power provides space for resistance becomes a little clearer. Butler (2004) argues that it is possible to read through Foucault (2002) that his theory of power becomes linked with recognition:

> Power can act upon a subject only if it imposes norms of recognisability on that subject's existence. Further, the subject must desire recognition, and so find himself or herself fundamentally attached to the categories that guarantee social existence ... We might say that conforming to the norm allows one to become, for the moment, fully recognisable, but since the norms at issue are constrained, one sees there, in the conformity, the sign of one's constraint. Indeed, perhaps we can speculate that the moment of resistance, of opposition, emerges precisely when we find ourselves attached to our constraint
>
> (Butler, 2004: 190–91)

So, to draw this back to my area of concern in this book, the moment law begins to define what it means to be lesbian or gay through the solidification and crystallisation of same-sex relationships (whether that be through marriage, civil partnership, domestic partnerships and so on), then resistance to law becomes possible. Resistance can only happen from within normative frameworks, not from outside. When positioned outside law, when formal equality is denied, resistance to the power of law has to be focused on gaining entry to law, otherwise resistance to (hetero)normative structures such as marriage has little potential to significantly impact on or transform the institution.

What, then, does this mean for lesbian and gay legal consciousness? In order to understand the ways in which lesbians and gay men are positioned 'against the law' the complex interplay of power and resistance is fundamental. Whereas the resistance described in Ewick and Silbey's (1998) text was concerned predominantly with ways of circumventing and avoiding law, lesbians and gay men need first to be recognised by law, before there is any substantive possibly of resistance that has the capacity to transform either explicitly legal frameworks, or normative conventions. The recognition and regulation of lesbian and gay families therefore allows the possibilities of resistance to come to the fore in a way that social movement organising for formally equal rights cannot. I return to the implications of this throughout the empirical chapters that follow but for now, I just want to take a look at how resistance becomes possible through legal recognition, by exploring the recent UK same-sex marriage case, *Wilkinson* v *Kitzinger*.[18]

Susan Wilkinson and Celia Kitzinger were legally married in British Columbia, Canada, on 26 August 2003, at which time there was no legal recognition of same-sex relationships in the UK. Their marriage is in accordance with, and is valid under the law of British Columbia. They applied to the High Court for a declaration that their marriage was valid under English law. The legal arguments in the case are not relevant to my discussion here,[19] but the reasoning for denying their claim provided by Sir Mark Potter, President of the Family Law Division, is key. Of particular interest is his 'justification' for the existence of discrimination under Article 14 ECHR[20]:

> It is apparent that the majority of people, or at least of governments, not only in England but Europe-wide, regard marriage as an age-old institution, valued and valuable, respectable and respected, as a means not only of encouraging monogamy but also the procreation of children and their development and nurture in a family unit (or 'nuclear family') in which both maternal and paternal influences are available in respect of their nurture and upbringing … If marriage is, by longstanding definition and acceptance, a formal relationship between a man and a woman, primarily (though not exclusively) with the aim of producing and rearing children as I have described it, and if that is the institution contemplated and safeguarded by Art. 12, then to accord a same-sex relationship the title and status of marriage would be to fly in the face of the Convention as well as to fail to recognize physical reality (at paras 118–20).

In this decision, we see that the legal 'truth' of marriage, as perceived by Potter J, is that it is a heterosexual, monogamous, life-long union, which is legally supported for the benefit of children of heterosexual parents. Leaving aside the obviously problematic nature of this 'justification' from both a legal and a feminist perspective,[21] the meanings attached to marriage here provide an interesting case study for considering the power of law to define the parameters of social structures. Drawing on Butler's (2004) reading of Foucault, the claim to recognition inherent in this marriage case can be read as an attempt to bring same-sex couples inside the norm of marriage. The court's denial of this same-sex couple's entry to the institution of marriage therefore serves to insulate marriage from the inevitable transformations (removing the heterosexual imperative) as well as other potential change that would flow from the recognition of same-sex marriage. By refusing recognition of same-sex marriage in this way, this lesbian couple are not only categorised as 'civil partners' rather than married, but are also refused their recognisability as subjects, or their admissibility into the norm of marriage.

The potential for resistance is not, however, fully constrained by this judicial denial of same-sex marriage. One can imagine a same-sex couple, who were married in one of the several countries worldwide that allow same-sex marriage, describing themselves as married, irrespective of whether their marriage is legally recognised as such in their country of residence. This could be described as stabilising resistance: they have a valid legal marriage in the country in which they married, they hold a marriage certificate, but their marriage exists outside the normative frame of marriage in their country of residence. By marrying in a different jurisdiction, they can be seen to resist the law by defying the limits of the norm. So a same-sex couple in a situation like that of Wilkinson and Kitzinger is, I would say, in a prime position to resist a number of different aspects of law's power.

Approaching this claim for recognition of a validly constituted same-sex marriage through the lens of legal consciousness, as I have proposed to develop it, allows for a much more nuanced understanding of the various power relations at work in this case. The parties can be described as holding a 'before the law' legal consciousness: they recognise the power that law has to recognise (or not) their relationship. They can also be said to be drawing on 'with the law' legal consciousness: by asking the courts to recognise their Canadian marriage, they are attempting to use the legal system for their own ends. They have access to legal representation and are attempting to resist the 'downgrading' of their marriage to a civil partnership. The parties' actions could also be described as moderating resistance, as by bringing their legal case, they emphatically wished to bring the issue of same-sex marriage into the public domain (Kitzinger & Wilkinson, 2004a). Another reading of this case is to think of it as an example of an attempt to resist the continued hetero-normativity of marriage, following the enactment of the Civil Partnership Act 2004. While the attempt to challenge the heteronormativity of marriage was perhaps ultimately unsuccessful, the heteronormative constructions of marriage and the family underpinning the judgement at the very least brought these ideas firmly into the public domain. It is also possible to describe this case as an example of fracturing resistance. By challenging the state to recognise a same-sex relationship in a way different from that which had been very recently legislated for, the applicants forced the State (both the Court and a branch of the Government) to engage with their issue. Indeed, as with all decisions of first impression, there was certainly a moment in which it was possible that the outcome of the case could have been different. As such, this provides a more concrete example of how taking a plural approach to legal consciousness, with a fine-grained analysis of the concepts of power and resistance develops the potential of legal consciousness studies, exposing not only the resistance inherent in 'against the law' legal consciousness, but also the power relations at work in all three of Ewick and Silbey's (1998) schema.

Concluding remarks

In this chapter, I have set out a method for providing a more nuanced exploration of power and resistance within legal consciousness studies. I explored the interlinked concepts of power and resistance, focusing on Foucault's 'new' conception of power as a technical, creative and productive mechanism and the implications this has for theorising power relations through a consideration of heteronormativity, governmentality and resistance. I outlined an approach to thinking about resistance that highlights the ways that resistance can be thought of as a form of power. I described three different types of resistance: stabilising resistance, moderating resistance and fracturing resistance. Stabilising resistance can be thought of as a type of resistance that exists alongside everyday disciplinary mechanisms of power; the everyday forms of resistance that work to stabilise the exercise of power. Moderating resistance is used to describe explicit forms of resistance that take place in public space – marches, demonstrations and other public expressions of dissatisfaction with the exercise of power by the 'powerful' – which seeks to change the course of the exercise of power, to tame power. Finally, I use fracturing resistance to describe resistant acts that cause momentary breaks in the flow of power; resistance that creates a space for a reversal or major change in power relations. Fracturing resistance does not necessarily have to *actually* change or break power; rather resistance of this type seeks to highlight not only those episodes of resistance that result in revolution, but also those that could (potentially) have had a major impact on power relations, whether they are ultimately successful or not.

In subsequent chapters, I develop and apply these concepts of power and resistance alongside the theoretical and methodological approach of legal consciousness studies, through an exploration of the place of law in the everyday lives of lesbians and gay men. In Chapter 5, for example, I argue that lesbian and gay parents often have to resist their legal and social categorisation as 'second-class' or 'illegitimate' parents, and that they do this through strategies of stabilising and moderating resistance. Also, in Chapter 6, I show that lesbians and gay men are resistant to the increased regulation that the introduction of legally recognised relationships has facilitated and I argue that stabilising and moderating forms of resistance are more easily found in lesbian and gay accounts of their lives than examples of fracturing resistance. In the next chapter, I explore lesbian and gay legal consciousness through analysis of a large-scale, quantitative and qualitative online survey of attitudes to the legal recognition of same-sex relationships.

Notes

1 For detailed consideration of Foucault's analytics of power as it relates to feminisms and lesbian and gay struggles, see *inter alia*: Bell (1993); Cooper (1995b); McNay (1992); Sawicki (1991); Smart (1989).

2 There is not space in this chapter to rehearse these critiques in detail – for an overview, see McLaren (2004).

3 By 'legal institutions', I mean not only courts and governmental law makers, but also the statutory and common law regimes under which they operate.

4 As evidenced by the wide disparities between, for example, the regulation of sexuality in the UK (civil partnership), Canada (equal access to marriage), and the US (with limited recognition of same-sex relationships, and the recent raft of State-level constitutional amendments defining marriage as heterosexual).

5 For example, through the repeal of anti-gay laws such as Section 28, or the reform of adoption to allow for joint and second parent adoption by same-sex couples.

6 I explore this issue in much more detail in Chapters 4 and 6.

7 I have dramatically over-simplified the complex physics of electromagnetism for my own purposes – but this is a metaphor, and not meant to be relied on in the creation of electronic circuits.

8 This example is complicated by the ways that many pride marches have been colonised by commercial interests, through sponsorship, and where they have local government support. Governmental support for such events can often be explained through the material benefits that large public events bring to urban space, because they bring people into the area, creating wealth and spending through accommodation and other 'tourist' expenditure (see Bell & Binnie, 2001). I return to issues of sexuality, space and governmentality in Chapters 6 and 7.

9 I would exclude prison riots from this form of resistance because, as Carrabine (2004) argues, prisoners are very limited in the opportunities for resistance that are open to them and the context of a prison riot cannot lead to a true break in the flow of power.

10 This example is, of course, complicated by the fact that the San Francisco same-sex marriages can also be read as resulting from an instance of resistance by one governmental institution (city of San Francisco) against another governmental institution (state of California).

11 The subsequent events around same-sex marriage in California, including the May 2008 court decision (*In re Marriage Cases* [2008]43 Cal.4th 757 [76 Cal.Rptr.3d 683, 183 P.3d 384]) which held that limiting marriage to heterosexual couples was in contravention of the state Constitution, the enactment of Proposition 8, amending the state Constitution to outlaw same-sex marriage in November 2008, and the ongoing legal challenges to Proposition 8 are also important in demonstrating the ongoing relations of power and resistance which characterise the current same-sex marriage movement in the US.

12 In this example, my main focus is on the ways this worked in most parts of 'the West', as it must be remembered that there are still a number of countries worldwide where homosexuality is not only still criminalised, but is also punishable in the most extreme cases by either corporal or capital punishment. It is also important to note that often lesbian sexuality was/is not necessarily criminalised in the same way as gay male sexuality.
13 Sexual Offences Act 1967.
14 Polari was a secret language used (predominantly by gay men in theatrical circles) to prevent outsiders from understanding what was being said.
15 It is important to note that clientele of the Stonewall Inn at the time of the riot included many of the most marginalised groups in the underground lesbian and gay community of the day – drag queens, transvestites, butch lesbians and homeless youth. For detailed historical accounts of the Stonewall Riots, and their impact on the emergent LGBT movements, see Carter (2004) and Duberman (1993).
16 Paradoxically, this argument is one which is used in similar (if not quite identical) ways by the more radical writers on same-sex marriage and relationship recognition (see Barker, 2006; Polikoff, 2003).
17 My use of the word 'oppositional' is not intended to imply a dichotomised or binary power relation, rather as a way of describing a multitude of differential positions and perspectives.
18 [2006] EWHC 2022 (Fam).
19 For a detailed analysis of many the issues raised by *Wilkinson* v *Kitzinger*, see Harding (2007).
20 'The enjoyment of the rights and freedoms set forth in this Convention shall be secured without discrimination on any ground such as sex, race, colour, language, religion, political or other opinion, national or social origin, association with a national minority, property, birth or other status.'
21 For more on this issue, see Harding (2007).

Chapter 4

From 'outlaws' to 'in-laws'?

I now turn to the empirical analysis that forms the backbone of this book. Through analysis of the qualitative comments from a large-scale online survey of attitudes to the legal recognition of same-sex relationships, I argue that in discourse around the introduction of same-sex marriage and civil partnership, formal equality is prioritised and reified by lesbians and gay men. Further, I contend that lesbians and gay men have complex perspectives on the relationship between law and social change. Finally, I argue that rights discourse and citizenship claims are common in lesbian and gay attitudes to the legal recognition of their relationships. I demonstrate that the 'right to marry' is seen by many as an important indicator of lesbian and gay human rights. I further argue that citizenship claims both facilitate the normalisation and assimilation of lesbians and gay men into heteronormative society and simultaneously draw attention to legalised forms of discrimination.

Throughout this analysis, I weave the theoretical approaches outlined in previous chapters into the empirical analysis. I argue that working my three 'types' of resistance (stabilising resistance, moderating resistance and fracturing resistance) into the 'against the law' category helps legal consciousness studies to be sensitive to the specific issues raised by sexuality. I demonstrate, through my analysis of the data presented here, that stabilising and moderating forms of resistance are drawn on by lesbians and gay men in their attitudes to, and engagement with, issues around the legal recognition of relationships.

Method: online methodology and legal consciousness

The qualitative data I analyse here originate from a large-scale multi-method online study of lesbians and gay men's perceptions of and attitudes towards equality and the legal recognition of same-sex relationships.[1] I had several reasons for using an internet-based form of data collection, including the potential for: access to a diverse range of participants, international scope, anonymity and confidentiality and access to a large number of respondents.[2] It is widely accepted within lesbian and gay social science research that achieving a 'representative sample' of lesbians and gay men is not a realistic possibility (Fish, 1999; Herek & Berrill, 1992), therefore, two methods of sampling were used: strategic opportunistic sampling; and snowball sampling. Strategic opportunistic sampling consisted of sending a recruitment email to 24 lesbian or gay organisations or email lists with a potential interest in the subject. Snowball sampling began with 20 emails to other contacts. The website was available online for six weeks (from April to June 2004).[3]

The survey was split into three sections. The first part of the survey was concerned with the relationship status of respondents, including whether or not they were in a same-sex relationship, the duration of their current relationship, how they would define their relationship, whether or not they lived with their partner, whether they had performed any form of commitment ceremony with their partner and general attitudes towards marriage. The final section of the survey included demographic options about gender, sexuality, age, location, and occupation. The main section of the survey contained 12 substantive statements that captured a range of (pro and anti) opinion about legal aspects of same-sex partnership recognition. In the quantitative portion of the survey, respondents were asked to indicate their view on a forced-choice Likert-type rating scale from strongly agree to strongly disagree. A total of 1538 respondents completed the questionnaire, the majority of whom identified as lesbian or gay (69.4%, n = 1050). Responses came from 27 different countries worldwide, with the majority from Australia, Canada, the UK and the US.

The quantitative results from the survey highlighted a number of key findings, including: first, that the legal recognition of same-sex relationships is seen to be a highly important equality issue for lesbians and gay men. Second, there was significantly more support from lesbians and gay men for marriage than for civil partnership. However, respondents who live in Canada or the US tended to support same-sex marriage more strongly than respondents from elsewhere in the world.[4] Third, liberal formal equality arguments were better understood and more accepted than substantive or radical equality arguments, and finally, contrary to previous assumptions concerning the differing attitudes of lesbians and gay men toward same-sex marriage, responses did not vary significantly by gender.[5]

After each quantitative statement there was space for respondents' to provide more in-depth responses to explain or justify their choice. Respondents were free to write as much or as little as they wished in the qualitative part of the survey and it is these responses that are my focus here. The survey generated a large number of comments, including lengthy narratives from respondents, which help to give an insight into *why* these lesbians and gay men were so supportive of the legal recognition of same-sex relationships generally, and specifically, same-sex marriage. For the purposes of this chapter and in order to gain a 'whole picture' view of these respondents' attitudes to the legal recognition of same-sex relationships, the qualitative responses analysed were limited to those comments from respondents who identified as lesbian (n = 173) or gay (n = 145) and who gave a qualitative response to all of the substantive questions. A total of 318 qualitative questionnaire responses (resulting in 737 pages of single-spaced data) were examined using thematic analysis (Braun & Clarke, 2006) to identify dominant themes within the comments. As is common with thematic analysis, the themes were selected not simply because of their prevalence in this data set, but rather because the themes demonstrate patterns emerging from the survey, which provide insights into lesbians and gay men's views about the regulation of relationships in their everyday lives.

The survey participants who are quoted in this chapter have a range of demographic characteristics. Table 4.1 shows the overall demographic characteristics of the participants quoted in this chapter. The demographics of the qualitative respondents broadly map on to the overall demographics of the full online survey sample, with: slightly more lesbian (n = 173, 54.4%) than gay (n = 145, 45.6%) respondents; the majority of respondents falling into the age range of between 25 and 44; and an over-representation from the 'professional' and 'student' occupational categories. Overall, however, the qualitative respondents have a broad range of demographic characteristics which therefore provide varied perspectives on the legal recognition of same-sex relationships in different legal systems.

It is important to note that this survey does not conform to the methodological approach of much of the recent legal consciousness literature.[6] Analysis of these data, however, shows that it is possible to glean some insights into lesbian and gay legal consciousness from data such as these. This approach therefore expands the methodological reach of legal consciousness studies. These data do, however, raise some questions about the ways in which the three 'types' of legal consciousness (Ewick & Silbey, 1998) 'fit' with lesbians and gay men's attitudes to and perceptions of law. I return to these issues in the conclusion.

Attitudes to and perceptions of same-sex relationship recognition

Five themes relevant to this study of legal consciousness were evident in these data. The first, and dominant, theme was a major attachment to arguments about the sameness of same-and different-sex relationships, which manifested itself in the form of support for formal equality and the entrenched nature of formal equality infused all of the responses. A second theme was the perceived power of legal change to create social change, and to 'normalise' same-sex relationships. The third theme concerned the idea that civil partnerships were not 'enough' for equality. A fourth theme evident in these data was that respondents often called on human rights rhetoric or discourses of common

Table 4.1 Demographic information for qualitative respondents

Demographic category	*Sub-category*	*Number*	*Percentage (%)*
Gender	Female	171	53.8
	Male	141	44.3
	Trans	6	1.9
	Total	318	100.0
Sexuality	Lesbian	173	54.4
	Gay	145	45.6
	Total	318	100.0
Age	Under 18	6	1.9
	18–24	46	14.5
	25–34	99	31.1
	35–44	81	25.5
	45–54	58	18.2
	55–64	24	7.5
	Over 65	4	1.3
	Total	318	100.0
Occupation	Not answered	3	0.9
	Admin/clerical	21	6.6
	Manual	2	0.6
	Professional	179	56.3
	Student	61	19.2
	Unemployed	6	1.9
	Retired	15	4.7
	Other	31	9.7
	Total	318	100.0
Country	Australia	102	32.1
	Canada	101	31.8
	UK	41	12.9
	USA	55	17.3
	Other EU	12	3.8
	Other rest of world	7	2.2
	Total	318	100.0

humanity as justification for the legal recognition of same-sex relationships. Finally, respondents invoked discourses of citizenship as another rationale for lesbian and gay legal equality.

Formal equality

The most common theme within respondents' views about the legal recognition of same-sex relationships was that formal equality should be the governing principle of relationship recognition and within legal frameworks more generally. For example, several of these respondents used statements like:[7]

— Everyone should be treated the same (R593);
— We are equal if we get the same legal rights as heterosexuals (R73); or
— Love is not different just because it is between two people of the same sex. Love is love is love (R485).

Statements of this nature implicitly accept that in order for lesbians and gay men to be eligible for the equal protection of law, the similarities between lesbians, gay men and heterosexual people must be emphasised. Interestingly, reliance on formal equality arguments such as these did not seem to vary between lesbian and gay respondents; there was no evidence in these data of a gendered difference in ways of conceptualising the meaning of equality. The last of these three examples highlights another type of engagement with the principles of equality: that words like 'love', 'equality' or 'equal rights' are self-defining, and therefore their meanings are inevitable. Tautological statements like these ('equality is equality', 'love is love', 'equal rights are equal rights') draw attention to the ways in which these concepts are entrenched within lesbian and gay rights struggles. The common perception is that they do and can only have one meaning; that equality means being treated the same, or that love between two women or two men is *the same* as love between a woman and a man, or that equal rights means that legal rights should not be in any way contingent on personal status, but rather always applicable to all.

As well as focusing on sameness as an essential component of equality, some respondents expressed the need for formal equality in terms of the lack of acceptability of different treatment, for example:

— As the saying goes, 'different is never equal'. If any distinction is made between the legal recognition of same-sex relationships and heterosexual relationships under the law, it will leave room for discrimination (R 103);
— It's important not to have different systems, different terminology as again, it emphasizes differences, 2nd class status & not equality which is the real issue (R180);
— It is the continuous labelling of difference that is most harmful to our community and the way it perceives itself and dangerous in the eyes of the heterosexual community and the way it perceives us. Diversity within the same category is important – creating new categories justifies discrimination based on difference (as recognized in the different label). Human should not be divided into black, white, yellow. Marriage should not be divided into gay, straight. Individual should not be divided into man, woman. The labelling of difference makes people think that way (R1321).

This emphasis on difference and different treatment as incompatible with equality is interesting because it draws attention to the ways that particular arguments for formal equality are reproduced in different social movement struggles. The comment from R1321 (a gay man from Australia) is interesting as he draws attention to the ways that sameness within equality is different from issues of diversity; he articulates that the naming of difference contributes to harmful discrimination, rather than promoting diversity.

Another facet of the ways in which these respondents conceptualised formal equality in relationship recognition was through comparisons with other minority groups. Several respondents from North America, for example, also analogised the exclusion of same-sex couples from marriage to race discrimination, anti-miscegentation laws or apartheid systems:

— It really isn't any different than a white man or woman marrying a man or woman who is black, mexican, chinese or any other minority. Why do people have to make such a big deal about it just because they don't understand it? (R1386);

— Unless it is called 'marriage', it is not equal, fair, just. It would be like saying black people can't marry but they can have a civil union. No one would stand for that (R440);

— Any term other than marriage is not equality. It's like saying to blacks in the American South in the 1960's, you can ride on our bus but you have to sit at the back of the bus and leave the front for those of us who are straight. Equality means equality. If heterosexuals have a problem with the term 'marriage', they are hiding behind historical prejudice and bigotry. Future generations will judge them accordingly (R418).

Comparisons like these are common in some of the academic literature on same-sex marriage (see e.g. Cox, 2000; Eskridge, 1996; Koppelman, 1988; Strasser, 1997; Wolfson, 2005). Barbara Cox (2000), for example, argues that the denial of same-sex marriage can be compared to race segregation policies in the US because 'centuries of power, control and social and psychological affirmation provide both whites and heterosexuals a comfort and expectation of rights benefits and protections' (Cox, 2000: 126). She then goes on to say that the creation of civil unions (specifically in relation to the Vermont civil unions) is a harm that is only thinly disguised as equality and 'having seen the negative effects of this "thin disguise" of equality in the race context, it is difficult to embrace the separate status offered by the Vermont Legislature' (Cox, 2000: 127–28). This particular analogy is controversial, however, with a number of commentators giving forceful reasons why restrictions on same-sex marriage cannot and should not be compared to anti-miscegenation laws (e.g. Coolidge, 1998; Halley, 1998).

The entrenched nature of formal equality within lesbian and gay struggles is understandable, especially given that lesbians and gay men have (so far) attained formal legal equality in very few jurisdictions across the world. This reification of formal equality, however, is somewhat problematic.

Experiences from other social movements, such as feminist and civil rights movements, show that formal equality is not the cure-all solution that reliance on the need for 'sameness' of legal provision may suggest (see e.g. Smart, 1989; Williams, 1992). The focus on formal equality in lesbian and gay struggles, therefore, may be more problematic than helpful. On a different view, it is difficult to conceptualise how any form of equality can be achieved where groups are not on an equivalent legal footing; substantive visions of equality build on, rather than replace, formal equality (Lessard, 2004). If the ultimate aim in egalitarian thinking is equality of power – more specifically the idea that no one should have 'an inherent right to impact more on their social and physical environment than anyone else' (Cooper, 2004: 77–78), then formal legal equality must be a necessary starting point.

Applying Ewick and Silbey's (1998) three schemas of legal consciousness[8] to these views about equality and the place of law in relationship recognition initially seems straightforward. For example, the 'before the law' type of legal consciousness is used by Ewick and Silbey to describe instances where the law is described as impartial, and that law 'achieves its impartiality and objectivity through a deliberate indifference to the particularities of biography or personality' (Ewick & Silbey, 1998: 76). Indifference to 'biography or personality' seems to be a strong reference to the need for formal equality before the law. It appears that these respondents were very clear that this impartial, objective law that is blind to difference is the ideal. By calling on ideas of blind justice, sameness of treatment and formal equality, these participants seem to view the power of law in a particular way. Rather than envisioning power as a relationship, the reification of formal equality seems to imply that 'law' has the 'power' to recognise the value of same-sex relationships, and therefore places emphasis on the juridical and sovereign power of law, rather than disciplinary power.

When it came to translating idealised notions of law into their own life situations, however, these respondents emphasised that, currently, the legal reality for lesbians and gay men is that the law is *not* blind to difference. Respondents achieved this by using terms like 'should' (e.g. R593) or 'if' (e.g. R73) to acknowledge the current limitations in legal 'protection' for same-sex relationships. These responses therefore show that these participants think that the law is currently not as 'just' or 'equal' as it 'should' be. This formulation of legal consciousness, then, seems to be closer to a 'with the law' consciousness, in that it is depicting the law as a terrain of contest, where lesbians and gay men are currently 'losers'. 'With the law' legal consciousness is defined by Ewick and Silbey as being 'less concerned about law's power than about the power of self or others to successfully deploy and engage with the law' (1998: 48). As discussed further in the next section, however, the ways in which lesbians and gay men formulate the relationship between positive legal change and social acceptance highlight that the 'with the law' type of legal consciousness does not necessarily 'fit' with lesbian and gay rights claims either. Rather, in spite of the entrenched nature of formal equality arguments in attitudes to same-sex marriage, these respondents' accounts are infused with forms of resistance. They resist the 'othering' of same-sex relationships by calling on entrenched conceptions of the power of law and the need for justice and fairness that is blind to difference, thus attempting to use the normative power of law to change law.

Legal change and social acceptance

The second theme in these respondents' accounts was the complex and contradictory relationship between social change and legal change. The relationship between legal change and social acceptance was described in three different ways by these respondents, all of which include an acknowledgement of the power and/or importance of law. First, legal change was conceptualised as a foundation for greater acceptance of lesbians and gay men in society. Second, positive legal change was described as evidence *of* social acceptance. Finally, some respondents reported that attaining legal rights was more important than achieving acceptance of lesbians and gay men in society.

The first of these conceptualisations of the relationship between legal change and social acceptance was highlighted through statements like:

— Acceptance by society can only come through recognition of our legal status (R81);
— You can't achieve societal acceptance when different laws apply for different people … it just emphasises difference (R180);
— Legal recognition would lead us to become accepted in society. If law reflects society, then by saying it's legal for gay couples to marry makes it 'socially acceptable' in turn (fingers crossed) (R1494).

These types of statement work on several different levels: they acknowledge the 'power' of law to determine what is, and is not, socially acceptable, while concurrently envisioning law as a separate and distinct entity from 'society'. Through the legal recognition of same-sex relationships, law is envisioned as something that is both important and capable of having the effect of normalising lesbians and gay men. For example:

— It's the laws that matter. But I guess the public view would be needing to see gay men and lesbians getting married for them to click 'oh, they are getting married, just like us, that makes them, us'(R812);
— Ultimately civil rights have everything to do with equality in the social sphere. As long as people are allowed and legally encouraged to see us as being lesser, they will be inclined to treat us that way. They will only begin to treat us equally (as in the case of women and people of colour) if they are legally required to (R592).

Comments like these also emphasise the ways in which 'laws' can impact on people's perceptions of who is 'the same', and therefore entitled to equal treatment. So, this first conceptualistion of the relationship between law and society in relation to positive legal change for lesbians and gay men highlights the perceived ability of legal change to influence public opinion. By telling people what to think, and delineating the extent of acceptable discrimination, these respondents posit that 'law' can have the effect of creating greater acceptance of marginalised individuals.

The second formulation of the relationship between law and society looks at this equation from the opposite angle: that rather than social acceptance following on from legal change, legal change only happens when 'society' already accepts lesbians and gay men as full members. The enactment of positive legal reform thus serves as evidence of greater acceptance. For example:

— Legal recognition IS-IS-IS 'being accepted in society' (R418);
— If society accepts lesbian & gay relationships then the law will follow (R714);
— If queers aren't accepted in society, then there's little point in working at a step up from that and trying to get our R'SHIPS accepted in society. Accept queers and there will be less problem getting legal recognition in the first place. then again, give us legal recognition of r'ship and we'll be a little protected against the unacceptance IN society (R967).

Statements of this kind seem to acknowledge that law is not the supreme, external body that has power to shape the views of society and decide what is 'objectively just' as envisioned in a 'before the law' legal consiousness. Instead, these statements acknowledge that 'society' has some impact on 'what the law is' and, that 'law' is reflective of 'society', rather then 'society' reflecting 'law'.

Finally, some respondents prioritised legal change over social acceptance, acknowledging that law does not have the capacity to change attitudes, but that it does have the ability to protect lesbians and gay men from discrimination and prejudice. For example:

— Some of society will never accept us ... just like other minorities ... at least this way we have legal rights (R844);
— There will always be people in this world that don't accept people who are different from them, but legal recognition will allow me to protect my loved ones, regardless of how someone else may feel about me (R532);
— I think that legalities and acceptance always have a tenuous relationship (that is, which one comes first?), however, if we wait until everyone in society is accepting of gays and lesbians before we achieve legal recognition, then it will never happen. We need to address both issues, in different but supporting ways. So, I think that, realistically, we need to

> keep pushing for rights and educate society along the way to also strive towards acceptance (R1345).

Statements such as these seem to conceptualise law as a weapon to be used against those who do not respect 'people who are different from them', or as a shield against arbitrary discrimination.

These three different conceptualisations of the relationship between legal change and social attitudes towards lesbians and gay men highlight some interesting points about lesbian and gay legal consciousness. Law has the 'power' to protect individuals against prejudice or discrimination, which seems to fit with a 'before the law' legal consciousness. But, as law's power (even after positive legal change) is not sufficient to achieve attitudinal change, a 'with the law' perspective is also evident. However, rather than these respondents being concerned with having the skills necessary to play the game of law, the need for legal change is emphasised as a precursor to full engagement with law. Arguably this shows evidence of a type of legal consciousness that is reminiscent of Ewick and Silbey's (1998) 'against the law' schema, as these respondents resist the current legal marginalisation of lesbians and gay men.

The form of resistance exemplified by these respondents' views about the relationship between legal and social change is most easily thought of as 'stabilising resistance',[9] in that it is resistance which does not necessarily have an immediate transformative effect, but rather it exists as a necessary element of power relations. That legal reform can be conceptualised as the precursor to social change, evidence of social change and as a defence against discrimination when social change does not happen, highlights the complexity of the ways in which people view law and legal processes. Legal consciousness is complex, and, as these data show, can be contradictory even within individual responses. This resistance to the positioning of lesbians and gay men as not entitled to the full protection of law is reinforced when considering respondents' views about the creation of a 'new' form of legal recognition (e.g. civil partnership/civil union/domestic partnership/registered partnership) for same-sex relationships.

Civil partnership is not enough

The third main theme in these participants' responses, which is closely linked to both formal equality and the relationship between legal and social change, was a focus on civil partnership not being good enough:

> Mmmm ... marriage-lite: same great taste, half the respect of regular marriage (R984).

This sarcastic, quasi-advertising slogan for civil partnership alludes to a number of the problems inherent in the creation of a 'new' form of legal recognition of relationships specifically for same-sex relationships. First, it highlights that civil partnership is considered 'marriage-lite' – reinforcing and adding another step to the traditional hierarchy of relationship forms, which places marriage at the top. Second, the reference to 'same great taste' alludes to the idea that although civil partnership is obviously something *different* from marriage it is designed to be as similar as possible, though (like low-fat foods) the thing that is missing is that which made the product 'great' – in this case, the social and cultural importance of marriage. This is reinforced by the third part of the statement which highlights that it is 'respect' which is missing from 'marriage-lite'.

These problems were expanded on by a number of other respondents. The first, that the creation of civil partnership creates another step in the hierarchy of relationship forms, can be found in references to inferiority, segregation and 'second-class' status:

> The intent behind creating the different label 'civil union' while retaining the label 'marriage' (for hetero's only) would imply inferiority, segregation, same but less. ... ie – it's meant to be inferior (R863).

In this excerpt, R863 calls on the power of law to create or entrench social attitudes. The lack of formal equality means that the creation of a different name for legally recognised same-sex relationships becomes seen as a legalised form of discrimination. Similarly, this respondent questions why marriage is not replaced wholesale with 'civil union':

> The term 'civil union' perpetuates the stigma of being different. Why doesn't the straight world abolish 'marriage' and adopt 'civil unions'? Because they see it as second-class. As do I. So why should gays and lesbians settle for second-class when the straight world doesn't? (R418)

This respondent highlights another problem related to naming:

> In Finland, we can have a 'registered partnership' – but I think that dogs are 'registered', people shouldn't be (R529).

In this case, the comparison of 'registered partnership' to registering a dog implies that not allowing same-sex couples access to marriage can work to de-humanise and degrade lesbians and gay men.

The cultural importance of naming was also expanded on by other respondents to highlight the less-than marriage status of civil parntership:

— Take the 'Spirit of Ecstacy' hood ornament from a Rolls Royce and put it on a Honda. Do you have the equivalent car? I think not. Civil Union does NOT equal marriage. Period. End of statement. 'Marriage' as I have stated earlier is a very powerful word. It has conotations, it has history. 'Civil Union' is ... what? It has no history, no visceral meaning, it is irrelevant (R17);

— What the heck are civil unions? Marriage has existed forever. Why would we create some new bizzare construct? (R51);

— Marriage (in the equal and full sense) provides an omnibus protection and in a single word identifies a whole set of cultural norms and expectations. I think a civil registry or civil union would be a never ending cycle of litigation for each and every perceived benefit or prejudice that this business or that organization feels they do not have to honor (R61).

These statements emphasise the cultural importance of calling legally recognised same-sex relationships marriage by invoking the socal capital embedded in the word 'marriage'. They draw attention to the universality of marriage as a social and cultural phenomenon, its history and the legal rights and responsibilities associated with it. The way R61 (above) conceptualises civil partnership as a continuing legal struggle is also interesting – it implies the continued presence of law in same-sex couples' lives, through a 'never ending cycle of litigation', despite legal recognition of the relationship. This suggests that whereas marriage is a socially and culturally understood concept, which would allow same-sex couples to live without constant interference from law, civil partnership should be resisted as it would emphasise the continuing relevance of law to same-sex couples. The view that civil partnership would lead to the continuing (negative) involvement of law in the everyday lives of lesbians and gay men is interesting because it shows a consciousness of law as a silent backdrop in everyday life, rather than something that should be directly relevant on a day to day level. In a sense, this respondent is suggesting that the appropriate place for law in everyday life is as a regulatory framework, rather than as an everyday terrain of contest.[10]

Finally, when commenting on the inadequacies of the (re)naming of same-sex marriage as 'marriage by another name', respondents also utilised sameness arguments:

— I don't mind if everyone then fell under this category, but to create two classes of relationship is doing just that – two classes. When we are trying to describe something different, with different outcomes in terms of rights etc., then different terminology should be used (eg de-facto or carers relationship, parent, guardian). However, if it's the same thing it is the same thing. To name the same thing something different could be done only for one reason – discrimination and admission of difference (R1321);

— We should have the same options as straight couples – if we want weddings with all the bells and whistles, we should have it. If we just want a registry office marriage, we should have it. If we want de facto rights, we should have it. What if straight people feel left out because they can't have

> 'civil unions'? The same name should apply to the same union no matter what the gender of those involved. Same name, same rights (R1244).

This emphasis on the importance of having the same options open to same- and different-sex couples is connected to a conceptualisation of equality as treating everyone the same, as discussed above. Rather than acknowledging any difference between same- and different-sex couples, respondents reinforce the similarities and name the creation of a new institution (like civil partnership) 'discrimination'. This type of argument also highlights the ways in which the creation of a new legal institution can feed into 'special rights' arguments (see e.g. Goldberg-Hiller, 2002) – indicating that problems could arise if 'straight people feel left out because they can't have "civil unions"'.

Again, this resistance to the re-naming of legally recognised same-sex relationships shows resistance to continued, adverse, legal presence in lesbian and gay lives, which could be described as an 'against the law' legal consciousness. Law is envisioned by these respondents as a political and social phenomenon, not an omnipotent presence. When faced with the potential of a new legal framework specifically for the legal recognition of same-sex relationships, lesbians and gay men speak out against the need to play the game of law. This, although showing elements of both before and with the law legal consciousness, is still typified by a resistance to different legal treatment of lesbians and gay men. I would argue that the form of resistance highlighted in these data is different from the forms of resistance defined by Ewick and Silbey (1998; 2003); rather than being concerned with 'rebellious acts' (Ewick & Silbey, 2003: 1336) or evasive or passive resistance, these respondents resist the different treatment of lesbians and gay men in law in a more active way. These respondents challenge law on its own terms, utilising the language of justice and equality to resist law, while simultaneously complying with legal rules. Ewick and Silbey's (1998) original typology does not seem to have a place for those who resist the law in this way – who resist the law but also wish to make the law fulfil its claims of justice and equity for all. This raises questions of whether there are intrinsic class and race implications embedded in Ewick and Silbey's (1998) category of 'against the law', rather than being reflective of the experience of 'marginalised individuals' more generally. I would call this type of active, equality-seeking resistance 'moderating resistance',[11] because conscious and public engagement with the problematic nature of discriminatory legal provision is evident in these respondents views. Further examples of this type of resistance are also highlighted in the ways rights claims are presented by these respondents.

Rights discourse: rights to equality and the right to marry

As can be expected when looking at arguments for the legal recognition of same-sex relationships, many respondents used rights rhetoric, or called on discourses of common humanity to argue for rights to equality and the right to marry. This forceful rhetoric has been present in lesbian and gay struggles for many years (Herman, 1994), but with the rise in the importance of international human rights norms, equal rights discourse has arguably become even more entrenched in Western societies (McGoldrick, 2001). Indeed, the argument that as humans we are all entitled to the equal protection of fundamental civil and political rights has reached such a state of ascendancy that almost all claims for lesbian and gay legal equality seem to find their basis within this framework:

— It is fundamental that we are afforded our right to equality on the basis that we are human (i.e. human rights = same rights for all) (R238);
— Everyone should be accorded the same human rights, regardless of their sexual orientation (R591);
— This is a matter of Human Rights and Equality before the law and in society (R401).

These statements highlight a number of interesting facets of lesbian and gay men's usage of human rights rhetoric to argue for legal change, including interesting differences arising from the differential treatment of lesbians and gay men in different jurisdictions. First, the 'right to equality' is posited by R238, a lesbian from the UK, as a stand-alone human right rather than (as is currently the case in UK and European human rights jurisprudence) a limited right which only applies in conjunction with another right. For instance, in the European Convention of Human Rights, there is no specific 'right to equality', but simply the guarantee under Article 14, that 'the enjoyment of the rights and freedoms set forth in this Convention shall be secured without discrimination on the grounds of … '.[12] Second, as in the second example above (R591), when using human rights as an argument for lesbian and gay equality, respondents sometimes almost mirror the language of human rights instruments, but specifically list sexual orientation as a ground on which discrimination is prohibited, inserting 'sexual orientation' as a ground of discrimination, even where it is not included in the 'official' list.[13] This technique is interesting because it shows that, in the UK context at least, lesbians and gay men continue to have to argue that 'human rights' apply in relation to sexual orientation. It may be, of course, that these statements are used as a result of ignorance of the detail of legal frameworks, but I would argue that this is again an example of moderating resistance. The lesbians and gay men who frame their arguments in this way are attempting to harness the rhetorical power of legal discourse to transform power relations and attain legal equality for lesbians and gay men.

These calls to equality also highlight the importance of human rights and equality arguments by placing emphasis on these words. In the extract above, R401 capitalises 'Human Rights' and 'Equality', giving these intangible legal ideals proper names, and therefore attempting to convert them into substantive 'things', stressing their structural significance. It is interesting to compare the categorical terms of R401's (who lives in Canada) comments with those of R238 and R591 (both resident in the UK) as this arguably reflects the legal differences in the treatment of lesbians and gay men in Canada and the UK in relation to human rights instruments. Whereas in the UK lesbians and gay men still often have to argue for inclusion in human rights protections, this is not necessary under the Canadian Charter constitutional rights framework (see e.g. Smith, 1999). Similarly, in the extract from R1405's comments (a lesbian from the UK) that follow now, the emphasis is placed on 'human' through the use of capital letters. This again serves as a strong statement of lesbian and gay claims to equality, by virtue of being human, even though this is not a fully realised legal 'truth' in the UK:

> Basic HUMAN rights – we're no different from heterosexuals. We should have the same rights as straight people (R1405).

Further, many respondents specifically formulated the 'right to marry' as a human right. For example:

— Denying our rights to get married is denying our human rights (R1168);
— All humans should have the right to marry the person that they love (R1487).

These claims for the lesbian and gay 'right to marry' again work on a number of different levels. Respondents position access to marriage as a 'human right' based on 'love', rather than as a special protection that is afforded to those who fit into the normative conception of the family.[14] Claims that the right to marry is a human right therefore look far more to the social and cultural significance of marriage than to the legal rights and responsibilities that stem from this state-supported institution. Access to marriage is, however, also perceived to have a multitude of different effects, not simply the upholding of a 'human right':

> Every major civil rights effort has required at the outset a recognition of basic human rights, such as the right of women to vote, or the right of interracial couples to marry. Our children need to have the social respect for their family lives that is afforded heterosexuals. Many people will recognize our relationships, especially over time, as being fundamentally no different from heterosexual relationships if we are allowed to marry (R592).

In the above example, the struggle for the 'right to marry' for lesbians and gay men is framed as having the ability to grant children from lesbian and gay families 'social respect' and to make possible the social acceptance of same-sex relationships. This excerpt also highlights the ways in which some respondents frame claims to human rights in terms of group discrimination – like women or racial or ethnic minorities, lesbians and gay men are an identifiable group, entitled to protection. Indeed, even those who disagree with marriage seem to emphasise the importance of upholding the lesbian and gay human right to marry:

> The right to marry, even though I don't agree with it, should be an option for everyone. The government, through its dismissal of human rights opens the door for others to openly abuse its citizens. It is still socially acceptable to publicly criticize gays and lesbians, we are one of the few groups that lack the validity and protection such that our protection can be transgressed without public/social censure (R196).

This example is not only concerned with lesbian and gay rights to marry, but also draws attention to the secondary problems of the denial of same-sex marriage. This respondent argues that by legally condoning a dismissal of human rights for lesbians and gay men, the state is complicit in continued discrimination against and abuse of lesbian and gay citizens. There are clear limitations to this argument, however, as it implies that other groups have been satisfactorily protected through existing anti-discrimination provision. For example, an extension of this argument would claim that as discrimination on the basis of race is outlawed, racism no longer exists, or, when racist views are expressed there is always public or social censure. The continued experience of racism in contemporary society clearly highlights the limitation of this line of argument. But this type of argument does show evidence of resistance to the construction of lesbians and gay men as undeserving of human rights protection. Rights discourse, therefore, rests on perceptions of law as a powerful force for recognition and respect, underpinned by the desire for formal equality in the form of 'equal rights' and 'human rights'.

Returning to legal consciousness then, these respondents' comments about the place of human rights and rights to equality within the same-sex marriage debate again reflects the forms of resistance outlined in Chapter 3. Where lesbians and gay men are not treated equally under the law (as is the case in the UK), they call on the universality of human rights language as a technique to claim the full 'protection' of law. Claims such as these seem to again display evidence of the complex combination of Ewick and Silbey's (1998) categories of 'before the law' and 'against the law' legal consciousness. In contrast, where same-sex couples have attained formally equal legal rights, the discourse becomes less concerned with arguing for lesbian and gay inclusion within rights protections and seems to display a 'with the law' type of legal consciousness. Respondents were able to unproblematically draw on legal terms (like 'human rights' and 'equality') to advance their perspective.

Geographical differences in legal provision for same-sex relationships seem, therefore, to affect the ways in which lesbians and gay men express their rights and rights claims. So, in these respondents' comments, where same-sex marriage is available, the discourse used is one which is 'with the law'; where there is either no formal recognition of same-sex relationships, or where there is a legal framework but this falls short of formal equality (e.g. civil partnership, domestic partnership or de facto recognition), respondents find themselves positioned 'against the law', but simultaneously draw on the power of law inherent in a 'before the law' legal consciousness to claim equal rights. This discourse is also reflected in respondents' use of citizenship as a facet of the legal recognition of same-sex relationships.

Relationship recognition and citizenship

The fifth and final theme in these respondents' views about the legal recognition of same-sex relationship was a discourse of citizenship. Within the debates surrounding same-sex marriage, citizenship claims take many forms, and are strongly linked to the other themes evident in these data – equality, rights, social attitudes and discrimination. In these data, respondents used several devices to claim citizenship, and interestingly the most dominant of these was concerned with taxation. The argument goes something like: lesbian and gay citizens are fulfilling their part of the bargain and being good citizens by paying their taxes so therefore are entitled to all of the benefits and protections of the state. Citizenship claims were expressed by these respondents in terms such as:

— I don't pay limited taxes, so therefore I shouldn't have limited rights (R617);
— It is an equality issue. We have to abide by the law in relation to taxes, compliance etc. so why should we be discriminated against? (R1055);
— Same-sex couples live ordinary, mundane lives, go to work, pay taxes, raise children the same as heterosexuals (R417);
— We are required to pay the same taxes as anybody else, therefore we deserve the same exact benefits of state (R424).

These respondents, by emphasising the relationship between tax-paying citizen and entitlement to 'benefits of the state', also draw attention to the the ways in which the state (as opposed to other citizens who have discriminatory/prejudiced views) is complicit in discrimination against lesbians and gay men. These arguments raise interesting questions about the concept of citizenship as it should apply to lesbians and gay men. For instance, what of those who are not in a position to pay taxes due to poverty or other circumstances? Are lesbians and gay men who are marginalised through class or race unentitled to citizenship and therefore same-sex marriage or other legal rights? What of those who truly are not 'citizens'? Arguably, this formulation of citizenship being specifically related to economic status is particularly exclusionary and ignores the importance of social and/or cultural citizenship claims.[15]

Other respondents took this state-sanctioned discrimination further, and provided it as evidence of the 'second-class status' of lesbians and gay men:

— I don't need a legal agency to legitimize my relationship, but I do feel like a second class citizen for having to settle for a domestic partnership, and not a marriage (R605);
— There is no logical or moral reason why any legal forms of discrimination should exist. To treat same sex couples differently is to enshrine prejudice in law and to send a message to society that queers are second class citizens (R1293);
— We deserve the same rights and respect that straight couples get. We are human beings and should not be treated as second class citizens (R77).

These citizenship claims show some of the ways in which lesbians and gay men are different from other socially marginalised groups. Law defined (and in many jurisdictions continues to define) lesbians and gay men as deviant, undeserving of legal rights and protections, or even criminal.[16] As a result, lesbians and gay men are positioned as outsiders in the realm of legal protection. By virtue of being 'legally' discriminated against, the power of law is evident: law (as a product of an intolerant society and/or social structure) has the power to discriminate and oppress – therefore lesbians and gay men hold on firmly to the principle of all human beings being inherently equal, as strong reasoning in favour of the attainment of legal equality. The calls to common humanity, citizenship and liberal sameness that are an intrinsic part of formal equality arguments allow the normalisation of lesbian and gay sexuality, while simultaneously vocalising the continued oppression of sexual minorities and claiming a 'rightful' place in society.

Concluding remarks

The above analysis has highlighted that the lesbians and gay men who responded to this survey conceptualised legal aspects of same-sex relationship recognition in ways that emphasised their desire for formal equality. By using a legal consciousness approach, I have brought the ways in which lesbians and gay men understand the legal recognition of same-sex relationships to the fore in the complex debates about same-sex marriage. These respondents seemed to view law as a predominantly regulatory framework, rather than purely the domain of the civil and criminal court system. Using a legal consciousness approach has highlighted the pervasiveness of formal equality discourse, but perhaps more importantly, it has shown the way in which law is viewed from the perspective of those who are positioned (at least in some respects) outside the legal sphere. Lesbians and gay men, as outsiders looking in at the benefits of the legal recognition of relationships, see the incongruity between law's external image (that of justice, blind to difference, fair and unbiased) and their everyday experience of being excluded from the 'protection' offered by law.

Despite these data being drawn from both lesbians and gay men, with a wide variety of geographical locations and ages, legal consciousness does not often appear to differ on the basis of these demographics.[17] Where some geographical variation in respondents' views could be found, these seemed to map closely to the different legal frameworks available to respondents in their country of residence. It seems odd that more gendered differences were not evident in these data, but there could be a number of reasons for the lack of difference between respondents' views in this research. One reason could be the ways in which same-sex marriage and the legal recognition of same-sex relationships had been represented in the world media, or the particular time frame in which these data were collected. The fact that these comments were collected through a survey tool, rather than a more researcher-led form of qualitative data collection may also have had an impact. Certainly, the presumption that these data raise that lesbians and gay men do not differ in their views about the legal recognition of same-sex relationships is complicated somewhat by the interview data analysed in Chapter 6. Perhaps the most interesting conclusion generated thorough a legal consciousness analysis of these data is the force and ubiquity of approaches to rights, equality and discrimination frameworks. My analysis of these data suggests that ideas around formal equality are hegemonic within lesbians and gay men's perceptions of and attitudes towards the legal recognition of same-sex relationships.[18]

From a legal consciousness perspective, these data suggest that while there are elements of both 'before' and 'with the law' legal consciousness evident in lesbian and gay men's attitudes to the legal recognition of same-sex relationships, the most dominant appears to be an unusual form of 'against the law' legal consciousness, which draws on both stabilising and moderating forms of resistance. A 'before the law' perspective can be discerned from the ways in which these respondents conceptualise how law should be: they utilise liberal notions of equality, human rights and citizenship to explain understandings of law. At the same time, however, these respondents highlight the lack of 'equality' evident in the current legal situation of lesbians and gay men. 'With the law' legal consciousness is invoked by those respondents for whom legal frameworks do feel equal, and for those who hold the view that law *can* be changed, whether through political, judicial or societal means. The focus of these respondents' views however is resistance: resistance to the naming of lesbian or gay sexuality as deviant or abnormal; resistance to legal formalisations of the differences between same- and different-sex relationships; and resistance to the lack of equality within the law as it relates to lesbians and gay men. This analysis also highlights the ways in which these forms of active, equality-seeking, resistance are missing from the tripartite typology of legal consciousness proposed by Ewick and Silbey (1998).

These data also suggest that forms of legal consciousness that do not easily fit within the three types set down by Ewick and Silbey (1998) can be found within lesbians' and gay men's accounts, even outside of the traditional methodological approach (the in-depth interview) used in previous legal consciousness research. As this was an anonymous internet-based study, the data are limited in that there was no place to follow up on interesting comments made by respondents, and the survey format relies on questions. It is hard to tell from these data, for example, how relations of power and resistance play out in the everyday lives of these respondents because the survey tool was not flexible enough to construct robust ways of accessing this type of information. More detailed demographic characteristics such as class, racial or ethnic origin or religious beliefs were not available through this survey, and may have highlighted other differences in perspective. As discussed above, there was an over-representation of people who described their occupation as 'professional' in this data set – but this category is arguably a very wide descriptor, and more detailed occupational or earnings information was not gathered. The sample is, therefore, assumed to be weighted towards middle-class perspectives.

The limitations of using an online form of data collection must, therefore, be taken into consideration in assessing the generalisability or representativeness of the views expressed. It is important to note, however, that using online methodologies has brought a new method to bear on legal consciousness studies. Rather than respondents' accounts being co-constructed by the interviewer and interviewee, as can be the case in interview research,[19] online methodologies seem to allow for less mediated narratives to become ascendant, and certainly allow for large numbers of respondents to be accessed quickly (Harding & Peel, 2007). The lack of identifiable differences between the perspectives offered by these respondents also highlights the ubiquity of the legal schemas and stories of law told by these respondents. In the following three chapters, I build on the perspectives offered by the respondents to this online survey by analysing different types of texts and cultural representations of law and legal consciousness in my exploration of the place of law in the everyday lives of lesbians and gay men.

Notes

1 The quantitative results from the survey have been published elsewhere (Harding & Peel, 2006).

2 For a more in-depth discussion of using online tools for data collection, see Harding & Peel (2007).

3 It must be remembered, therefore, that there may be discourses present in these data that are specific to the time that the online survey was carried out. Same-sex marriage was, for example, not yet available across the whole of Canada, but only

in Ontario and British Columbia, and in the UK, the Civil Partnership Act 2004 was still on its passage through Parliament.

4 Note that this is a difference of degree, that is, more likely to 'strongly agree' rather than 'agree'; not a difference between agree and disagree.

5 For a full statistical analysis of the quantitative results, alongside a reproduction of the full survey, see Harding and Peel (2006).

6 As outlined in Chapter 2, legal consciousness studies have developed to primarily draw on in-depth interview method, generally where the 'legal' focus of the project was not made explicit to the interviewees (see e.g. Ewick & Silbey, 1998; Nielsen, 2004).

7 Data extracts have been reproduced verbatim, with correction of minor spelling errors.

8 'Before the law', 'with the law' and 'against the law'.

9 'Stabilising resistance' is the term I use to describe every day, mundane forms of resistant practices; those forms of resistance that serve as the constant counter-balance to power relations – see Chapter 3.

10 This view of law as a regulatory framework, rather than an intrinsic part of every-day life could be considered a particularly middle-class view of the place of law. I return to this issue in more detail in Chapter 6, where an interview participant explores her views about the ways that working-class people are more used to being subjected to interference from state actors in their everyday lives.

11 'Moderating resistance' is the term I use to describe conscious and public attempts to transform power relations, or to resist the exercise of power by law or the state.

12 A stand-alone right to equality has been included into the ECHR through Protocol 12, but the UK has not yet ratified this protocol.

13 Although sexual orientation is included in the European Charter of Human Rights (which is currently unenforceable) it is not specifically listed in, for example, the European Convention on Human Rights (Article 14) and the Universal Declaration of Human Rights (Article 2).

14 See, for example, UDHR Article 16 (3): 'The family is the natural and fundamental group unit of society and is entitled to protection by society and the State.'

15 It is important to note that the prevalence of this 'tax-payer' discourse may be due to the over-representation of 'professional' lesbians and gay men within the sample.

16 Although, of course, lesbians have been historically less likely to be criminalised than gay men.

17 Again, the over-representation of respondents identifying their occupation as 'professional' or 'student' may have created a class bias in this sample. Had there been more 'working-class' respondents, examples of different varieties of legal con-sciousness may have been more prevalent.

18 The hegemony of formal equality in lesbian and gay views about same-sex marriage is also discussed in detail in my analysis of the quantitative aspects of this survey (Harding & Peel, 2006).

19 See, further, Chapter 6.

Chapter 5

Stories of law

> Society itself may be seen as a textured but seamless web of stories emerging everywhere through interaction: holding people together, pulling people apart, making societies work.
>
> (Plummer, 1995: 5)

I now turn to the second empirical lens in my exploration of legal consciousness and sexuality, by examining lesbians' and gay men's stories of parenting. Specifically, the moments within these parenting narratives where law or legality is mentioned, invoked, questioned or described. In contrast to the legal recognition of same-sex relationships, the regulation of lesbian and gay parenting is, in many respects, a less analysed facet of lesbian and gay family life. As discussed in Chapter 4, same-sex relationship recognition has attracted a great deal of attention from lesbian and gay activist groups and the media and has faced strong opposition from conservative and religious groups and individuals. Lesbian and gay parenting, on the other hand, seems not to have had the same level of either support or opposition. There have, of course, been times when lesbian and gay parenting has been in the media spotlight, for example in debates about whether same-sex couples should be able to adopt jointly (see Hicks, 2005), or whether lesbian couples and single women should be entitled to access assisted conception services (see Jackson, 2002; Robinson, 1997). But these sorts of debate seem to cohere more around the moral arguments for and against allowing lesbians and gay men to become parents, rather than how law and legal regulation affect the everyday experiences of those lesbians and gay men who *are* parents. My concern in this chapter, then, is to explore published narratives from lesbian and gay parents, and the place of law in their experience of being parents.

Stories[1] are everywhere. They are told and re-told, written down, published in books or passed on orally from person to person. Stories come in many forms – they are fictitious, factual, personal, political, biographical, autobiographical, all these things, none of them, and can also take an almost infinite variety of other forms. In some respects, stories can be so individual and specific, that it could be difficult to see where different stories are linked. But each and all stories either contribute to normative visions of society or are counter-stories, working from outside or underneath the dominant cultural understandings present in society (Harris et al., 2001). Each story also has its own situation in a time, space and place and, as a result, has the capacity to reflect the social world from which the story was born (Plummer, 1995). Since at least the mid-twentieth century, stories have become a focus for social thought and academic research in the social sciences (Orbuch, 1997).

Much sociological and literary research into narrative has taken narrative structure as a focus of investigation (see e.g. Maines, 1993; Roof, 1996) and has mapped the ways in which narrative is constructed, including exploring the need for a story, a plot and a linear progression through time (Maines, 1993: 21). Other narrative research, however, has taken the content of stories as the focus of analysis, 'inspecting the social role of stories: the ways they are produced, the ways they are read, the work they perform in the wider social order, how they change, and their role in the political process' (Plummer, 1995: 19). It is this latter form of narrative inquiry that will be my focus in this chapter.

Although a number of scholars have used narrative to elucidate the position(s) of lesbians and gay men in law (e.g. Eskridge, 1994; Fajer, 1992; Robson, 1997), none of these analyses has taken lesbian and gay parenting as their starting point. My concern is primarily with the way(s) in which legal rules impact on the everyday lives of lesbians and gay men who are parents (and, by extension, the lives of their children), and the perceptions of and attitudes towards 'law' that are present in lesbian and gay parenting stories. Specifically, it is the ways in which relationships of power and resistance are highlighted and exposed by these stories that I find interesting from a legal consciousness perspective. I begin by outlining some of the ways in which storytelling and narrative have been used in legal scholarship, with an exploration of the ways narratives of law can be used with legal consciousness studies in order to understand perceptions of and attitudes towards law in everyday life, and to highlight relations of power and resistance. I then turn to a discussion of the stories of law that can be found within lesbian and gay parents' published stories, with specific regard to legal consciousness, perceptions of the power of law and examples of resistance to law. I conclude with an overview of gender and legal and social change in lesbian and gay parenting as expressed through these personal narratives. I argue that similar discourse about the place of law in everyday life for lesbians and gay men can be found in these stories of law as were evident in the analysis of attitudes to the legal recognition of same-sex relationships in Chapter 4.

Narrative and law

> Stories are ... attempts to explain social action. They locate characters in times and space, describing both what enables and what constrains action.

> In other words, they point to the sources and limits of agency that exist within social structures.
>
> (Ewick & Silbey, 2003: 1342)

Although storytelling and personal narrative may not, at first, seem to be an intrinsic part of legal scholarship, stories and narrative have been used by a wide variety of scholars, including legal historians (e.g. Ball, 1989), legal anthropologists (e.g. Lopez, 1984), law and literature scholars (e.g. Thomson, 2001), critical race theorists (e.g. Williams, 1992), feminist scholars (e.g. Abrams, 1991) and lesbian and gay legal scholars (e.g. Eskridge, 1994; Robson, 1997). Narrative and stories have been used for any number of different purposes within legal scholarship – to introduce experiential accounts into a legal analysis of a particular crime (e.g. Estrich, 1986 [rape]; Mahoney, 1991 [domestic violence]); to enrich legal analysis of the problems of racial justice (e.g. Bell, 1987; Williams, 1992); or to draw attention to the contradictions in anti-gay law, such as the ban on lesbians and gay men in the military (Eskridge, 1994). Indeed the connection between stories and law is not confined to the pages of academic journals or books – storytelling has always been part of the adversarial process (Robson, 1997).

A number of scholars have used narrative in relation to sexuality, often focusing on coming out stories (e.g. Cossman, 2002b; Herman, 2005; Jolly, 2001; Munt et al., 2002; Phelan, 1993). Other approaches include exposing the heterosexuality of narrative structure (Roof, 1996), the ways in which sexual stories are told, and understandings of contemporary attitudes towards sex and sexuality through their intersection with storytelling (Plummer, 1995). In law, narrative accounts have been used sparingly in relation to lesbians and gay men and the law, although several interesting articles have approached legal scholarship with illustrations of personal narrative from the author's own experience (see e.g. Eskridge, 1994; Fajer, 1992; Robson, 1997).

It is important to remember that narrative plays a major role in legal consciousness studies. It is through the stories that people tell about their experiences of law and legal process that insights into the place of law in everyday life are given. Further, Ewick and Silbey (2003) argue that:

> Stories people tell about themselves and their lives both constitute and interpret those lives; stories are media through which identities are negotiated ... stories enact and construct, as they describe, the world as it is lived and is understood by the storyteller.
>
> (Ewick & Silbey, 2003: 1341)

In other words, the telling and writing of personal stories not only produces a window on the experiences of the storyteller, but also reflects and refracts society. Stories of resistance, Ewick and Silbey (2003: 1346) argue, 'transcend the subjective and the personal, implicating and inciting the audience in the acts of resistance'.

In the remainder of this chapter, I seek to highlight some of the legal issues facing lesbian and gay parents by drawing on examples from already published personal narratives. In the previous chapter, I began combining legal consciousness approaches with a theoretically informed analysis of power relations, and argued that the three schemas of legal consciousness created by Ewick and Silbey (1998) – 'before the law', 'with the law' and 'against the law' – were useful in describing the content of peoples' stories of law, but that these categories can also help to highlight the relationships of power and resistance within accounts of attitudes to and perceptions of law. In this chapter, I again use the theoretical toolbox of legal consciousness as a prism through which to view the relationships of power and resistance that are present in lesbian and gay parents' stories of law. My focus is therefore on the ways these parents describe the effects of the 'power of law' in their everyday lives, and moments of resistance to law that can be found in their stories.

Legal consciousness and lesbian and gay parents

In this section, I turn to personal narratives about parenting, as told by lesbian and gay parents. The narrative accounts that I rely on here differ in a number of ways from the types of narrative used in both legal narrative research and legal consciousness studies, as they are neither my own stories, nor narratives told to me in the context of an in-depth interview or other method of qualitative data collection. Rather, these parents' stories are excerpts from eight edited collections of stories about lesbian and gay lives. Four books have an explicitly lesbian focus (Abbot & Farmer, 1995; Aizley, 2006; Pollack & Vaughn, 1987; Saffron, 1994), three take gay fathers as their subject (Barret & Robinson, 2000; Mallon, 2004; Strah & Margolis, 2003) and the final collection has stories from both lesbians and gay men (Hicks & McDermott, 1999).[2] In some cases, the author uses the first person (I/we) to tell their story; in other cases, the author uses the third person (they) to tell their story. In each of these collections of personal narratives, however, the stories have been told by the lesbian or gay parents themselves and as such they are the narrators' constructions of the events they recount, rather than accounts modified by or co-constructed through the research process. In some of the collections (Abbot & Farmer, 1995; Aizley, 2006; Pollack & Vaughn, 1987), the stories are explicitly written by the lesbian or gay parents themselves, and therefore their authorship is acknowledged. In the others (Barret & Robinson, 2000; Hicks & McDermott, 1999; Mallon, 2004; Saffron, 1994; Strah & Margolis, 2003), the storytellers have been anonymised, or their stories told in the third person.[3] The quotes I provide in the analysis that follows are illustrative examples, taken from the wider context of the experiential stories related by these lesbian and gay parents. As such, my analysis necessarily draws not only on the content of the extracts provided, but also the broader themes and perspectives evident in the wider narratives, all of which are available in the public domain.

Published narratives are not, of course, completely raw, because they have been prepared for publication. Such published narratives are revised, refined and edited and the final published version of the story is always directed at a particular audience. It is important to note, therefore, that narrative is always 'constructed through transactions between speaker and audience, text and reader ... [and are] ... collaborative productions offered within overlapping relational contexts' (Ewick & Silbey, 2003: 1343). The narratives analysed here are stories written for audiences including lesbians and gay men who wish to become parents, professionals such as social workers, psychologists or lawyers who are interested in the issues relating to lesbian and gay families, and even as a way of convincing those who are less than certain of the validity or even existence of lesbian and gay families.

In closely reading these collections of personal narratives from lesbian and gay parents, I highlight three dominant themes within lesbian mothers' and gay fathers' stories about parenting: first, the difficulties of parenting outside the law and the lack of legal rules for lesbian and gay families; second, legal and social constructions of 'real' or 'illegitimate' parents; and, third, social and legal constructions of lesbians and gay men as second-class parents to second-class children. In each of these themes, these lesbian and gay parents invoke discourses about the power of law, and outline their moments of resistance to (hetero)normative constructions of parenting.

Parenting outside the law

The first main theme within these published narratives of lesbian and gay parenting is the problems associated with parenting outside the normative heterosexual framework. In their stories, lesbian and gay parents regularly draw attention to the difficulties of negotiating rules in the absence of (official) law, and the problematic effects of heterosexist laws relating to the family:

> When Clause 28 identified 'pretend families', it hit a raw nerve. We know we are different, but in order to be supportive to us, 'real' nuclear families tend to overlook the differences and *they* 'pretend' we are just like them.
>
> (Saffron, 1994: 101)

In the above extract, a lesbian mother highlights that she feels lesbian families are different from their heterosexual counterparts, but concurrently acknowledges that in order for her family to be understood, the differences between them and 'real' nuclear families are overlooked. Interestingly, this narrator attributes the reluctance of her heterosexual friends to notice the differences between their families to the effects of the notorious (and now repealed) Section 28, which was enacted to prevent local authorities from 'promoting homosexuality' or promoting 'the acceptability of homosexuality as a pretended family relationship'.[4] That this lesbian parent accredits the enactment of anti-gay law with creating a stressful parenting environment is interesting in that it shows a certain amount of acknowledgement of the 'power' that law has over her everyday life.[5]

The most straightforward reading of this story would be to describe it as an example of 'before the law' legal consciousness, as the narrator describes the effect of a particular law as extremely wide-reaching. However, the reification of law in this story is very limited, and it is the relations of power and resistance that are illuminated by these parents' narrative that I find more interesting. Here, the power that law holds is not attributed directly to the content of Section 28 and the fact that the state described lesbian/gay families as 'pretend' but rather through the ways in which that legislative provision impacted on how heterosexual people viewed lesbian families. As such, this is an example of power at the 'extreme points of its exercise ... where it is less legal in character' (Foucault, 1980: 97). As it applied only to local authorities, and therefore did not include private individuals, Section 28 did not have any direct *legal* impact on lesbian/gay parents, but for the narrator of the above extract, it had a power over her life that was far greater than the content of the law.

In some stories from lesbian mothers, a more simple approach to the power of law is evident, in particular the legal exclusion of lesbian mother as a valid category of parent. For example, in this extract from the story of a mother who lost custody of her children when she left her husband, the potential for legal power to be coercive and discriminatory is highlighted:

> I came out during a time when the courts couldn't see past my sexual orientation to my worth as a loving mother and a decent human being ... I was *forced* out of the closet in the divorce court.
>
> (Knight-Lopez, S. in Abbot & Farmer, 1995: 255)

By describing her experience in court as one of being 'forced' out of the closet, this narrator implies that she had no choice but to declare her lesbianism, and that law is a powerful force, in the face of which she was powerless. Feelings of powerlessness in relation to legal processes are not unique to lesbian mothers – this phenomenon has been noted in a number of legal consciousness studies (see e.g. Cowan, 2004; Merry, 1990). In some respects, this is a classic example of juridical or sovereign power, where power is something that one party holds over another – in this instance, that the court holds over the formerly heterosexually married lesbian mother. From a different perspective, the power that is being exercised by the court in this instance, is also to do with the disciplinary power of the state – a form of disciplinary power that dictates who can legitimately be described as a parent and who cannot. It is implicit in this woman's story that she felt that she may have been able to (re)gain custody of her children if she had been able to place more emphasis on her identity as a parent, and not on her sexuality.

Another context in which the power of law is evident is in relation to lesbians and gay men who choose to become parents through adoption or fostering. Adoptive and foster parents have no choice but to work within the (sometimes restrictive) rules that official law lays down in order to achieve their dreams of becoming parents. In the words of one adoptive gay father: 'what an amazing cleaver and bonder of families the law is' (Strah & Margolis, 2003: 92). Or, from the story of a lesbian couple who became parents through adoption:

> As the words droned on, Nita and Clare realized the enormity of the moment. This man [the judge] was God. He could make or break their dreams.
>
> (Hicks & McDermott, 1999: 27)

Here, law is a powerful force in the lives of alternative families. The adoptive lesbian mothers in the above extract again described their feelings of powerlessness in the face of the potential for a deified judge to 'make or break their dreams'. In the event, the adoption order (in favour of 'Nita') and a joint residence order in the names of both women were granted, and the power of law was therefore rendered somewhat benign.

Similarly, in another story by adoptive lesbian mothers from the UK, only one partner is legally able to be named as the adoptive parent:[6]

> The girls have been with us for three years now and we're waiting to adopt. Ideally we'd both like to be legal parents but, unfortunately, the law, as it stands at the moment, means that only one of us can adopt. One decision we made fairly early on – years before we were even offered the girls – was that we weren't going to tell them which of us will be their legal parent. They've got two mums, that's all they need to know. They don't need to know the legal details.
>
> (Hicks & McDermott, 1999: 96)

This extract highlights a form of resistance to legal power, showing the techniques that one lesbian couple uses in an attempt to negate the problem of not being able to legally adopt jointly. They do this by determining that they will not place any extra status on the 'legal parent' within their family. This is an example of resistance being a way of attempting to exercise power over law's power. By making the decision not to disclose the differential legal status of each parent, these prospective adoptive mothers are simultaneously acknowledging the power of law and attempting to produce effects on that power. They imply that knowing which one of them was legally defined as the parent could be harmful to their family (through the potential for one of them to be perceived as a lesser parent by their children), so by not disclosing their different legal statuses, they are circumventing that possibility. By refusing to acknowledge the potential power that law has over them as adoptive parents, they are attempting to resist the inappropriate legal provision by creating their own rules. The form of resistance implicit in this situation is interesting because it highlights the different, cross-cutting power relations at work in families. I would describe this type of resistance as 'moderating resistance' because the aim is to change the effects of legal power or legal truth on their family. This is also an example of resistance as a form of the exercise of power; the effect of these parents' moderating resistance is the creation of another power relation between them and their children. Through their resistant act of deliberately keeping the 'truth' of their differential legal status from their children, they are also, therefore, exercising their power over those less powerful than them, their children.

There is now an added dimension to these parents' story, because since December 2005 same-sex couples in the UK have been able to adopt jointly, and if they are civil partners, the non-legal status parent can adopt their partner's child through step-parent adoption processes.[7] These new legal developments can be read in two distinct ways. In one view, these legal developments mean that lesbian and gay parenting no longer exists 'outside the law', meaning that there is no need for lesbian and gay parents who live and parent in couple relationships to create their own legal rules in relation to their children. On a different reading of the impact of these new legal frameworks, however, some element of agency may have been removed by the formalisation of lesbian and gay parenting. Prior to the introduction of civil partnership and joint adoption by same-sex couples lesbian and gay parents had a wide degree of flexibility in respect to deciding how to organise their lives 'outside the law'. The creation of legal rules stipulating that same-sex couples can both be parents (the governmentalisation of lesbian and gay parenting) could, by way of contrast, mean that the possibilities for radical disruption of legalised forms of 'the family' are closed off to lesbian and gay families who do not conform to the norm of the nuclear family.

Examples of 'moderating resistance' can also be found in stories where biological lesbian parents highlight difficulties in parenting outside the law, particularly in relation to negotiating the lack of formal legal rules surrounding the creation of lesbian families. So, inappropriate or undesirable laws are also an issue when children are conceived through self-insemination from known sperm donors:

> When we started out, they specified that they only wanted to be donors, and we left it unwritten for a long time. We were uncertain whether it was desirable to write a contract and see whether it is honoured, or whether to acknowledge on paper the fact that they are the fathers. We didn't put their names on the birth certificate. One of the men was

> concerned about child support, and he wanted an understanding that he wouldn't have to be responsible for child support.
>
> (Pollack & Vaughn, 1987: 122)

In this extract, the lesbian mothers explain that they were unsure of whether it was 'desirable' to enter into a legal contract with their donors, as this would necessarily mean acknowledging 'on paper' that the donors were the biological fathers of their children. This seems to show a resistance to the formalisation of the agreement between the parties, and that writing down that the donors were the biological fathers of the children would, in some way, transform the donors from having no legal relationship to the children into the children's 'fathers'. The power of writing, in relation to legal matters, is another common theme within legal consciousness studies, and has been highlighted by other research (e.g. Ewick & Silbey, 1998; Merry, 1990). Writing does not always continue to be a negative force, however, as this lesbian couple's story continues with an explanation of how they resolved tensions between them and the donors after the birth of the children:

> But then when the children were born ... at that point we wrote up an agreement. A very basic agreement. We did it without a lawyer. We got some sample contracts and wrote a simple contract that said we would never sue them for child support and that they would never sue us for custody, and that if Beth or I died, they would honor, and never challenge, the surviving member's guardianship of the child. They waived their rights of guardianship. It was very simple, but it was very difficult for them to see it on paper.
>
> (Pollack & Vaughn, 1987: 122)

So, these lesbian mothers decided that in order to work around the legal presumptions concerning child support, custody and guardianship they would create their own explicit rules, setting out the relationship between them, as parents, the donors and the children. By creating their own rules, they believed that they successfully negotiated the legal presumptions surrounding the parentage of their children and as such, resisted the power of law to decide what the 'truth' is in relation to their children. It is important to consider here the 'audience' that these parents had for their 'contract'. Should the issues of child support, custody or guardianship arise within the context of a legal battle, their attempt to construct their own rules through their 'very basic agreement' would, in all likelihood, not have been legally enforceable.

But if none of the parties involved ever challenges this agreement (in a legal context), the strategy of creating their own rules will be effective resistance against the power of law, and a form of counter to the problems of parenting outside of the law. This sort of resistance strategy, using a contract of explicitly no official legal value to resist unsatisfactory official legal provision, raises some interesting legal consciousness issues. First, it could be seen as similar to a 'with the law' legal consciousness, in that these lesbian mothers use legal form (in spite of the lack of legal validity) to solidify their relationship with the donor fathers. Thinking of this approach in these terms, however, does not take sufficient account of the 'outside' or 'up against' the law position of these women. Rather, they imply that the formal legal definitions of 'family' did not adequately address their situation, so created their own version of law to regulate their familial relationship. To label this 'very basic contract' as 'legal' seems to draw clearly on a plural conception of law, one that allows for that which people identify, and use in their social practices, as 'law' to be seen as an alternative to official law.

In summary, for these lesbian and gay parents, the problems of parenting outside the law include experiencing the negative effects of the exercise of legal power, the difficulties of negotiating rules in the absence of (official) law, and the problematic effects of heterosexist laws relating to the family. The resistance strategies used by these lesbian and gay parents to counter the negative effects of 'parenting outside the law' include elements of Ewick and Silbey's (1998) 'against the law' category of legal consciousness, but also include both stabilising and moderating forms of resistance. Stabilising resistance is evident in lesbian and gay families where they do not explicitly challenge legal provision, but rather they simply live their lives outside 'official' legal frameworks. Moderating resistance appears where lesbian and gay parents respond to the problems created by law through resisting official legal constructions of what makes a family 'real' or 'pretend' and creating their own rules, contracts and legal frameworks that more adequately and accurately reflect their everyday lives. The difficulties of inappropriate legal provision are also highlighted in the second theme in these narratives.

'Real' and 'illegitimate' parents

The second theme common to published stories of lesbian and gay parenting concerns the distinction made between 'real' and 'illegitimate' parents – in other words, the different social and legal status granted to co-parents depending on the legal relationship they have to their children. In the past, children who were born outside legally married heterosexual relationships were labelled as 'illegitimate' – they were subjected to social stigma and their rights to inheritance were limited (Nygren, 2003). In the second half of the twentieth century, however, the legal distinctions between children born in and out of marriage were eroded to the point of (near) extinction. In more recent times a variety of legal changes have allowed unmarried (genetic) fathers to be easily recognised as legal parents, and they can also obtain parental responsibility more easily than in the past (Smart & Neale, 1999). In the context of lesbian and gay families, however, the problems of 'illegitimacy' appear to subsist, where one parent is classed as the 'real' parent and the other has no legal relationship to their child(ren), and consequently, the child has no legal relationship to one of their parents:

> People always ask, 'Who are you? Are you his dad?' Legally, we are not family, but in reality we are. We have a father-and-son relationship. Look at us and tell me that we are not.
>
> (Mallon, 2004: 78)

In the above extract, a gay father who does not have a legal relationship to his son emphasises the *de facto* relationship that he has with his son as a way of countering the difficulties inherent in being an 'illegitimate' parent. While he acknowledges the lack of legal bond between them, he attempts to circumvent this through focusing on the reality of his parenting situation. However, by drawing attention to the ways in which 'people always ask' about the technicalities of his relationship with his child, and the legal 'truth' of his status as a parent, he is both noting the power of law to create a 'truth' about who is a parent while attempting to resist this through de-emphasising the ability of the restrictive legal framework to accurately describe his role as a parent. Similarly, another gay father talks about the problems his lack of legal status as a parent could have 'in the event that something should happen, but love is stronger than paper' (Mallon, 2004: 78). Through his assertion that 'love' is more important than legal technicalities ('paper'), he is again contesting the ability of law to construct an accurate 'truth' about his life as a parent.

These examples highlight a different side to the discussion of 'paper' and 'writing' than in the first theme above. Whereas the creation of a quasi-legal document was empowering for the lesbian mothers discussed above, the lack of legal writing is problematic for these gay fathers. As these fathers do not have a legally recognised relationship with their children, they have to resist law's version of their family status. Rather than allowing the 'truth' of their lack of legal status to define their relationships with their children, they resist this by emphasising their own version of the 'truth' of their situation. These truth claims seem to create space outside the power relations imposed by legal definitions of who is and is not a parent. This discourse seems to have elements of 'against the law' legal consciousness: in this situation, law is something that should and must be avoided; 'illegitimate' (lesbian and) gay parents use strategies of stabilising resistance to balance the asymmetrical power relations imposed by legal structures.

On occasion, the difficulties facing 'illegitimate' parents become less abstract and more real:

> Sometimes, when I have felt the weight of hatred – after a carload of young men has driven by my lover and me and yelled 'What you

> need is a good fuck' after I was denied recognition as a parent because I was not the 'real' mom; I wish for a life without the tensions of discrimination.
>
> (Richmond, M. in Abbot & Farmer, 1995: 153)

As the above extract shows, one facet of heterosexism and homophobia confronting lesbian and gay families arises when parents, who have *de facto* relationships with their children, but no legal status, can be 'denied recognition' of their status as parents. This can, in part, be attributed to the ways in which society constructs who does and does not count as a parent. Culturally embedded constructions (both 'common sense' and biological 'fact')[8] determine who is a parent: children have one mother and one father, and they are genetically related to both.[9] The legal definitions of 'parent' are highly important in the context of lesbian and gay families, as all too often the non-legal status ('illegitimate') parent is sidelined, especially in times of emergency:

> When Drew fell and we had to rush him to the hospital, we were really scared, I mean, our kid was bleeding and we were a mess. When we ran into the emergency room, the first thing we were confronted with was, 'Which one of you is the dad?' Legally, my partner was the parent, so, right then and there, even in this emergency situation, and even though I was holding Drew, I had to back off and let my partner take charge because of his legal status. It was so upsetting to me and to Drew too.
>
> (Mallon, 2004: 125)

Interestingly, in the above extract, the narrator highlights the ways in which legal status interacts with the everyday life of this family. He emphasises that the episode was upsetting both to him, as a parent, and to their injured child. Rather than being able to claim equal status with his partner, his lack of legal status caused him to feel that he had no legitimate role when interacting with the officials at the hospital. This is another example of the ways that people who are subjected to the power of law to decide the 'truth' of their lives are made to feel powerless in everyday situations. The effect of laws which only acknowledge the legitimacy of one parent in a lesbian/gay co-parenting relationship is, therefore, to make 'illegitimate' parents feel unable to participate in the official interactions that are an inevitable part of parenting.

In some situations 'illegitimate' parents can contest or resist the ways in which they are sidelined by restrictive legal provision, through emphasising the reality of their situation over legal constructions. At other times, however, the power of law remains ascendant, and 'illegitimate' parents feel disempowered and unable to help their children. That this father felt unable to speak what he knew to be a legal 'untruth' is a very interesting part of his narrative. He is clear that he is a father, that his son is his son and yet he was unwilling to simply state 'I am' when confronted with a direct question about his parental status. On one reading, the hospital officials may not even have been asking about the legal truth of their relationships, but the effect of normative conceptions of what constitutes a family seems to be that without legal status, lesbian and gay parents feel unable to claim their *de facto* status as parents.

The following extract provides another example of why lesbian and gay parents who lack legal status may be wary of claiming to be a parent in emergency situations. In the following extract, a lesbian mother describes how she felt when she was refused entry to see her partner in the hospital ward shortly after she had given birth by caesarean section:

> In this moment I begin to understand how illegitimate I am. Although Julie and I have been a committed couple in love for eight years, to the staff she is simply my roommate. I have no blood nor legal tie to either her or Annie; despite that I was there when Annie was conceived and have been speaking to her for eight months ... there really is nothing I can show them that tells them who I am.
>
> (Goodridge, H. in Aizley, 2006: 33)

For this woman, who was denied access to both her partner and her child by nursing staff, the status of 'illegitimate' parent is all too real.[10] Later in her story, she describes how she managed to get past the nurse on a different occasion:

> Later, I walk down the hall to be with them [her partner and child].
> A nurse stops me.
> 'Who are you here to see?'
> 'Julie Goodridge,' I say.
> 'And you are?'
> 'Hillary Goodridge, her sister.'
> 'Go right in,' the nurse says with a smile.
>
> (Goodridge, H. in Aizley, 2006: 34)

This part of her story describes a resistant act; lying to the nurse to avoid having to explain her relationship to her partner again. By telling this part of her story, the author highlights the moment of resistance against the heterosexism of the hospital staff. As Ewick and Silbey (2003) argue, telling a resistance story transforms the original act into another form of resistance. By narrating an act of resistance, the resistant act is taken out of its initial time and place, and becomes a tool for others to use. The initial resistant act could be described as 'stabilising resistance', but through narrative it is transformed into a public act of moderating resistance – with the potential for wider effects.

Another feature of lesbian and gay parents' stories of law and the problems of being an 'illegitimate' parent is the invisibility of the parent without legal status:

> In some ways I think I have gotten used to being unrecognized, being the invisible dad. But I hate feeling that way, because, God knows, I do my share of parenting. I really hate it when someone asks, 'Which one of you is the real dad?' The kids have my partner's last name, so in some ways it is already set. It also becomes a challenge when I have to sign something for the kids from school or at the doctor's office – it really gets to me.
>
> (Mallon, 2004: 78)

Here, the lack of legal status of the 'illegitimate' parent is placed very much within the bounds of everyday life – parents are often required to sign consent forms for school trips, or medical treatment. The mismatch between doing his 'share of parenting' and feeling invisible, or finding it a 'challenge' when parental consent is required in an official setting (as a result of his lack of legal status) is something that 'really gets to' this father. Rather than describing resistance to the law in this context, however, this gay father seems to internalise the problems of being an invisible 'illegitimate' parent. His use of phrases like 'I really hate it' or 'it really gets to me' again highlights his feelings of powerlessness in the face of legal constructions of who is a parent.

The following extract highlights a slightly different problem confronting the 'illegitimate' lesbian or gay parent, taken from the perspective of the 'real' parent:

> We don't have a contract. We do have a verbal agreement. I told her when I was pregnant, and I still believe it, that I would honor whatever her real relationship was to this child. The fact of the matter is she's an equal parent like I am. I don't think that I'm the kind of person who could break up with her and not honor that.
>
> (Pollack & Vaughn, 1987: 119)

In this extract, the biological mother in a lesbian co-parenting arrangement states that, she would always honour her partner's 'real relationship' to their child, and says that her partner is an 'equal parent', even if their couple relationship were to end. However, she then proceeds to go into more detail about how she thinks the co-parenting relationship would continue if the relationship were to end:

> I mean she's the coparent, and if we divorce, we would have to work out timing and visitation. I think while Megan is small, I would want the bulk of time with her, but certainly Jean would go on being her parent. I think while she's young, I could provide a better home, make sure meals were

> ready on time, that I was home and there were fresh cookies. I'm more like that than Jean is. I don't think it means I'm a better parent or Jean shouldn't have equal rights to Megan. It just means that at this point in our relationship our roles are different.
>
> (Pollack & Vaughn, 1987: 119)

She states that they have 'different roles' and that she would 'want the bulk of time' with the child – this shows an interesting disjunction between her description of 'equal parent' and her (implicit) view that as the 'real' (biological) parent of their daughter, she is better placed than the other, 'illegitimate', parent, to decide on what would be in the child's best interests, should the adult relationship break down. Also, by specifically mentioning 'timing' and 'visitation', and not mentioning custody, she implies that there would be no question about who would have custody of their child. In this sort of situation, it is unlikely that there would be a question over who would be favoured by a court, should a contested custody situation arise. In some respects this 'real' mother is empowered by her knowledge of the law in relation to child custody, at the expense of the 'illegitimate' mother, leading to an imbalance of power relations between the co-parents, as well as in their differential legal status. So, this example shows another place where law interacts with everyday life, in that because legal frameworks place more value on the 'real' parent than the 'illegitimate' parent, this creates differential power relationships between co-parents, compounding the difficulties of one parent having a stronger legal claim to the status of parent. The differential legal status of parents in stories such as this one seems to have a clear impact on their legal consciousness.

Inevitably, the legal status of each parent becomes highly important when same-sex couples with children split up. The ways in which the different status of each parent creates an unequal balance of power in same-sex co-parenting relationships is commented on in this extract:

> The child loses and the non-adoptive or non-bio mom – the non legal status mom – has to fight for every single inch she gets. And the bio moms, in all the vitriol and negativity of the breakups, or simply because the conditioning of the culture, have the power and sometimes keep it.
>
> (Loulan, J. in Abbot & Farmer, 1995: 264–65)

Here, the difficulties of not having legal status in relation to the children of a same-sex relationship are highlighted. In this extract, like in the example above, rather than power being directly attributed to law or legal actors, the power relationship that comes into focus is the effects of the different legal status of the adoptive or biological parent and the 'other' parent. In the context of the breakdown of same-sex relationships, the parent with legal status becomes the powerful, normalised parent – the one who has the 'right' to say what happens to their child(ren). The 'other' parent then becomes the one who must resist their categorisation as un-entitled to custody or contact, much in the same way as lesbian mothers had to resist the law's conception of 'lesbian mother' as an oxymoron. This echoes the situations that arose when lesbian mothers had to fight in court to try to retain custody of the children they had while in a heterosexual relationship, when 'the very notion of *lesbian* and *mother* was a contradiction in terms to the average judge' (Pollack & Vaughn, 1987: 44).

This problematic, of what happens when same-sex parents' relationships end, is one that is echoed in a number of the personal stories published in these books about lesbian and gay parenting:

> We finally decided to separate after a lot of painful discussion, once again, we had to figure out everything about being divorced gay parents by ourselves. It's not like with straight couples, where they can go to an attorney and have someone mediate the separation agreement. Since gay people do not have sanctioned, legally recognized, unions, they once again have to figure out how to do things without sanctioned legal guidance.
>
> (Mallon, 2004: 83)

The above extract highlights again the problems of the 'lack' of law for lesbian/gay parents. Like in the examples of parenting outside the law under the first theme, when co-parenting adult relationships end, the absence of law can be a real problem, especially for the 'illegitimate' parent. It is interesting that this gay man attributes the problems that can occur when same-sex co-parenting relationships break down to the lack of legal recognition of same-sex relationships. This highlights the interwoven nature of adult relationship recognition/regulation and parental status, and that same-sex marriage or civil partnership is construed as having the potential to make life easier for lesbian and gay parents.[11] Similarly, in this extract, one gay father, who was not the 'legally recognised parent' expressed his anxiety at the potential that his ex-partner could prevent him from continuing to be an active parent in his children's lives:

> Paul was the legal parent. When we adopted, he felt so strongly about it that we decided that he should be the legally recognized parent. We both equally financed the adoption, and we had always both been very involved in the children's lives, and the legal issue was never really an issue for us until we separated. As the legal parent, he had all the rights and I had none. It was as if I had no say whatsoever over my own child. It was terrible. I was so afraid that he wouldn't let me be a part of their lives, and he could have [done that], if he wanted to. Fortunately we worked

> things out, and we share custody of our children through a mediated agreement with staff at the Lesbian and Gay Center.
>
> (Mallon, 2004: 77–78)

In this example they 'worked things out', coming to their own arrangement without legal intervention, by drawing on the community resources available through their local lesbian and gay centre, creating their own rules. This again draws on a legal pluralist viewpoint – the rules they have created are just as necessary and valid in their lives as any rules from 'official' law. However, in other cases, the 'illegitimate' parent may not be able to come to an agreement with the 'real' parent which reflects their feelings of equal entitlement (see e.g. Barret & Robinson, 2000: 111; Pollack & Vaughn, 1987: 27; Saffron, 1994: 149).[12] Another important aspect of this gay parent's story is that he states that he and his ex-partner 'both equally financed the adoption'. This highlights a disjunction, that while both parties may contribute equally (both in financial and caring terms) to the parent/child relationship, the operation of legal frameworks means that only one is recognised as a legal parent.

By focusing on an equal caring contribution, the non-legal status parent is making a specific claim to the child that can be viewed as a form of stabilising resistance – by claiming to do an equal amount of parenting labour, the normative vision of family life as gendered and with an unequal distribution of childcare is resisted. The effect of mentioning equal *financial* contributions, on the other hand implicitly makes a different sort of legal claim, one based in property law rather than child law. It is interesting to note that discourses about equal financing of the family seem to be much more prevalent in gay male parenting narratives than in lesbian parenting narratives. This may, of course, be due simply to the different methods of creating a family that are open to gay men and lesbian women. Whereas lesbians have the potential to conceive through donor self-insemination, which can be a low- or no-cost route to becoming a parent, the options that are available to gay men are generally limited to surrogacy and adoption or fostering. Different legal frameworks around adoption and surrogacy in different jurisdictions[13] mean that surrogacy and adoption can be very expensive methods of creating a family. The difference between lesbian and gay accounts could, however, be attributed to a different source, that of the historical claim that a father had to ownership of his children.[14]

In summary, as Susan Boyd has argued, 'legal definitions of who constitutes a "parent" often do not accord with personal understandings of familial relations' (Boyd, 2007: 22). The privileging of genetic (such as those between a birth mother and child) or legal (such as those created when only one same-sex partner can legally adopt) familial ties over those formed through social parenting leads to a hierarchy of parents in lesbian and gay families. This hierarchy means that in (equal, co-parenting) lesbian and gay families one parent is often the 'real' parent, and another the 'illegitimate' parent. The legal position of the 'illegitimate' parent can be precarious, and often seems to result in the non-legal status parent being sidelined in times of emergency or relationship breakdown and therefore necessitates ongoing resistance from 'illegitimate' parents to their legal marginality.

Second-class parents to second-class children

The third theme that was evident in these personal stories of lesbian and gay parenting is that lesbian and gay parents are constructed as 'second-class' parents to 'second-class' children. Hierarchies and power imbalances, therefore, are not only evident within lesbian and gay families as between 'real' and 'illegitimate' parents, but the 'second-class status' of lesbian and gay parents more generally is apparent, particularly in relation to adoption and fostering. This may, of course, be because lesbians and gay men who adopt or foster have no choice but to interact with 'officials' of one variety or another in order to become parents. Where (prospective) lesbian and gay parents decide to opt for adoption or fostering in the UK, they experience a hierarchy of both parents and children in the state care system. For example:

> Before embarking on our quest [to adopt] we had never been made to feel as much like second-class citizens as we were now being treated. We exposed ourselves to the worst insults and bigotry we had ever encountered. No one had any qualms about telling us that we were unfit or unsuitable or had no right to think we might be suitable.
>
> (Hicks & McDermott, 1999: 49)

In the above extract, two lesbian mothers describe the homophobic and heterosexist 'insults' and 'bigotry' they were subjected to by officials in relation to their decision to adopt. The reference to 'second-class citizens' echoes some of the discourses surrounding the legal recognition of same-sex relationships, discussed in Chapter 4. Here, again, lesbian and gay parents strive against their construction as second-class citizens, or as un-entitled to equal treatment from state actors. As with the legal recognition of relationships, however, constructions of lesbians and gay men as less deserving of rights are pervasive. The effects of the prior criminalisation of homosexuality, public social censure of lesbian and gay sexuality and the lack of legal protection against discrimination on the basis of sexual orientation all arguably contribute to the construction of (potential and actual) lesbian and gay parents as 'second-class citizens'. That lesbians and gay men continue to challenge the attitudes of social workers and adoption agencies is, however, a form of resistance against the pervasiveness of the construction of lesbians and gay men as 'second class'.

Another facet of the construction of lesbian and gay parents as second class within the adoption and fostering system relates to the 'types of children' that are available for adoption by them and the hierarchy of children that exists within the adoption system. For example, the same lesbian couple notes that:

> She [the social worker] told us about the process and the types of children that might be available; she confirmed that there would be no possibility of a baby ... We knew that as a lesbian couple we would only be considered for the most difficult-to-place children – children with learning difficulties, severe physical problems/illnesses, or sibling groups.
>
> (Hicks & McDermott, 1999: 49–50)

In their case, they decided to opt for a sibling group, but in the remainder of their story they explain that it took a total of eight and a half years from their first enquiries into adoption to actually having children placed with them, a delay that they attribute entirely to their sexuality and the heterosexist attitudes of the officials involved in the fostering and adoption process (Hicks & McDermott, 1999: 51–52).[15]

Their story is echoed by other potential foster/adoptive parents:

> Paul and I were offering ourselves for the so-called 'hard-to-place' older children where potential homes were few and far between. Nonetheless, it seemed that a children's home was preferable for some agencies (and probably for many more if the truth was known behind the reasons they gave) than taking the chance of placing with a gay couple.
>
> (Hicks & McDermott, 1999: 57)

This British gay couple again attributed the reticence of adoption agencies to place children with gay foster parents to the effects of anti-gay law and Section 28:

> The government had set the tone with Clause 28 of the Local Government Act in 1988. Even reasonable people in social services departments, or on their fostering panels, didn't believe that they could look at the situation after that with an open, enquiring mind.
>
> (Hicks & McDermott, 1999: 57)

Here, as with the issues of parenting outside the law which were raised above, the enactment of this anti-gay law which applied to local authorities was felt to have a direct impact on the lives and aspirations of lesbian and gay parents. Rather than accepting 'defeat' at the hands of this restrictive law, however, these prospective foster parents accepted their situation as 'up against the law' (Ewick & Silbey, 1998) but continued to work within the system for some form of fostering responsibility. They eventually succeeded in having a child (with behavioural problems and learning difficulties) for whom they had been providing respite care placed with them on a permanent basis. The story told by these gay foster parents again, therefore, highlights a form of resistance to the ways in which they were labelled as unsuitable, less deserving or 'second-class' parents.

Another example of this sort of resistance can be found in this narrative from another lesbian mother:

> The practice of placing 'hard to place' or 'difficult' children with lesbians and gay men has been going on for years and that is what happened in my case ... I have to ask the question that, no doubt, many other lesbians and gay men have asked: If there are such anxieties around our sexuality and we are considered to be inferior or second-class citizens, why place children who need extra special care and attention with us? I would like to believe that it is because social workers feel we may empathize more because of our own experiences of being treated differently. However, I wonder if that is really the case or are we seen as the last resort?
>
> (Hicks & McDermott, 1999: 82–83)

This woman initially heard about the child she has since adopted 18 months before she was placed with her. The reason for the delay was that a heterosexual couple who had been 'earmarked to adopt' the child 'decided not to pursue it because, amongst other reasons, she had a very obvious squint' (Hicks & McDermott, 1999: 83). Later, the child was diagnosed with a number of learning disabilities. This woman's story does, however, raise some serious questions surrounding the value placed on lesbians and gay men as parents within the fostering and adoption system as well as around the different value judgements made about children and parents on the basis of other factors such as race and disability.

The effects of the creation of this hierarchy of children and parents as constructed by social workers is commented on by a number of the lesbian and gay parents who have told their stories. One gay couple from the US talks about the way the possibilities for adoption were described to them by a social worker who was addressing a gay parenting conference:

> They went along to learn what they could. They 'learned' that their 'only option,' according to the social worker at the lectern, was 'to adopt a special-needs child.' Marc raised his hand. 'What about open adoption?' he asked. 'Good luck,' retorted the social worker. 'No one will turn over a baby to a gay couple.'
>
> (Strah & Margolis, 2003: 9)

Here, the social worker assumed that all people will hold the same views about gay parents as s/he and the professionals in social services more generally did. Arguably, this shows the pervasiveness of heterosexist or homophobic attitudes within social services, as well as contributing to the construction of lesbians and gay men as second-class citizens. Again, however, these prospective gay dads managed to resist the subjugation of gay parents by social services and did, eventually, adopt twins through open adoption.

The construction (by legal actors) of lesbian and gay adoptive parents and the children they adopt as second-class citizens is an extremely troubling problem for many lesbian/gay adoptive and foster parents. The law here is not only perceived as a powerful force, but is concurrently seen as a discriminatory and unfair. In some ways, this sort of view of law fits with Ewick and Silbey's (1998) 'against the law' schema – prospective adoptive parents are positioned as both marginalised and up against an all powerful legal system. However, there is more to the stories of law from lesbian/gay adoptive parents than attempts to avoid law's power. The lesbian and gay parents quoted above have succeeded in negotiating the difficult terrain provided by discriminatory laws, and have become adoptive or foster parents. They have exercised their power to resist law's power to decide who can and cannot be a parent, or who is appropriate to be a parent.

This type of resistance is not one which could be described as working 'against' the system, as adoptive/foster parents have no choice but to work within the framework of rules set down by governmental actors such as social services, social workers and adoption panels. Rather, the resistance here is more simple and yet more complex. All these parents have had to battle against discriminatory provision, and have succeeded in their desire to become parents.[16] By trying, sometimes for many years, to become parents in the face of strong opposition, discrimination and inadequate legal frameworks, they have successfully resisted the power of law to decide who is, or is not, a suitable adoptive or foster parent. These lesbian and gay parents' stories expose the relational nature of the power of law and the ways in which marginalised individuals can and do exercise their own power (through resistance) over legal actors and legal rules.

What 'the law' is for adoptive and foster parents, however, is not always clear, and strategies of resistance can also vary from minor deceits in order to avoid the restrictive legal provision through to the reification of a particular agent of the law:

> I was told by my mentor, 'You can be out, but you won't get a child.' People who knew about foster care were very clear about that … We talked three times, and then she [my caseworker] finally came to my house, and I knew that they were interested. She said about halfway through the process, 'You know, it's really unfortunate that a number of people can't adopt – including lesbian and gay people.' I didn't say anything, but it was her hint to me to say, 'If you're gonna say you're gay, then we can't do this.' I mean, I could read the cards very quickly.
>
> (Mallon, 2004: 39)

In the above extract, this prospective gay adoptive father chose not to disclose his sexuality to the caseworker who interviewed him at his home, rather than admit that he was a gay man, in order to avoid being told he could not adopt. This form of minor deceit[17] (not volunteering information, rather than lying) seems to be quite a common form of resistance to legal authority within gay men's accounts of negotiating the adoption process (see also Barret & Robinson, 2000: 2–3; Strah & Margolis, 2003: 145). In these cases, the form of resistance used echoes Ewick and Silbey's (1998) description of resistance by those who find themselves 'up against the law' more closely than in the other stories above.

A very different form of resistance against the power of legal actors within the adoption and fostering system was described by another adoptive gay father, a qualified social worker and former manager of a children's home, who had fostered a child from the children's home he used to manage. He experienced a number of incidents of discrimination on the basis of his sexuality from the local authority and some incidents of mis-management of his application to foster and a lack of support from the council in relation to the care plan of his foster son:

> I later lodged a complaint against the council for not properly considering my earlier complaint about the implementation of Ismail's care plan. This was upheld by the ombudsman and amounted to maladministration for the second time. I complained that the department had not properly considered my complaint that I was dealt with inappropriately when I disclosed my sexuality. Again, the council were found guilty of maladministration. I argued that they had not properly considered our request for Ismail's sister to come live with the family. The ombudsman concluded that the decision to place Nazan elsewhere was reasonable and not taken with bias. However, the process involved amounted to maladministration. Finally, we received compensation.
>
> (Hicks & McDermott, 1999: 104)

This story highlights a very different approach to the problems encountered by lesbian/gay adoptive and foster parents. Rather than work within the system in the ways outlined above, or attempt to circumvent the problems by not being 'out', this foster father used his skills and knowledge of the system to resist, confront and challenge the problems he experienced. This could be an example of a 'with the law' legal consciousness, in that he used the legal means available to him (the local government ombudsman) to challenge the actions and decisions of the council. Arguably, however, although he eventually received compensation for the council's 'maladministration' of his case, this form of resistance was perhaps not as effective as some of the others highlighted above, as his success was only partial and his aim of trying to have the sister of his foster son placed with him was, in the end, unsuccessful.

In summary, lesbians' and gay men's narratives about becoming parents by fostering and adoption included two distinct forms of 'second-class status': lesbian and gay parents as 'second-class parents' and the children placed with lesbian and gay parents as 'second-class children'. The notions of lesbians and gay men being 'second-class parents' were evident through the ways in which these parents wrote of their difficulties in becoming parents. The 'second-class' status of lesbians and gay men as adoptive and foster parents were described through reference to overt homophobia and heterosexism, extensive delays in the fostering and adoption process, and the 'types of children' who were offered to them and eventually placed with them. The 'second-class' status of the children adopted by lesbian and gay parents was alluded to through descriptions of 'difficult' 'hard-to-place' children: older children, children with physical and mental disabilities, and sibling groups. These lesbian and gay parents did, however, write of the ways in which they resisted their categorisation as 'second class'. Forms of resistance included continuing to work towards adopting for extensive periods of time, in some cases for nearly a decade; by challenging the homophobia, heterosexism and other prejudices of official actors in the adoption process; and by challenging unfair or unjust decisions through judicial means, including institutions such as the local government ombudsman service.

Changing times for lesbian and gay parents?

In the final section of this chapter, I now turn to a broader analysis of changes over time in lesbian and gay parenting narratives, focusing on gendered (and other) differences between the experiences of lesbian mothers and gay fathers. Whereas in the analysis above my focus was on thematic similarities between and across accounts, my concern here is to map out some of the discontinuities, conflicts and complexities within lesbians' and gay men's stories of being and becoming parents. In the following analysis, I chart some of the changes over time in the regulation and recognition of lesbian and gay parenting, to highlight the issues of gender difference that intersect with lesbian and gay experiences of being a parent, and to draw out the different ways that contrasting discourse appears and disappears in parenting narratives. This section is split into two sub-sections: gender in lesbian and gay families, and legal and social changes in the makeup of lesbian and gay families.

Gender in lesbian and gay families

The first point to note here is that perhaps the most startling difference between lesbian mothers' and gay fathers' narratives is highlighted by the differential quantities of published narratives that exist about lesbian mothers' and gay fathers' experiences. Whereas experiential accounts (e.g. Pollack & Vaughn, 1987) and academic studies of lesbian motherhood (e.g. Tasker & Golombok, 1997) have been in print for nearly two decades, books about gay fathers (e.g. Mallon, 2004; Strah & Margolis, 2003) seem to be a relatively recent phenomenon. There could be any number of reasons for this discrepancy, including: the ways in which lesbians and gay men become parents,[18] socio-cultural prejudice and fears of paedophilia (Arnup, 1999), the effects of the HIV/AIDS epidemic on gay male communities and societal constructions of childrearing as 'women's work'. Lesbian motherhood has often been described as invisible, particularly from the perspective of the non-biological mother (see Aizley, 2006), but the comparative lack of stories from gay fathers draws even more attention to the invisibility of parenting outside of the normative, heterosexual family unit.

The different numbers of published narratives from lesbian mothers and gay fathers are not, however, the only manifestation of gender difference in accounts of lesbian and gay parenting. There are two other areas in which gender becomes extremely important in these stories: first, providing appropriate gendered role models, and second, the gender of children placed for fostering or adoption in lesbian and gay families. Consider these two excerpts:

> The social worker felt that they [a previous lesbian couple who had been approved] had been easier to approve as they fitted into more stereotypical male/female, butch/femme roles which the adoption panel could relate to. We did not present this type of relationship so we underwent a lot of questioning about how jobs around the house were divided and also how we would provide positive male role models for children. The discussion about male role models went on for some time. For some years our social circle had been entirely female. I even worked in an all-women environment.
>
> (Hicks & McDermott, 1999: 50)

> There were a few points on which they had lengthy discussion, the most thorny being the male role models in their lives and whether or not they would adopt a boy.
>
> (Hicks & McDermott, 1999: 21–22)

As is clear from these two extracts, there seems to be an obvious concern that lesbian mothers provide appropriate male role models for the children whom they may have placed with them through adoption.[19] The issue of appropriate gender role models did not, however, seem to be raised in the same way for prospective gay fathers. Interestingly, there does not seem to be a concern for finding appropriate *female* role models for the children of gay fathers, either from these personal narratives or in scholarship on lesbian and gay parenting more generally.[20]

A second complication in this area is the gender of the children placed with lesbian and gay male parents. Consider these two excerpts, the first from a gay man and the second from a lesbian:

> I was approved for two boys aged nought to eighteen years. I hadn't bothered to specify an age range. I was also approved for one 'special needs' boy aged eight to eighteen years. It was their decision to specify boys but I was happy with that because I didn't feel it appropriate for me to care for young women.
>
> (Hicks & McDermott, 1999: 32)

> There were also lengthy discussions around the gender of the children we wanted. We initially dodged the issue, feeling that if we declared an interest only in girls, this would be disapproved of, but after two sessions the social worker herself said that she felt we had far more to offer girls than boys and that she would be recommending that we be considered for girls only. I had also felt very uncomfortable about expressing a preference as, if I had become pregnant, I would have not had this option.
>
> (Hicks & McDermott, 1999: 50)

In both of these excerpts, the prospective adoptive/foster parents are only approved for children of the same gender as them. This arguably highlights the continuing relevance of gendered and heteronormative societal understandings of the family. The practice of placing girls with lesbian (adoptive/foster) mothers and boys with gay (adoptive/foster) fathers seems to draw on understandings that female children need female parents and male children need male parents. Gender, gender difference and gender roles, therefore, seem to continue to be of immense importance in the family. This may seem a little like stating the obvious, but my concern in highlighting these issues in relation to lesbian and gay parenting is to draw attention to the difficulties inherent in disrupting the ideological force of socio-biological understandings of sex and gender within the family (see, further, Malone & Cleary, 2002).

Legal and social changes

The second area in which inconsistencies and incongruities appear in these narratives from lesbian and gay parents is in relation to the social and legal conditions in which lesbian and gay families exist. There are two issues in particular I would like to highlight here: first, the changing ways in which lesbians and gay men become parents, and the discourse used to describe the formation of lesbian and gay families and, second, the changing legal status of lesbian and gay parents.

As I noted above, many of the earlier lesbian parenting narratives in the collections analysed here are concerned with lesbian mothers who initially had their children within heterosexual relationships. The transition from heterosexual family to lesbian family was often experienced by these women as a difficult road, with some tales recounting difficulty in retaining custody of children, having to live closeted lives (whether for fear of their children being taken away by some other power, or through fear of rejection by children themselves), and the difficulties of navigating parenthood when lesbian families were either rare or invisible. I also noted above that the options for gay men in relation to becoming parents are often very different from those open to lesbians; while both lesbians and gay men can have children from a previous (heterosexual) relationship, adoption, fostering and surrogacy are the main options for gay fathers planning children within the context of a same-sex relationship, whereas lesbians may conceive through known or anonymous donor insemination, or through the adoption/fostering route.

Second, in many of these published narratives, the differential legal status of parents within lesbian and gay families was a major issue. As I dealt with this issue of 'real' and 'illegitimate' parents in detail above, I do not wish to revisit this point in depth, but it is worth noting a couple of interesting themes in some of the more recent stories. Consider this example:

> Given our status as registered domestic partners in the state of California, legal parental rights would default to me if anything ever happened to Dana, just as they do for married heterosexual couples. But our domestic partnership isn't recognized federally, so if we're traveling out of state and had a car accident, depending on whether that state's medical community chose to honor my relationship with my son, I might or might not be able to make medical decisions for [him]. To assure our best legal protection, we are going through an expensive and sometimes humiliating adoption process ... While the adoption process is the same for heterosexual coparents, I often find myself stewing over the fact that when any two straight people have sex and make a baby, they instantly become legal parents with full rights and privileges under the law.
>
> (Hill, M. in Aizley, 2006: 65)

This excerpt from the narrative of a non-biological lesbian mother[21] highlights the problematic effects of differences in the recognition and regulation of lesbian (and gay) families in different jurisdictions. While she is able to gain legal status from the state jurisdiction, her fears cohere around the lack of federal (and international) recognition of their family. The most interesting point in this narrative, however, is the way that she compares her situation to that of 'any two straight people' who produce a child. The use of this comparison is reminiscent of the emphasis placed on 'sameness' in formal equality arguments. Even though it is possible for these lesbian parents to gain equal legal standing in their home jurisdiction, the financial and emotional difficulties of accessing second parent adoption highlights the continued lack of 'equality' between different family forms. This discourse therefore implies that much more wide-ranging legal and social change is necessary before lesbian (and gay) parents feel as if they have achieved any semblance of 'equality' as compared to the normative (heterosexual) family.

In summary, although there does appear to have been a number of changes over time in the legal and social situations of lesbian and gay parents, it seems that social and cultural understandings of gender and sexuality in the family continue to infuse the experiences of lesbian and gay families. Even progressive law reform, such as same-sex second or step-parent adoption, or legally recognised same-sex relationships, have not (yet) sufficiently disrupted the heteronormative assumptions that underpin the ideological force of 'the family'.

Concluding remarks

The lesbian and gay parents who have written their personal stories down or told them to the editors, researchers or writers of these eight books about lesbian and gay parenting have highlighted a number of issues related to the legal situation of lesbian and gay parents. By identifying the stories of law (whether 'official' or otherwise) contained within these personal narratives, I have drawn attention to certain aspects of the ways in which law impacts on the everyday lives of these parents. The concerns of lesbians and gay men who parent outside the law have highlighted the power of law in the everyday lives of lesbian and gay parents, including the problems caused by anti-gay legislation and both official and unofficial rules. Indeed, the power inherent in law for these men and women seems to be evident even (or perhaps especially) when there is a lack of law that accurately reflects their everyday lived experiences, or no rules to govern the breakdown of their personal relationships.

In some tales, judges are given 'god-like' status – they, as the physical manifestation of the law, have the power to make or break people's families. Acknowledgement of the power of law is not the only way in which these lesbian and gay parents experience law in their everyday lives, however. They also tell stories of resistance to law: small deceits like not being 'out' to social workers or adoption agencies; or resistance to the rules around the different legal statuses of the parents where only one partner can 'legally' adopt the child(ren). This analysis has shown the tensions, upset and anxiety experienced by 'illegitimate' parents – those lesbians and gay men who have no legal relationship to the children that they love and care for. I have highlighted the ways in which 'illegitimate' parents resist legal constructions of who is a parent by focusing on the *de facto* relationships they have with their children. Finally, these extracts have exposed the ways in which lesbian and gay parents resist their and their children's categorisation as second-class citizens. Through the insights into the ways law interacts with the everyday lives of these lesbians and gay men, I have discussed their strategies of resistance to arbitrary decisions by legal actors and the continuing fight for recognition of lesbian and gay parents as 'real' parents.

In conclusion, my analysis in this chapter demonstrates that in stories of parenting, lesbians and gay men draw on experiences of stabilising and moderating resistance in their stories of law. This has parallels with attitudes to the legal recognition and regulation of same-sex relationships discussed in Chapter 4. The legal consciousness expressed by these lesbian and gay parents again draws on forms of 'before the law', 'with the law' and 'against the law' legal consciousness, highlighting the complex relationships of power and resistance in lesbians', and gay men's experience of the place of law in their everyday lives. That similar ways of expressing legal consciousness and experiences of power and resistance appear in both the survey data analysed in Chapter 4 and the published personal narratives analysed in this chapter highlights the pervasiveness of these layered attitudes to the place of law in everyday life. In the next chapter, I again consider accounts of parenting, alongside attitudes to civil partnership and marriage, through analysis of in-depth interviews with lesbians and gay men.

Notes

1 In this chapter, I use the terms 'stories' and 'narratives' interchangeably.
2 As with the survey respondents in Chapter 4, the perspectives in these stories come from a range of geographical locations and therefore refer to a range of different legal frameworks.
3 For clarity, where the author is available, I show this through secondary referencing, for example: (Goodridge, H. in Aizley, 2006).
4 Local Government Act 1988, s.28, repealed by the Local Government Act 2003, s. 122.
5 The political conditions that gave rise to this provision and the lasting effects of Section 28 have been discussed and analysed elsewhere (see e.g. Cooper & Herman, 1991; Jeffrey-Poulter, 1991; Monk, 1998).
6 This was the case in England and Wales until the Adoption and Children Act 2002 came into force in December 2005. Same-sex couples can now adopt jointly.
7 This has been made possible through the changes introduced by the Adoption and Children Act 2002 and the Civil Partnership Act 2004.
8 There are scientific advances using cloning technology and embryonic stem cells that have the potential to change the need for both female and male gametes in reproduction (Connor, 2007); but the likelihood of these advances being licensed for and utilised by lesbian (and gay) prospective parents seems slim.
9 It is important to note that only gestational/birth motherhood is absolutely certain to give rise to legal status as a parent, and even this can, on occasion (e.g. surrogacy arrangements) be disrupted (Boyd, 2007).
10 Interestingly, the author of this story is Hillary Goodridge, one of the litigants in the successful Massachusetts same-sex marriage case from 2003, *Hillary Goodridge & Others vs Department of Public Health & Another* SJC-08860. While it is impossible to say here what motivated this individual to campaign for access to marriage, it is certainly plausible to suppose that her experiences as a non-biological

('illegitimate') lesbian mother contributed to her decision to participate in that court action – the story that she tells here is from a significant period of time before either the same-sex marriage court case, or the publication of her story.

11 The interconnectedness of relationship recognition and parenting is also referred to when lesbians and gay men talk about the need for relationship recognition – see Chapters 4 and 6 for more discussion of this issue.

12 For an exploration of these problems in the context of US custody case law, see Robson (1994), and for analysis of recent litigation between lesbian mothers, see Millbank (2008).

13 For example, whereas in the UK adoption is almost exclusively accessed through the state social services system and payments to surrogate mothers are limited to payment of reasonable expenses, the US system allows for payments to surrogate mothers and payments to birth mothers through the 'open adoption' process.

14 Discourses of 'ownership' of children, particularly when tied to financial contributions are, of course problematic. This issue has most clearly been considered in literature examining the Father's Rights movement (see e.g. Boyd, 2006).

15 That this lesbian couple decided to opt for a 'sibling group' is interesting, as it shows that they needed to engage with the hierarchy of children, in that they chose what they felt would be the 'best' option for them given their limited choices. So, a sibling group was their idea of the 'best' option, rather than children with learning disabilities, severe physical disabilities or other health problems.

16 There are, of course, therefore perspectives missing from these accounts – the stories of those lesbians and gay men who would have wanted to become parents, but who did not succeed. Stories from these (much harder to reach) lesbians and gay men would undoubtedly bring different experiences to light.

17 I use the phrase 'minor deceit' here in reference to the list of resistant practices outlined by Ewick and Silbey (1998) in their discussion of 'against the law' legal consciousness.

18 Many of the earlier narratives from lesbian mothers, for example, are concerned with coming out as a lesbian after being heterosexually married or having children in the context of a heterosexual relationship (see Abbot & Farmer, 1995; Pollack & Vaughn, 1987).

19 Issues of male role models are also important for lesbian families when children are conceived through donor insemination at an HFEA licensed clinic. For more discussion of this, see Harding (2005).

20 I return to this issue in Chapter 6.

21 This woman's partner gave birth following donor insemination.

Chapter 6

Recognising regulation

In this chapter, the third of four empirically grounded chapters, I explore lesbians' and gay men's views about the impact and effects of new legal developments in the regulation of relationships and parenting on their everyday lives from accounts solicited through in-depth interviews. I argue here that in interviews about relationship recognition and parenting, lesbians and gay men draw on similar discourses around power, resistance and equality to those found in survey research (as detailed in Chapter 4) and published personal narratives (as per Chapter 5). I also argue that in-depth interviews allow for gendered differences to become more apparent in lesbian and gay legal consciousness: first, regarding the negative, assimilationist possibilities of legal recognition of same-sex relationships; and second, with respect to the issue of appropriately gendered role models for children.

The chapter is in three parts. I begin by outlining the methods used for this chapter and the demographic profile of the interviewees, before moving on to explore participants' views about the legal recognition of same-sex relationships, focusing on four themes: whether legal recognition is 'good' for lesbians and gay men; pragmatic and financial benefits of legal recognition; the complex interplays between recognition and regulation; and, finally, participants' views about civil partnership as against marriage. In the third part, I turn my attention to participants' views of law and legal process in relation to lesbian and gay parenting. These participants' views about parenting again cohered around four themes: the challenges of thinking about becoming a parent as a lesbian or gay man; the practical difficulties faced by lesbians and gay men who wish to become parents; the ways lesbian parents manage societal norms; and the effects of legal regulation on lesbian parents. I conclude with a discussion of the ways in which legal consciousness and stories of power and resistance run through these participants' accounts of their attitudes towards law and the place of law in their everyday lives.

Method: in-depth interviews

The interview material foregrounding this chapter concerns lesbians and gay men's views about, perceptions of and experience of the place of law in their everyday lives. As such, the methods used in this chapter conform more closely to the methodological approach of legal consciousness studies. I interviewed ten lesbians and gay men[1] about their attitudes to and views about these areas of life. The interviews were semi-structured in their approach, with a set of questions that I modified depending on the personal circumstances of the interviewee. There were, for example, different sets of questions depending on whether the interviewee was in a relationship or not, and whether or not they had children. The interviews each lasted approximately one hour. Interviews took place in the respondents' homes or in another mutually convenient location.

As discussed in Chapters 1 and 4, attempting to obtain a representative sample in sexualities research is a near-impossibility, as non-heterosexual people make up an undefined and difficult to represent population. As such, I have not attempted to create a representative sample of participants in this study. Rather, participants were recruited through strategic opportunistic sampling through informal networks within lesbian and gay communities. Six interviews were carried out in Edinburgh, two in the Midlands and two in London. All of the participants in this interview study were white. Table 6.1 shows the demographic details for the participants.

I am conscious that this small-scale examination of lesbian and gay views about the effects of legal change on their lives cannot compare to the large legal consciousness investigations that have characterised the field of legal consciousness studies. This study does, therefore, differs in a number of important respects from Patricia Ewick and Susan Silbey's (1998) study. In the study that formed the basis of *The Commonplace of Law*, Ewick and Silbey included a number of standardised questions related to legal knowledge, experience of and familiarity with legal institutions (e.g. courts) and specific questions about perceptions of legal authorities and legal procedures. In my study, no questions about legal knowledge were included – the aim of the

Table 6.1 Interview participants' demographic information

Pseudonym	*Age*	*Gender*	*Occupation*	*Sexual identity*	*Class identity*
Madge	32	Female	Teacher	Lesbian	Middle class
Kay	31	Female	Admin officer	Gay	Middle class
Angus	30	Male	Marketing director	n/a	'Abc1'
Michael	28	Male	Bar manager	Gay	'I don't'
Gillian	27	Female	Assistant solicitor	Gay	Middle class
Nicola	33	Female	Full-time mother	Bisexual	Middle class
Peter	24	Male	Press & promotions manager	Gay	'Not a chav'
Louise	43	Female	Social worker	Lesbian	Lower middle class
Elizabeth	45	Female	Social work manager	Lesbian	Middle class
Tom	21	Male	Student	Gay	Middle class

interview was solely to collect data in the form of personal narratives, not to evaluate how much legal knowledge interviewees had or to assess whether respondents' knowledge of law was 'correct'. Rather, I am interested in the narratives that are produced during the interview as texts. I do not claim that interview accounts are a method of accessing some kind of empirical 'truth' or as a window to some higher 'reality', but rather I see the interview as a place where stories are solicited by the interviewer and told by the interviewee – a space where co-constructed accounts of the relationship between law and everyday life are produced.

Moreover, whereas previous legal consciousness studies have drawn on very large numbers of interviews, for this chapter, I have interviewed just a small number of people (ten) about their views. I am not looking to people's perceptions of law to expose master narratives of the stories that people tell about law (e.g. the three types of legal consciousness described by Ewick and Silbey); rather, I am interested in individual narratives as texts, the stories that each individual tells of their perspective on the legal regulation of non-normative sexuality. For me, legal consciousness is a method of exposing the micro-interactions that happen at the level of everyday life, with individual experiences and stories of law being the focus of research, rather than broad legal systems and structures. I am also interested in the ways in which stories told in interviews reflect discourse around the issues of same-sex relationship recognition and lesbian and gay parenting using different methodological approaches.

Relationships: recognition or regulation?

The first section of the interview focused on attitudes to, and perceptions of, the legal recognition and regulation of same-sex relationships. None of these interviewees had entered into any opt-in form of legal recognition,[2] neither did any of them have plans to do so in the near future, although entering into a civil partnership was something that some participants had thought about doing at some unspecified future time. All these participants supported the introduction of civil partnership for same-sex couples, saying things like: 'I think it's a really good thing for lesbians and gay men and bisexuals' (Tom), 'it's so obviously a good thing' (Kay), and 'after Section 28 and all those dreadful things in the 80s I was just absolutely bowled over by it – the fact that it could ever happen [it's] just radical and fantastic, so it's brilliant, really brilliant' (Louise). But these participants' positive perceptions of the legal recognition of same-sex relationships were also complex, contradictory and mediated by very real concerns about: first, whether same-sex marriage or civil partnership was good for same-sex relationships; second, the pragmatic and financial benefits of relationship recognition; and third, the relationship between recognition and regulation. In this section, I explore each of these themes, drawing out examples of these participants' 'legal consciousness' and the understandings of equality and relations of power and resistance that are highlighted in their accounts.

Legal recognition: good for gays?

The first theme in these participants' accounts of the legal recognition of same-sex relationships cohered around why and whether legal recognition was good for lesbians and gay men. Generally, these participants were supportive of the introduction of civil partnership, although some participants saw the potential drawbacks of the introduction of legal recognition for same-sex relationships. Some of these participants were very much in favour of the legal recognition of same-sex relationships. Michael, for example, offers the perspective that civil partnership is a good thing for gay men:

> It is something I would like to do, yeah. I think it's good for the binding of two people legally, y'know when it comes to building a life together. When people get mortgages together, I think it's a safeguard, I think it's good for that. I think it's good for our culture, um our own society because it is so baby-like in comparison to the norm. I'm not saying that being gay is a new thing, but I think the way that we've integrated into society is still quite young and I think it's important for us. It's an important step for us to do that because marriage, civil partnership, which are all just words anyway, it's a commitment between two people and they're acknowledging that, and I think it's very good foundational step for two people when they choose to spend their lives together – stops them running.
>
> (Michael)

In this excerpt, Michael attributes both the longevity of relationships and financial protection to 'the binding of two people legally', which is an interesting perspective on the function of law. For Michael, legal recognition is important for the protection of people in relationships, because 'love doesn't conquer all' and so 'any sense of security or backup is always good' (Michael). He also comments on what he calls the 'baby-like' nature of same-sex relationships, as he perceives gay (male) culture to be like 'kids in candy stores with everyone doing everything', and that the legal recognition of same-sex relationships has the potential to make gay male culture 'grow up'.

This perception of legal recognition as having the potential to make gay male culture more 'emotionally mature' can, in part, be read as evidence of a 'before the law' (Ewick & Silbey, 1998) perspective on the function of law in society, as it sees law as a distinct sphere from society that has the potential to dramatically affect the ways that people live their lives. Ewick and Silbey's 'before the law' perspective, however, does not fully explain this attitude to the function and possibilities of legal recognition of same-sex relationships. Rather, Michael describes law and society as being far more entwined than a 'before the law' perspective can allow. He claims that legal change has the capacity to catalyse wide-ranging changes *within* gay male culture – so that same-sex relationships become more like the norm of heterosexual relationships. He is, in a sense, reflecting the 'conservative' argument that gay marriage will tame and domesticate gay men, stop them from being promiscuous and encourage them to become more emotionally mature (Sullivan, 1997). Jonathan Rauch (2004) presents a similar type of argument. He contests that marriage would be 'good for gays' because it would make gay culture 'which seemed to suffer from an advanced case of Peter Pan syndrome' (Rauch, 2004: 66) grow up. This perspective of law's power to change the way in which people act and behave cannot fully be attributed to any of the three schemas of legal consciousness, as it shows awareness of the more diffuse, regulatory effects of law, law outside the confines of the judicial system, where governance, regulation and social as well as legal rules are the crux of the place of law in everyday life. Alongside this, Michael's perspective on the place of law in people's personal relationships focuses on law as protecting people, as backup for when things go wrong.

Similarly, Gillian likens civil partnership to marriage, and makes it clear that she believes that being in a legally recognised relationship gives people 'more incentive to work it out':

> I suppose I have a bit of an old fashioned view about marriage being a union for life and all that sort of thing I think if there was someone that I'd like to do that with then like if you take your marriage vows seriously, then if you're having a difficult spell in your relationship you've got more incentive to work it out and all that sort of thing.
>
> (Gillian)

This argument seems again to be indicative of a socially conservative approach to why the legal regulation and recognition of relationships is a beneficial thing for society – that being married or in a civil partnership gives people a reason to work through difficult periods in their relationships. She does not give any reasons why people should stay in a relationship that is not going well; rather, she accepts that people should live in couples, and that the longstanding coupled relationship is a sensible way to live one's life and is an organising principle of our society.

For both Michael and Gillian, introducing the legal recognition of relationships involves the production of effects on the ways that same-sex couples live their lives. This perception of legal recognition to change the behaviour of people in same-sex relationships has echoes of Foucault's (1998) conceptualisation of the disciplinary mechanisms of power. The regulation of same-sex relationships in this way disciplines lesbians and gay men into conforming to normative ways of living. But, in Foucault's account of the disciplinary mechanisms of power, wherever there is power there is resistance. So, even with the introduction of creative, disciplining forms of regulation for same-sex relationships, there should also be scope for resistance to these disciplinary effects.

Resistance to the disciplinary effects of civil partnership was expressed by some of these participants. Louise, for example, spoke of the possibility of civil partnership creating a hierarchy of lesbian and gay relationships:

> I hope it doesn't create a hierarchy in lesbian and gay relationships, that we're not in a similar position in say 20 years as the heterosexual community have found themselves at different points where there is a difference between people who are married and not, so I hope it doesn't do that ... That's my only fear, that [there] won't become a situation where you have to do it in order to be valid as a couple. I want us to have the same thing we've always had, but also to have the choice to have a civil partnership if we want it.
>
> (Louise)

In the above extract, Louise challenges the notion that legal recognition is inherently a good thing for lesbians and gay men, by highlighting the possible negative societal effects that the legal recognition of relationships could have on same-sex couples. This perspective has echoes of Paula Ettelbrick's (1992) argument that same-sex marriage would create a double standard for lesbian and gay relationships, where a same-sex couple is socially acceptable if they are married, and not if they are not. Louise's concern that the introduction of a legal framework for the recognition of same-sex relationships could impose a new hierarchy, where the only socially acceptable form of relationship is one that has been legally recognised draws on an interesting conceptualisation of the power of law as a producer of new social norms. By creating a legal framework for the recognition of same-sex relationships, a social norm that same-sex couples should enter into this legal relationship is created – thus encouraging same-sex couples to live their lives in a particular way. The specific nature of this societal contribution seems to be that of the privatised couple as an economically interdependent unit within neo-liberal capitalist society (Cossman, 2002a).

Gillian and Michael's view of the legally recognised couple unit as an unqualified good is also challenged by the perspectives of another participant, Madge:

> Recognition of same sex relationships seems to have the potential to shift the binary, in a sense, that y'know people talk about a binary of straight/ gay whereas recognition seems to have the potential to shift the binary from heteronormative to non-normative so everyone that's willing

> to participate in relationship recognition or recognition-like relationships so relationships that kinda fit in that model. So both straight people and lesbians and gay men are on one side of the binary and then on the other side of the binary are the people that don't want legal recognition or don't want to organize their relationships in those particular ways so people who are non-monogamous, who are single, who don't share domestic space with a partner, y'know all those kinda forms of relationship.
>
> (Madge)

For Madge then, the introduction of civil partnership (or the extension of marriage to include same-sex couples) is potentially problematic in that it may place too much emphasis on monogamy and continue to privilege the couple relationship above all other relationship forms. She posits that this has the potential to shift the same amount of social censure that has, until now, been directed at lesbians and gay men as well as those who live in alternative relationship structures onto just those people who choose to live outside the coupled relationship norm. Again, this perspective on same-sex marriage reflects radical feminist arguments about the dangers of same-sex marriage, most notably Nancy Polikoff's (2003) argument that a focus on same-sex marriage pushes law 'in the wrong direction by widening the divide between the status of marriage and the status of other relationships' (Polikoff, 2003: 225).

It is important that these critiques of marriage (and other forms of legal regulation of same-sex relationships) continue to be heard within the same-sex marriage debates, but feminist critiques of marriage are not the only function of the vocalisation of potentially detrimental effects of the legal recognition of same-sex relationships by Madge and Louise. Rather, making these arguments also opens up space for resistance to the potentially damaging effects of legal recognition on lesbians and gay men. By highlighting the creation of new norms through relationship regulation, Madge and Louise open up space for critical reflection on the effects of power – a space that can be filled with resistance. As with the moments of resistance discussed in Chapters 4 and 5, the types of resistance that are most commonly draw on in discussion about whether the introduction of legally recognised same-sex relationships will be 'good' for lesbians and gay men are forms of resistance that I would describe as stabilising and moderating.

These contrasting perceptions of the connection between legal recognition of relationships and the privileging of the coupled relationship also have echoes of the 'before the law' perspective, but allude to a different perspective on the place of law in everyday life. Michael and Gillian's perspectives that the existence of a legal relationship between a couple will encourage them to try to 'work it out' in difficult times seems to include the view that law is a useful set of rules which should be respected. Madge and Louise, on the other hand, are much more critical of the rules that are laid out through legal regulation – especially through their concern about the potential for widening legal 'protections' to further marginalise others who choose not to live in the way that civil partnership proscribes. The nuances of these views about how law works in everyday life through the legal recognition of relationships envision law as a part of society entwined with social values and entrusted with the regulation of the ways that individuals live their lives. Whereas Gillian and Michael see the power of law to change the lives of same-sex couples (all be it in a positive way), Louise and Madge both draw attention to the problems associated with power's effects in this area, and create space for resistance to law's power.

Pragmatic and financial benefits?

The second theme in these participants' accounts of the legal recognition of same-sex relationships was a more pragmatic one – the protection of personal and financial interests. Kay, for example, focused on the financial and practical implications as a reason for entering into a civil partnership:

> I think that we *might* do. It is something that I've been thinking more about. Probably more because of thinking 'are we going to buy property at some point' so having something a bit more in terms of kinda a legal issue or something like that ... It is a bit bad that you start thinking of civil partnerships as y'know 'when things go wrong' [but] at least if a partner dies there is some kind of y'know legal framework there to ensure that they're not just ignored.
>
> (Kay)

Here, Kay highlights potential benefits that entering into a legally recognised relationship might have for the individual. In a sense this is a 'with the law' perspective, because it is about using the law for one's own aims, taking advantage of the protections that legal rules and regulation can give the individual. But this is not about playing the 'game' of law; rather, it is an example of an awareness of the potential that entering into the arena of legal recognition could provide benefits. Essentially, it is the potential for civil partnership/same-sex marriage to have beneficial practical effects for individual lesbians and gay men that makes entering into a civil partnership an attractive prospect for same-sex couples. Without the potential for individual benefits of legal recognition, there would be no incentive for same-sex couples to enter into legally recognised relationships. The practical 'rights and responsibilities' nature of civil partnership could be described as a technique of governance; a way of bribing lesbians and gay men into participation in the neo-liberal privatisation of caring and economic responsibilities into the family.

Interestingly, the actual scope of the perceived 'benefits' of entering into a civil partnership is not always clear to these participants, as this excerpt from Peter's interview shows:

> I think that er ... the real benefit to it would be in terms of ... erm ... having um rights in terms of hospitals ... erm ... and ... erm ... and things like that and I know it would've absolutely broken my heart not to be able to do that and find somebody's family rejected you if there was ever a situation like that with your partner. ... Um ... um and maybe in the future it will be y'know have financial benefits for me.
>
> (Peter)

In the above excerpt, Peter struggled to find practical or pragmatic reasons for entering into a civil partnership; he paused frequently and finally settled on the issue of hospital visitation. So, rather than the legal benefits and 'protections' available to lesbians and gay men being clear, they are vague, almost mysterious things – but things which (without legal regulation) could be frightening or upsetting – like 'being ignored' if one's partner dies, or being rejected by a partner's family (and prevented from visiting) if a partner fell ill and was in hospital.[3] Similarly, Elizabeth mentions inheritance, but then finds it difficult to think of any other 'rights and responsibilities' associated with civil partnership, while reflexively noting the strangeness of this:

> I think that the rights and responsibilities that go alongside it are important. Things like um ... inheritance um and um ... I was thinking about things like ... this is ridiculous! I can't think of the words!
>
> (Elizabeth)

One explanation for these participants' difficulties in explicating the practical advantages of entering into a civil partnership could be that the involvement of law in personal relationships is entrenched within the legal and social norms of our society – we are used to being told what is good for us by the state. The official governmental discourse on civil partnership, for example, was far more concerned with abstract principles such as 'equality' and 'fairness'. It is interesting to note, however, that in the consultation paper on civil partnership, the Government made clear that one of the aims of the introduction of civil partnership was the extension of familial rights and responsibilities to same-sex couples in order to 'encourage more stable family life' (Women and Equality Unit, 2003: 13). In a sense, then, the difficulties that these participants had in elucidating real, substantive practical benefits of entering into civil partnership is linked to the introduction of civil partnership as a mode of governance (Stychin, 2003). By a 'mode of governance' I mean a way of including same-sex couples within the competence of state regulation – shifting relationships that were previously outside the reach of law's regulatory power to within the competence of state regulation.

This governmentalisation of same-sex relationships did not go unnoticed by these respondents. Rather, some concerns were expressed about the wider-reaching effects of legal recognition, especially in relation to the changing status of lesbians, gay men and same-sex relationships within society:

> I think in talking to others, I'm not sure that I really share this, but there is a worry about sameness and assimilation ... I know that a lot of our friends are concerned about this, like saying it's the same as marriage and therefore defining your relationship in a way that they perhaps didn't want it to be defined
>
> (Elizabeth)

This excerpt from Elizabeth's interview is interesting because she explains one of the main arguments against the legal recognition of same-sex relationships, while concurrently distancing herself from this viewpoint. One explanation for this is that, like many lesbians and gay men, Elizabeth had formerly been heterosexually married:

> I did value being married for those reasons of making that public statement and some of the systems and rules are sort of set up and not having to think through every single thing. Like at the moment we're thinking 'oh, we must make a will, we must do this, we must do that', so I see those things as being positive benefits, and maybe because I come into this at a slightly different moment in history.
>
> (Elizabeth)

For Elizabeth, then, the package of rights and responsibilities that come along with marriage and civil partnership are useful, in that it allows for the easier day to day organisation of one's affairs – there's no need to think through every single aspect of 'what will happen if ... '. This is certainly an important aspect of the legal recognition of relationships, particularly as it allows those who may not have the economic resources or legal knowledge to deal with these aspects of life on an ad hoc basis access to a way of ensuring that their loved one is provided for in the face of adverse circumstances (Peel & Harding, 2004).

Elizabeth's comment about approaching the issue of the recognition of same-sex relationships 'at a slightly different moment in history' is also significant, as it shows the differences between people who have come out more recently and those who have identified as lesbian or gay for a longer period of time. Kay, for example, talks about being gay as a rebellious lifestyle:

> This might be quite an old fashioned view of it but this idea that to be gay is to rebel slightly from-to not be part of general society. It's to be a bit on

> the outside. But I think maybe the attitudes have moved beyond that now, y'know it's the [laughs] creeping suburbanisation kind of y'know. But at the same time it's difficult to argue against, it's difficult to see anything that-if that's what people have been fighting for then would necessarily be a good thing.
>
> (Kay)

This attitude, that being gay is 'a bit on the outside', throws some light on the more insidious and less obvious aspects of the increase in recognition of same-sex relationships – that recognition also inevitably involves regulation and normalisation. The argument that same-sex marriage will 'normalise' lesbians and gay men and 'assimilate' them into heterosexual society is one which has been well rehearsed in (particularly) feminist and lesbian and gay scholarship (see, for example, Boyd & Young, 2003; Butler, 2002; Herman, 1994; Polikoff, 2000b). But the 'creeping suburbanisation' described by Kay seems to be alluding to something more than a reflection of the assimilation discourse around the legal recognition of same-sex relationships. She is drawing attention to the ways in which recognition necessarily also includes regulation; that equality for lesbians and gay men comes at a price – the potential dismantling of gay culture. Kay's approach to this issue could be described as a version of 'against the law' legal consciousness, because she is describing law as something that has the potential to have negative effects on lesbians and gay men: effects that could problematically redefine what it means to have a lesbian or gay identity.

This awareness of the potentially problematic aspects that exist alongside the benefits of civil partnership again highlight forms of stabilising and moderating resistance. None of the participants in this study had either entered into a civil partnership; neither did they have specific plans to do so. For some of these participants this was based on reasons like feeling that their current relationship was not one that they would like to commit to in that way. But for other interviewees, their reasons for not entering into a civil partnership were more complex and were infused with resistance to the governmentalisation of lesbian and gay lives. The concerns expressed by these participants about assimilation and normalisation of lesbian and gay relationships are interesting as they highlight the less positive side of same-sex relationships coming under the gaze of regulation and the continued scope for individual agency and resistance to the (hetero)normalisation of lesbian and gay lives.

In summary, these respondents were less than clear about the practical and financial benefits of civil partnership. When thinking in abstract terms about 'protection' for 'when things go wrong', they viewed civil partnership as a good thing for lesbians and gay men. When considering civil partnership in more concrete terms, however, they were less willing to accept that the privatisation, domestication and assimilation of lesbian and gay identities into mainstream society were positive moves. From a legal consciousness perspective, these participants were, on balance, suspicious of the effects of the introduction of civil partnership, but they showed evidence of 'before the law', 'with the law' and 'against the law' legal consciousness. The 'before the law' perspective, in relation to the pragmatic and financial benefits of the legal recognition of same-sex relationships was evident through an unquestioning approach to the place of law in regulating interpersonal relationships. 'With the law' legal consciousness showed through in many of these participants' acceptance that they could use the benefits of civil partnership for their own aims, to save them time, money and effort, or to ensure that they were not 'ignored' by their partner's families if their partner was ill or died suddenly.

What is most interesting to me, however, is the way an 'against the law' legal consciousness intersects with these participants' accounts of the practical and financial benefits of legal recognition: the way Kay spoke of the 'creeping suburbanisation' of lesbian and gay lives, or Elizabeth's vocalisation of others' fears around assimilation. This 'against the law' perspective highlights resistance – resistance to law's power to demand that in return for legal recognition, lesbians and gay men should become more like the idealised heterosexual norm and participate in the promotion of the stable, (hetero)normative, privatised family.

Recognition or regulation?

Following on from, and connected to, the potential assimilatory effects of the introduction of civil partnership, the third theme in these participants' accounts was a concern that the introduction of legal recognition of same-sex relationships would act as a catalyst for increased legal regulation of lesbians and gay men. Madge pointed out that civil partnership will not only affect those who choose to enter into a legally recognised relationship, but rather that it will have an impact on everyone:

> What civil partnership allows the government to do is to regulate *everyone* y'know and I guess that's what bothers me about it. That whether or not you want part of it you that you are going to [be] ... I mean it's naïve to think that legal recognition only regulates the people who participate in it. It is a form of regulation for all society and for everyone that's in society.
>
> (Madge)

As this extract shows, Madge sees a negative side to the opening up of legal recognition of same-sex relationships, in that the introduction of recognition for some means regulation for others. Similarly, Tom noted that 'when I think of the word regulation and I think of relationships, I don't particularly like the two things together.' What these participants have highlighted is that recognition and regulation are two sides of the same thing – what constitutes recognition for some (in this case those who opt in to civil partnership) becomes unwanted regulation for others.

This, again, brings to mind Foucault's (2002) concept of governmentality. If the object of government is the regulation of 'each and all' then the introduction of legal recognition of same-sex relationships can be seen as a governmentalising move. Thus, whether through civil partnership or same-sex marriage, the introduction of state recognition (through an opt-in framework) that allows (predominantly) middle-class or wealthy lesbians and gay men to avoid inheritance tax, also inevitably brings non-registered, unmarried, low-income same-sex couples under the gaze of regulation. It allows the regulation of the *entire* population of non-heterosexual people whether or not they wish to be known by or regulated by government.

Nicola's experience of the effects of the introduction of civil partnership brings this issue sharply into focus:

> Along with that has come the change in the law that living together, that if you're unmarried or not in a civil partnership, that it affects all your money and all your benefits and all of that ... I'm a total casualty – I'm like, not supposed to be claiming any money now ... and I do, because we-I didn't actually realise and the law changed. I think it changed last December the terms for the benefits and everything. So previously I was treated as a single person and now I'm-would be treated as if I'm living as a civil partner. And I'm not in a position to be honest about that ... because materially-if I-well, if my money were to be stopped, we wouldn't be able to afford to pay the rent, for example. Huge. Phenomenal. A phenomenally huge impact. Huge. Scary. Worries me all the time.
>
> (Nicola)

For Nicola, the introduction of recognition for same-sex relationship has had the effect of a drastic change in the level of regulation in her life. Prior to the introduction of civil partnership, her same-sex partner was ignored by the benefits agency and so she was able to claim benefits as a single person. After civil partnership was introduced, her relationship suddenly became relevant to the state, because one of the legal reforms associated with the Civil Partnership Act (CPA) was that same-sex couples who were living together and claiming state benefits (even if they were not in a civil partnership) changed from being assessed as individuals to being assessed as a couple.[4] According to government information (Department of Work and Pensions, 2005), same-sex couples in this situation were supposed to contact their benefits office and simply accept that they were no longer entitled to any social security benefits. Nicola did not do this – and she therefore resisted the introduction of this form of regulation into her life. Her resistance arose not because she particularly wanted to avoid state regulation or because she disagreed that same-sex couples should be treated 'equally' in law, but because if she did 'confess' to the benefits agency, she would not be able to afford to pay her rent. In some respects, Nicola's story is a classic example of 'against the law' legal consciousness – she is a marginalised individual (because she relies on social security benefits) and she is avoiding legal regulation through small deceits (not contacting the benefits office). But she was scared – scared of being found out – and it was a cause of daily worry for her. Even though Nicola resisted the regulation of her life as a result of the introduction of civil partnership, she also saw the law as powerful, frightening and worrisome.

The very real financial impact of the introduction of civil partnership for Nicola is not an unexpected result of the introduction of civil partnership; rather, it is reminiscent of the warnings from feminist scholars that the neo-liberal privatisation effects of the formal legal recognition of same-sex relationships will be experienced most strongly by those who are already disadvantaged by class, race or gender (Cossman, 2002a; Fineman, 2004; Polikoff, 2000b; Young & Boyd, 2006). In reference to the major changes in the recognition of same-sex relationships in Canada, Claire Young and Susan Boyd noted that extending spousal status to lesbians and gay men reinforces the neo-liberal privatisation of economic responsibility, by placing it on family members, rather than the state (Young & Boyd, 2006). Similarly, Brenda Cossman (2002a) argued that 'family law is becoming a more important regulatory instrument for the enforcement of private support obligations for economically dependent family members' (p. 169). Interestingly, just as these critiques of the neo-liberal privatisation of the family and the differential impact on those who are already disadvantaged through the operation of class or gender norms have been predominantly expressed by feminist scholars, reference to the negative economic potential of same-sex relationship recognition was only made by lesbian participants in this study.

A second issue related to the relationship between recognition and regulation of same-sex relationships through civil partnership is alluded to by Kay:

> That's also of course something that makes me shy away from it slightly, because for that very reason the fact that there's some kind of third party involved, y'know. But I suppose that's one of the things I quite like about gay relationships is that they can sometimes be seen as a bit under the radar or not something that's fixed and that they don't have a framework and you are kinda making it up as you go along whereas with a civil partnership it's more a fixing of things really and again putting it in that broader framework.
>
> (Kay)

The creation of an opt-in framework for the legal recognition/regulation of same-sex relationships is seen by Kay as a way of 'fixing things' rather than people in same-sex relationships being able to make things up as they go along. This again goes back to the idea of the legal recognition of same-sex relationships as a technique of government – a way of bringing lesbians and gay men under the control of law. The creation of a legal framework for same-sex relationships becomes a mapping out of how things are supposed to go – two people meet, fall in love, enter into a civil partnership, become more emotionally mature, become financially dependent on each other, and so on – mirroring heteronormative discourse around heterosexual marriage.

The solidification of same-sex relationships is not the only way that these participants thought that civil partnership could work. There is an alternative to this framework, as Peter pointed out:

> Well, It depends how it pans out really, because it's either something that you can do for a couple or three years, and it doesn't have the same stigma as marriage or that it does have the same stigma as marriage and I know that a lot of marriages break up but the intention behind marriage is that it's for ever and ever amen and that y'know. But it might be that over the next little while we see that civil partnerships actually become viewed as a means to an end in terms of the benefits that they bring to people and that there's no stigma about getting in and out of them at short notice and people don't think 'oh, you've been divorced, oh dear' (laughs) and [doesn't have] the same constructs around it as marriage has ... I'd probably call it gay wedding and gay marriage, but it's *gay* marriage, it's not marriage, it's still essentially a different thing.
>
> (Peter)

This excerpt suggests that the creation of civil partnership for lesbians and gay men does not necessarily have to act on lesbians and gay men in the same way as marriage does on individuals within heterosexual culture. While the creation of civil partnership can be seen as an example of governmentality, there still exists within the framework of civil partnership possibilities for individual agency, and the possibilities for lesbians and gay men to resist the neo-liberal privatisation of same-sex relationships. This conceptualisation of civil partnership highlights that the regulatory effects of civil partnership could not be as problematic as some of these participants feared. Peter's perspective highlights the potential for civil partnership to be developed by ordinary lesbians and gay men in ways that were not intended by either the government, with their focus on neo-liberal privatisation of caring responsibilities in the family (see Women and Equality Unit, 2003) or lesbian and gay pressure groups like Stonewall, whose focus in the civil partnership debates was one of formal equality and recognition rights (Stonewall, 2003).

It is too soon to tell whether the assimilatory and normalising aspects of civil partnership (as a 'gay' version of marriage) will be ascendant or whether civil partnership will actually mean something different to marriage for lesbians and gay men. Certainly, for Peter, the fact that civil partnership is not called marriage, and is perceived as something different from heterosexual marriage opens up the possibility of it not having the 'same constructs around it' as marriage. The fact, therefore, that governmental actors were reluctant to afford same-sex relationships 'equal' status to different-sex relationships allows lesbians, gay men and bisexual people the opportunity to do something different with this new legal institution than simply accept it as a 'gay' version of marriage. Civil partnership could, potentially, be a substantively different form of organising relationships, even though it has been modelled on marriage and in many respects legally mirrors marriage law (Peel & Harding, 2004).

In summary, some of these participants were concerned about the potential for the introduction of civil partnership to increase state regulation of same-sex couples, highlighting that recognition and regulation are inextricably linked when thinking of the family in society. What is perhaps most interesting in this theme, however, is that whereas the gay male participants were generally more concerned about the formal equality aspects and the financial and practical benefits of civil partnership, the lesbians who participated in this study seemed to have a different approach. Most of the women interviewed in this study could see that civil partnership could have potentially damaging effects on lesbians (and gay men), through the potential for assimilation of same-sex relationships into dominant (heterosexual) societal norms, the possibility that such assimilation will shift social censure onto those lesbians and gay men who choose not to enter into a civil partnership, and by highlighting the very real financial problems faced by same-sex couples at the lower end of the socio-economic spectrum.

Civil partnership or marriage?

The fourth theme in these participants' attitudes towards the introduction of civil partnership was the troubled interaction of civil partnership and marriage. Alongside the potential for civil partnership to become something very different from marriage, these participants also noted the difficulties associated with the creation of not-marriage for same-sex couples. The uneasy relationship between civil partnership and marriage was approached in three distinct ways by these participants – first, the difficulties of reconciling civil partnership with an understanding of equality as formal equality; second, participants had reservations about the relationship between civil partnership, marriage and religion; and, third, some participants objected to the whole idea of marriage, and were grateful for civil partnership as a real alternative.

The difficulties in reconciling the creation of civil partnership with a belief in formal equality were described by Angus, in his discussion of the way talked about the way he saw civil partnership being 'sold' to the public as gay marriage:

> My problem with it is that it is being sold to folk as gay marriage and it's not ... So in a way I think it's iniquitous. If you really want equality,

> then everyone should have the same thing, and this isn't the same thing, it's like I said [...] buying a car and running a car is the same as inventing something that runs on petrol and has four wheels but is called a gar or a par; it's a car, whether you call it something different it's still a car.
>
> (Angus)

There is an element of contradiction in Angus' attitude towards civil partnership – he thinks that everyone should have access to the same institution(s), but also that inventing something that is essentially the same but called something different is nonsense – so in essence civil partnership and marriage *are* the same thing with different names. He views civil partnership as a form of inequality enshrined in law, not just because same-sex couples are still excluded from the legal institution of marriage, but also because different-sex couples are excluded from civil partnership. His understanding of equality seems to have no space for different legal treatment of same- and different-sex couples. This way of viewing the legal regulation of same-sex relationships is reminiscent of the formal equality discourse discussed in Chapter 4, and again has elements of a 'before the law' legal consciousness, but is not fully explained by this descriptive category. Ewick and Silbey's (1998) category of 'before the law' focuses heavily on the impartiality and objectivity of law, the way that law is 'blind' to difference. As I argued in Chapter 4, lesbians and gay men's perceptions of legal equality seem to see objective, impartial law as an ideal, but do not necessarily see this reflected in the ways that they are treated in law. Similarly, Angus sees civil partnership as unjust, unequal and unfair and the creation of it as making a mockery of the objectivity of law – making up something that is the same as marriage but has a different name for same-sex couples is therefore in direct conflict with his conceptualisation of what equality means.

Other participants also spoke of resistance to civil partnership – this legal fiction made up especially for same-sex relationships. Tom, for example, said:

> I don't particularly like the word marriage, and I don't like all the values that necessarily people assume, I think, when you say the word marriage. But then again I don't particularly like the fact that we're being denied marriage, because I don't think they've given us civil partnership in some kind of radical 'let's give you something different' kind of way, but that they've done it because they don't want us to have marriage.
>
> (Tom)

In contrast to Angus, Tom does see the potential for civil partnership to be something different from marriage, but again views the continuing exclusion of same-sex couples from marriage as problematic. He expressed a desire for a different way of regulating relationships, but did not consider civil partnership as a real alternative to the marriage model:

> I know that heterosexuals complain that they don't have access to it, and siblings do too, and sometimes I feel that's kinda drawing attention away from lesbian and gay relationship recognition, but at the same time I think that there is a case for it being a lot more open to things like that and perhaps being widened away from just the couple relationship.
>
> (Tom)

Tom's views about civil partnership and marriage are in many ways more complex than Angus' perception that unless everyone has access to the same things, then it is iniquitous. By acknowledging that 'there is a case' for the de-privileging of the conjugal couple model of relationship recognition through extending the option to opt in to a legally recognised relationship to heterosexual people, siblings and 'widened away' from the couple, Tom draws attention to the ways that he envisages that civil partnership could have been more 'radical' and therefore a better alternative to marriage.

Gillian, on the other hand, while supporting the introduction of civil partnership sees a lack or 'gap' in the creation of a 'separate but equal status':[5]

> I think it's a good thing in a way, it's a step in the right direction. I mean obviously there's still a distinction between it and marriage as defined by church and state or whatever, but I think it's definitely a step in the right direction.
>
> (Gillian)

This perception that civil partnership is a 'step in the right direction' recalls the arguments of scholars like Kees Waaldijk (2001) and William Eskridge (2002) who argue that civil partnership is part of an identifiable sequence of events starting with the decriminalisation of same-sex sexual activity that will, eventually, lead to same-sex marriage (Waaldijk, 2001). Eskridge (2002) argues that civil partnership or civil union are 'stepping stones' and 'equality practice' – a method of testing and training the general (heterosexual) public to treat lesbians and gay men equally, before same-sex marriage can be achieved. There is a certain appeal to these arguments, but the idea that there is always a forward march of 'progress', which will eventually lead to 'equality' seems a little simplistic, as it does not factor in some of the more complex societal barriers to same-sex marriage.

One such barrier is the almost constant battle between organised religion and lesbian and gay equality-seeking movements. For some of these participants, the relationship between marriage as a religious concept and civil partnership as a specifically secular institution was a cause for concern.

> I did think it was really wrong actually that the government should specifically say that you can't have it in a religious place, and it kinda says that being gay and being religious is incompatible, which I don't think is their right to talk about. I mean obviously if they weren't to say that then religious organisations wouldn't have been forced to do them anyway – the Church of England wouldn't have been forced to perform them, but the very fact that the government is saying 'you cannot' I think is wrong, especially as other religious organisations would perhaps be more open to it.
>
> (Tom)

For Tom, the specific exclusion of civil partnership from anything religious is something that he sees as a negative that has been built into the framework of civil partnership. Nicola also saw the exclusion of religion from civil partnership as a negative aspect of the legislation:

> I don't think it's good that you can't have a marriage and a religious ceremony if you want one – I think that's bad, and I think that its bad how there's all the (och) priests and people who're refusing to […] so I don't like that, I don't think that's very nice.
>
> (Nicola)

Similarly, Madge points out that while she is not a religious person herself, she thinks that the exclusion of religion from civil partnership could be problematic for those lesbians and gay men for whom religion is a part of their lives:

> I know that if you are religious that one of the most important things about relationship recognition is having a form of recognition that is wedded to religion – to be poetic about language-because marriage is you know in a religious context is a religious practice and so even though I'm not religious, and I think religion is in general a pile of poo, it feels very discriminatory for lesbians and gay men and bisexuals in a same sex relationship who are Christian or Muslim or Jewish and they cannot have that dimension as part of their relationship.
>
> (Madge)

The forced separation of same-sex relationship recognition and religion contained within the CPA highlights the difficulties with imagining civil partnership as a stepping stone on the way to full (formal) equality for same-sex couples. There were, undoubtedly, particular concerns in the Government's exclusion of religion from civil partnership, one of which was a fear that if these exclusions were not included in the CPA the legislation would have faced greater opposition from religious organisations, and perhaps even an out and out battle along the frontiers of a conflict of rights. The concern expressed by Tom and Madge, however, is that by specifically excluding religious ceremonies and the use of religious premises, the Government has assumed that the right to freedom of religion does not apply to lesbians and gay men. As Tom points out, there are religious organisations that do not discriminate against lesbian, gay, bisexual and trans people, and places of worship that have been happy to conduct civil partnership ceremonies, or have them conducted by a registrar on their premises.

Not all of these participants saw the exclusion of religion from civil partnership in a negative way; rather, some were happy that civil partnership does not have the religious undertones of marriage, and viewed this as a positive aspect of civil partnership. Louise, for example, was pleased that civil partnership doesn't have the religious history of marriage:

> It's always been very important to me that we don't kinda 'ape' the heterosexual model. I think that for me, my identity as a lesbian is a different identity to a heterosexual woman and so therefore when I make a commitment to my partner I don't make the same commitment as a marriage. I also, personally, don't want something that had a religious history, so therefore for me that's also important, so the difference for me, that's fundamental for me. If it were marriage I wouldn't want it, although I'd be pleased for the people who did. But I wouldn't want it personally.
>
> (Louise)

This perspective, that the separation of religion and the legal recognition of same-sex relationships is a positive move seems to show a willingness and desire from (some) lesbians and gay men to retain some sort of distinction between same- and different-sex relationships. The issue of religion and lesbian and gay identity is a very complex one, and there is not the space in this book to do it justice. My concern with this aspect of the uneasy relationship between civil partnership and marriage is that it seems to be related to the resistance expressed by some of these participants to the assimilation of same-sex relationships into heteronormative models of relationships. The move from outlaw status to 'in-laws' is seen by these participants as a difficult road – one where it is important to retain the distinctive features of same-sex relationships, especially in the face of the neo-liberal privatisation of same-sex relationships and the blurring of lines of difference between same- and different-sex couples.

A further aspect of resistance to the naming of same-sex relationships as the same as heterosexual marriage comes in the form of feminist objections to the institution of marriage; Madge, for example, objects to marriage because of:

> The patriarchal heritage of marriage, the fact that marriage stems from a society where women are property and chattel, that marriage is structured

> around inequality and oppression, that marriage is a site of violence and abuse and degradation both for women and for children, that marriage represents a very normative and restrictive and repressive way of organizing relational and family and domestic space um that there's a hierarchy within society around different forms of relationships and marriage sets the tone and is at the pinnacle, that marriage also reinforces the organisation of society around 'the couple' so that 'the couple' become privileged above all other forms of relationship.
>
> (Madge)

And yet Madge described civil partnership as an 'amazing transformation', and agreed that equality for same-sex couples is reflected in the opening up of marriage to same-sex couples. This, I would say is an example of legal consciousness that includes all three of Ewick and Silbey's (1998) types of legal consciousness, 'before the law', 'with the law' and 'against the law', but which again also includes both stabilising and moderating forms of resistance. The 'before the law' perspective is visible through her perception of the introduction of civil partnership as an 'amazing transformation' – law has the power to transform the lives of lesbians and gay men and to transform wider societal attitudes to same-sex relationships. 'With the law' legal consciousness is evidenced through her reasoning around why law should be involved in people's relationships:

> Society is about money and economy, and even though relationships might be about love and romance, they are also about money and economy. You know because as individuals we own property, and some of us are fortunate enough to earn salaries that are big enough to accumulate savings and assets and they are fundamentally part of relationships then for that reason the law should impinge and regulate.
>
> (Madge)

Madge's reasoning for law being involved in people's relationships – that it is necessary to have rules about money, property and economy – highlights that legal recognition of relationships includes protective measures to prevent individuals being harmed financially as well as emotionally if a relationship breaks down. So Madge displays a 'with the law' legal consciousness in that she believes legal regulation is the best way to protect financial interests in relationships, and she also hints at the need for law to regulate and tax higher earners. But 'against the law' legal consciousness is also evident in Madge's account:

> Marriage law doesn't say you have to live together, marriage law doesn't say you have to organize your finances in a particular way it-it is suggestive of particular forms of organisation but you can resist that. But I think

> the problem is – is that the law becomes to be seen more that it is so that um you know in order to get married you know you should be living together, you should be monogamous, you should you know conform to these particular sets of norms which in many ways have got nothing to do with marriage law as I understand it.
>
> (Madge)

So, for Madge, the more insidious effects of legal recognition, those related to the normalisation of relationships, can and should be resisted. Rather than same-sex marriage or civil partnership necessarily involving assimilation or normalisation of same-sex relationships into heteronormative ways of living, or result in what Kay called the 'creeping suburbanisation' of lesbians and gay men, the introduction of the legal recognition of same-sex relationships could also leave room for wider transformative effects in society.

In summary, these participants see the introduction of opt-in legal recognition/regulation of same-sex relationships through civil partnership in complex and sometimes contradictory ways. Civil partnership was seen as potentially both good and bad for lesbians and gay men, by virtue of the disciplinary and normalising effects of recognition and regulation. Practical, pragmatic and financial reasons for entering into civil partnerships are also considered by these participants, but not in a purely uncritical way – the potential for wide-reaching regulation of lesbian and gay lives was considered alongside the beneficial effects of legal recognition. These participants drew attention to both the recognition and regulation aspects of civil partnership – highlighting that there are problems associated with civil partnership, especially for those at the lower end of the socio-economic scale. But, through strategies of resistance to the regulatory and disciplinary effects of marriage and civil partnership, and the legacy of different relationship forms within non-heterosexual communities, these participants highlight that space can be created within the disciplinary mechanisms of power for alternative ways of living.

Lesbian and gay parenting

The second section of these interviews focused on lesbian and gay parenting. Of the ten participants in this study, only three, Nicola, Louise and Elizabeth were parents at the time of the interviews. One other respondent, Madge, had given a substantial amount of thought to becoming a parent, and expressed a desire to do so in the near future. Most participants had given some thought to having children, and it was something that most had thought about doing in the future. But for the majority of these participants, parenting was not something that they had any specific plans to do, and for some it was something that they simply could not imagine doing as a lesbian or gay man. These participants' accounts focused on three aspects of becoming a parent as a lesbian or as a gay man: first, the difficulties of thinking about becoming a parent; second, the practical difficulties of becoming a parent; and, third, experiences of managing the heterosexual familial norms in society as a lesbian parent. Finally, I turn to look more closely at Nicola's account of being a parent who is reliant on state benefits.

Thinking about parenting

For most of the participants in this study, having children was something that they had only thought about in an abstract sense. Kay, for example, suggested that being gay in some way reduces the pressure on women to think about having children:

> I've thought about it, but not seriously. I used to think that was one of the good things about being gay was that you didn't have to think about that sort of thing-there wasn't that sort of pressure ... I do think that if I were straight there would be a different set of pressures. I don't know how much of it is because I thought well, it's just not a question because I'm never going to be in a relationship where that could [laughs] y'know accidentally happen, so it's not something that's ever been an issue. I've been surprised actually that a lot of my straight women friends, if they are in a relationship, it is something that is kinda there at the back of their minds, I think, and also there has been that pressure previously and that assumption that if they're going to – or if they're not going to get married then they might have kids. I've never had that pressure, never felt it at all.
>
> (Kay)

So, Kay feels that because she is not heterosexual and would never be in a position where she could 'accidentally' become pregnant, she's not really given much thought to the possibility of having children. Interestingly, Kay compares her situation to those of her straight female friends, for whom she senses having children to be 'there at the back of their minds' and who she feels are under pressure (from family, friends and society more generally) to have children. One explanation for this lack of familial or societal pressure on lesbians and gay men to have children, in contrast to the expectations placed on heterosexual people, could be the continued importance placed on children having appropriately gendered role models. Take, for example, this excerpt from Michael's interview:

> When I was engaged to be married it impacted on me then because I started to think of how is this going to work with you because even with a female, well y'know she was a lesbian and I was a gay boy and we kinda met and then something happened and we don't know what happened and

> four years later of this relationship and it was amazing but y'know I thought about genetics, I thought about lots of different things-I thought how that would affect-about how I am, with my mannerisms and I thought am I capable of raising a man, but then I couldn't come up with the answer to whether that was myself or whether that was society telling me that.
>
> (Michael)

For Michael, the issue of whether he was 'capable of raising a man' was a consideration when thinking about the possibility of becoming a father. It is noteworthy that he stresses that he was not sure whether the questions in his mind about his parental capabilities were rooted in what he thought, or whether it 'was society telling [him] that'. This is one area where there is an obvious gendered difference between the male participants in this study and the women. For the women I interviewed, the idea of whether they were capable of raising a child with an 'appropriately' gendered identity was not an issue for them; rather, it was a concern imposed on them from above. Nicola, for example, talked about the counselling that she and her partner were required to have before accessing assisted conception services at a clinic:

> I had to go to counselling, I think before they would accept us-but everybody does, anyone that's entering into the process, I think, has to go to counselling. And that's to do with the HFEA thing for the welfare of the child, and it just felt like jumping through hoops. The counsellor didn't really have clue what she was talking about while she was talking to us two. She was asking us things like 'how will you feel if you were to have a boy?' – my memory of it is her asking 'how will you feel if you have a boy?', but yeah, they asked about male role models, am I close to my dad, or is there men – and it was short and it wasn't particularly intrusive, but she clearly thought that y'know lesbians have a problem with men, and was worried in case we were-would be hostile to having a boy, but of course [my partner] was like 'I want a boy' and I was like 'I want a girl', but I kept my trap shut because I thought she'd totally psychoanalyse me if I said I want a girl.
>
> (Nicola)

Nicola's overriding memory of the counselling that she and her partner had to have before being accepted on the clinic's waiting list was this question of whether they would have a problem with having a male child, and whether there were appropriate male role models in their wider familial networks. This resonates with Michael's thoughts about whether he would be an appropriate male role model if he were to have a child, but highlights that it is wider legal and societal pressure and the Human Fertilisation and Embryology Authority (HFEA) frameworks surrounding the 'need for a father' and the 'welfare of the child' about who or what constitutes an appropriately gendered role model that is key here. Similarly, Louise, another participant who conceived using anonymous donor sperm, recounted her experience of counselling prior to donor insemination treatment:

> We then went to the counselling session that we had to have, which was hilarious, because we-we really prepared for it, y'know we really thought about 'what questions are they gonna ask?', 'are they really gonna put us through the mill?', and we need to make sure that we had a good list of male role models that we could list off for ways it was gonna be if it was a boy or if it was a girl, good role models and it was absolutely hilarious, we went to this counselling session thinking 'are we going to get through this' and this counsellor just stumbled her way through about 15 minutes of not knowing what to say and how to say it, and we just looked at each other, and it was hysterical. So we got through that terribly difficult barrier [laughs].
>
> (Louise)

That both Louise and Nicola were concerned about the counselling session is an interesting aspect of the ways that same-sex couples have to emphasise the similarities of lesbian families and heterosexual families in interactions with governmental actors in order to access infertility treatment. The contrast between these two women's accounts of counselling prior to accessing donor insemination services at a clinic is also interesting, given that they accessed these services at very different times. Louise accessed assisted conception services in the 1990s, before much of the recent positive legal change for lesbians and gay men. Nicola, on the other hand, accessed a clinic in the early 2000s, once the issue of lesbians having children had become more widely acknowledged in the public domain. Arguably, Nicola's experience of the counsellor's questions about male role models and how she and her partner would feel about having a boy child was so different to Louise's experience (of the counsellor not knowing quite what to say to a lesbian couple) because of the increased visibility of lesbian families and increased public and media attention given to the issue of lesbians raising children.

Certainly Nicola's impression that the counsellor thought that 'lesbians have a problem with men' resonates with much of the psychological literature on lesbian parenting, particularly the literature addressing representations of lesbian parenting in the popular media (see, for example, Chrisp, 2001; Clarke & Kitzinger, 2005). Interestingly, however, the issue of whether a gay man would be able to raise a girl and the issue of appropriate *female* role models was not mentioned by any of these participants. The question of appropriate female role models does not seem to be an issue – or at least has not received anywhere like the amount of academic attention that has been focused on concerns about appropriate male role models. This absence suggests that stereotypes around gender and sexuality are still very much in existence in relation to lesbian and gay parenting, and that the regulation of the family is still concerned with ensuring that family and society remains predominantly heterosexual. The stereotype of gay men as effeminate, for example, which is the basis for questions of whether gay men can be appropriate male role models for children (especially boys), seems to work to reinstate and reinforce social constructions of appropriate masculinity and femininity.

Practical difficulties in becoming a parent

Alongside the issue of appropriate gendered role models in parenting and the social construction of who can be an appropriate parent that informed these accounts of parenting from lesbians and gay men, more practical issues about becoming a parent were also mentioned. Madge, for example, spoke about why she would rather not have a child through assisted conception services at a clinic:

> I thought about going to a clinic but I'm primarily repelled by the cost and the idea of paying a ridiculous sum of money for something that you could just kinda get for free if you are willing to go to a horrible nightclub. I am also repelled by the regulation involved in getting pregnant through a clinic, both in the sense of being part of the medical system, having been quite seriously ill in the past, and hating being y'know subject to that process and I know that most clinics would ask loads of nosy questions and you have to have counselling and I just wanna say 'fuck off and die' I'm more than capable of being a parent don't-I mean I guess it's middle class privilege isn't it – being a middle class person and the idea of being subject to the forms of regulation and intrusion that working class people are subjected to all the time y'know in terms of having social workers for your kids and y'know that form of state intrusion, y'know as someone that has, up until now, had no reason for that form of state intrusion feels incredibly resentful about it which I know is a form of privilege, but at the same time I still feel bloody resentful about it.
>
> (Madge)

So, Madge is reticent about going to a clinic for assisted conception services for two reasons – first, that donor insemination is expensive; and second, that she feels that getting treatment would leave her open to intrusive forms of regulation, both from the medical system and 'state intrusion' into her life. The second of her reasons for not wanting to go to a clinic is noteworthy, as it highlights her perceptions of the regulation involved in becoming a parent without a partner. She notes that the sort of regulation that she does not want to be subjected to is that which 'working class people are subjected to all the time'. This highlights a new perspective on resistance to law in everyday life – while Madge sees law here as something to be avoided, as in Ewick and Silbey's (1998) category of 'against the law' legal consciousness, it is not because she sees herself as in any way a marginalised person. Rather, Madge's perspective on the regulation involved in accessing assisted conception services at a clinic highlights that she sees less privileged people being subject to much more regulation (both from the state and from the medical professions) than 'middle class' people. She sees herself as having the option to resist this form of state intervention in her life.

Madge then goes on to talk about some more practical difficulties related to being treated at a clinic:

> It's very difficult to get sperm as a single woman but it's hard to get sperm as a lesbian couple because of the Human Fertilisation and Embryology Act and the welfare clause that says that clinics have to consider the need of um the children's need for a father, which obviously leaves clinics open to make their own decisions about whether or not they're going to open up their services to lesbian couples and single women. And it seems that a lot of clinics err on the side of caution and are not willing to provide services to lesbian couples and they're not willing to provide services to single women although it – to my surprise, after phoning around a few clinics, it's a lot harder to get access to services as a single woman than it is as a lesbian couple. And the other practical issue is they don't have any sperm because of the changes to the law about sperm donation which means that sperm donors have to be willing to be identified to any offspring they produce. So sperm has gone down drastically. And based on the clinics I spoke to, lesbians and single women are not on the top of the list of people they want to give sperm to ... shock horror there!
>
> (Madge)

Here, Madge attributes the reasons for it being difficult for single women and lesbian couples to access assisted conception services as being directly related to the 'need for a father' clause of the Human Fertilisation and Embryology Act 1990,[6] and the discretion that is given to clinics to decide whether or not they treat single women and lesbians. It is also important to note that in the interactions she had with clinics, Madge reports being told that it is even more difficult to access assisted conception services as a single woman than it would be if she were in a same-sex relationship. This resonates with the discussion above of the potential for the introduction of civil partnership to increase the regulation, governmentalisation and normalisation of same-sex couples. As civil partnership makes same-sex couples more acceptable in society, the social censure that was placed on same-sex couples as well as others who do not conform to the heteronormative ideal of the coupled relationship shifts even more onto single women with children.[7] This also, again, brings into focus the neo-liberal privatisation of the family – the reticence of clinics to provide assisted conception services to single women undoubtedly reflects and refracts public discourse that single mothers are a real 'problem' for society.

It is important to note, however, that even with the increasing acceptability of same-sex relationships as brought about by the introduction of civil partnership and other associated legal changes, lesbians still experience very real instances of discrimination when attempting to access fertility treatments:

> When I was phoning up clinics to see if they would treat me and one was in [City], and I wanted to go there because it's near some relatives, and I said 'is it a problem that I'm in a same sex relationship?' and she said 'oh yes, the doctor won't treat you.' I've had that, the door slammed. Full stop. He doesn't agree with same sex – he's very religious – won't treat you. And I was really really upset by that.
>
> (Nicola)

This excerpt from Nicola's interview refers to an incident that took place quite recently, when she was trying to access assisted conception services to have another child. It is interesting, again, that religious views were used as the reason why the doctor at this clinic refused to treat same-sex couples. In circumstances like this one, it is almost impossible for lesbians to challenge the overtly discriminatory beliefs of some medical practitioners – the use of religion as a reason for refusing to treat same-sex couples effectively insulates the clinic from any accusation of unfair treatment, by relying on individuals' rights to freedom of religion. What this sort of incident draws attention to, however, is not only the way that religious beliefs continue to be used as an excuse for discriminatory views and behaviour, but also the ways in which providers of assisted conception services act as gatekeepers to who can and cannot have children.

Managing familial norms in society

Alongside continuing discrimination against lesbians from healthcare practitioners, the lesbian parents who participated in this study also talked about their ongoing struggles against normative expectations of the family in society. Nicola, for example, who has chosen to be a 'full time mum' spoke of the way she feels that society frowns on this choice, places no value on parenting as a social good, and expects her to return to work:

> Society places no value on it whatsoever, no value. The whole system is geared for having a baby, putting them in nursery and getting back to work. So you have your child, you get back into earning, and then you pay for someone else to bring up or to look after your child.
>
> (Nicola)

This is a difficult area, as there are obvious conflicts between the 'individual choice' of some mothers to stay at home and look after their children, societal expectations that everyone should work, and feminist arguments about the lack of value placed on domestic labour as an essential part of society (e.g. Fineman, 2004). In Nicola's case, these conflicts are exacerbated by her economic status as a woman claiming benefits as, the pariah of neo-liberal society, a single mother. Similarly, Louise also experienced the societal pressure to return to work and the pressures to pay the economic costs of having children from within the private family after she had her baby:

> Once, when I was on maternity leave, I asked [my bank manager] for an extension of my overdraft – I think I wanted to take another month off with [baby] to help him settle in to nursery and childminding – and he just went into one about how – 'why was I coming to him for money? Why wasn't I asking the father of the child? And I'd opted for there not to be a father of the child and therefore it was up to me wasn't it? And why should the bank bail me out?' And it wasn't about bailing me out it was about lending me a bit more money before I went back to work.
>
> (Louise)

Louise's experience of being lambasted by her bank manager for choosing to have a child without a father is an exceptionally clear example of the operation of social norms around the economically independent, privatised family.

The most important and interesting thing around both Nicola and Louise's experiences as lesbian mothers is the way that social norms are just as much a part of the regulatory framework governing their lives as the official rules of the legal system. Whereas the recognition/regulation of same-sex relationships has become overtly and obviously a part of the system of governance through the introduction of civil partnership, the regulation of and modes of governance of 'the family' as a social entity are much more opaque. There is no law stating that children should only be born into a (heterosexual) couple relationship, but there is an insidious and deep-rooted presumption that 'the family' is heterosexual. As a formerly heterosexually married woman, Elizabeth explains the differences between her new family setup and her previous experience of family life:

> How my family was before was very much more represented in normal pictures of society, which is that there's a mum and a dad and children, and I think y'know I see it in my own eyes, but also the eyes of the children who're very keen to name the relationships very quickly and even before we lived together we spent a lot of time together, they started to want to say y'know 'who is [my partner] to them?' and 'who are [my partner's children]?' um and feel that they are a part of the family.
>
> (Elizabeth)

One interesting aspect of this excerpt is that not only does Elizabeth notice that her new family structure is less obvious and less represented in society at large, but that her children were very keen to name their relationships with Elizabeth's partner and her partner's children as familial relationships. If nothing else, this sort of understanding of family life shows how easily children can accept non-normative familial relationships. The difficulty, however, comes through the ways that the (hetero)normative family is held up as the ideal and policed by society:

> I was a bit surprised recently when [my youngest child] brought home a piece of work – they were doing family trees at school and I felt the way it was presented was incredibly on a heterosexual model-but even that felt terribly stereotyped, the people who were on this tree, and I thought that really must not fit with probably the majority of children in the school, so that was a bit odd ... We live in an area where there are many same sex families, so it's not at all unusual for the children to have friends whose parents y'know have a same sex partnership, or have other differences, like [one child] lives with her dad and her granny, so lots and lots of difference, so it's much harder to say that 'this is the norm' really.
>
> (Elizabeth)

As Elizabeth notes in this extract, lesbian and gay families are not the only ones that do not conform to normative conceptions of the family as represented in the ways in which children are taught about family at school. Rather, many children grow up in different family structures, and yet the teaching materials seem to almost enforce the heteronormative ideal of the family onto children, even where their own experience of family life does not fit that model.

In many ways, the position of lesbian (and gay) parents in society falls very much into the realm of the marginalised and therefore, according to Ewick and Silbey's (1998) typology of legal consciousness, persons in this situation would be expected to display 'against the law' legal consciousness, typified by resistance. One example of resistance to the unspoken, unwritten 'law' that the family is a heterosexual institution is the way in which lesbian parents must challenge the assumptions of teachers, children and other parents when their children are at school. Take, for example, this story from Louise:

> I had a situation at [my child's] nursery where he came out of nursery one day with a father's day card and I went back in with it and said 'what's this' and the nursery said 'we didn't want him to feel left out' I said 'alright fine – you don't want him to feel left out, so you got him to make a father's day card for a father that you know he hasn't got.' So we had

> that out with nursery, about how you couldn't make him feel more left out so I was really angry about that, but I went back in and had a debate with them and they got it right the next year.
>
> (Louise)

In this instance, Louise directly challenged the heteronormativity of the nursery by explaining the effects of their actions in relation to her son, who does not have a father (because he was conceived through anonymous donor insemination).[8] This explicit resistant act does not sit easily with the forms of resistance illustrated by Ewick and Silbey (1998) in their study of legal consciousness, as it is not exemplified by avoidance or deceit, but rather through a proactive attempt to explain the potential damage that can be wrought through over-reliance on societal norms of the heterosexual family. I would describe this as an example of moderating resistance. By challenging the heteronormative assumptions of the nursery teachers Louise ensured that they were more sensitive to the needs of her child in the future – thus modifying the power of heteronormative conceptions of family life. The effects of such everyday resistant acts should not be underestimated – they may not have the revolutionary characteristics of full-scale resistant struggle, but they are undoubtedly transformative of power relations, even if only at specific times and in particular spaces.

A second aspect of the societal norms of the idealised heterosexual family are the difficulties that are presented through the operation of legal rules governing who is a 'parent' and who is not, and consequently who has 'parental responsibility' and who does not.[9] Louise talked at length of the difficulties of being a *de facto* parent of her ex-partner's birth children without the legal status of parental responsibility:

> She had particular ideas about the children's education and she wanted to pursue those and she just began to exclude me. She didn't let me know when parents evenings were, she didn't invite me. There'd be a drama production, and there'd be two tickets, and so she'd get one for their dad and one for her and stuff like that began to happen, and it's very difficult to challenge it, very difficult to do anything about it – you can't get beyond having a row really, because if somebody isn't going to listen then it gets more difficult, so I think it's about the power of making decisions and directing somebody in a particular way … I think the time where it's been very stark is the time since we've been apart, because she has not wanted me to spend time with them, and that's been very hard, and part of that is about not having a legitimate role as she sees it and the difference between me and their dad, and how she sees it even though I have parented them on a day to day basis much much longer than he has. Not that he's not [an] important man in their lives, he's a great great guy, and he's really nice and he's a great dad and I think it's really important

> that he does have a big part in their lives, but she wouldn't give me parity with him, even though I did live with them for much longer.
>
> (Louise)

In this extract, Louise explains how she had to struggle not only against the heteronormative assumptions that are present in wider society about who counts as a parent, but also the relative value that her ex-partner attributed to Louise and to the biological father of her two birth children. In certain respects, Louise has been invalidated as a *de facto* parent of these two children since the relationship between her and the children's biological mother ended. She went on to explain that:

> I hardly see them. I see [younger child] once a week, but it's a fight. I mean he's 17 and it's still a fight. [Older child]'s at university now, so I only see him when he's on holiday, but that's fine – nobody sees him very much so in many ways it's up to him now, but for [younger child] it puts him under quite a lot of pressure ... I think it's fair to say that I've taken a very different tack in relation to [my birth child], because as far as I'm concerned [my ex] is his parent. I don't give her full consultation on decision making, I do take most of the decisions, but I do make sure that he has a lot of contact with her. He spends every other weekend and every Monday and Tuesday evening and night with her so she sees him a lot, so despite the provocation that she gives me, I've really tried hard not to misuse my parental responsibility, but I could do – I really could say to her 'forget it – you give me an awful lot of grief' ... and I could take all the power. I could, I think, misuse it because I could just say no, but I don't really do it for me, it's for him.
>
> (Louise)

For Louise, then, one of the difficulties of being a lesbian parent is the way legal rules have created an automatic imbalance of power within the family. At the time Louise's family was created, while the birth mother automatically had parental responsibility, the non-birth mother has no automatic legal relationship with the child(ren).[10] Louise is in the unusual position of seeing this from both sides – being the parent with parental responsibility for her birth child, and being a *de facto* parent without parental responsibility for her ex-partner's two birth children. It is interesting that Louise conceptualises the status of being a parent with parental responsibility as being the more powerful party in the relationship. The operation of power relations in this form of relationship almost acts as a microcosm of wider society in relation to lesbian and gay parents. The heteronormativity of family life is such that it is the parent who has the stronger claim to a socially recognised familial role who is in the more powerful position; the socially unrecognised, invisible, parent bears the burden of having to resist societal constructions of their unusual or non-normative status in relation to their children. Interestingly, Louise's story is very reminiscent of the published personal narratives discussed in Chapter 5 and the imbalance of power that exists between lesbian and gay parents where one is socially and legally considered to be the 'real' parent and the other is 'illegitimate'.

Experiences of regulation as a lesbian mother

Societal understandings of who does and does not count as a parent pervade lesbian mothers' experiences of parenting. In this story about an interaction with the Child Support Agency (CSA), the invisibility of the non-birth parent is used to the advantage of the birth parent. Here, Nicola, who is currently unemployed and a full-time mother to her two-year-old son,[11] describes how she discovered that the rules surrounding benefits had changed after the implementation of the Civil Partnership Act:

> The only reason I ended up finding out about it was I had a run in with the Child Support Agency. They phoned – I mean it's like two years now since he's been born, and when I went along to the office to say about the father of the child, because it was donor sperm, which is totally true. Now I wish that I'd just said I had a one night stand because I was basically-not investigated but they phoned up and this guy said 'can you prove that it was donor sperm?' and I said 'yeah, I'll get a letter organised,' which I did and I said 'what'll happen then,' and he said 'well, has anybody adopted [the child]?' and I said no, and he's like 'are you-have you married or are you in a relationship?' And I said no, because I'm treating myself as being single and he said 'right, well that would be the end of it.'
>
> So I sent this letter off confirming that I'd conceived through donor sperm and then they phoned me back and said they'd been on the phone to the Clinic, because it was Clinic paper, saying 'you couldn't have gone through treatment on the NHS unless you're in a relationship.' Now I never said it was on the NHS, because it wasn't, what I actually ended up getting, so they make assumptions left right and centre and he was saying 'you must've been in a relationship,' and I was like, by this point, I was getting upset, going 'oh my god, my life's falling apart.' And I said I was in a relationship, but with a woman, and I knew that they had no case, but they didn't know that they had no case. And I had to get this guy to sort of be an advocate on my behalf and contact them on my behalf so that they would stop – they were phoning me at like half past 7, 8 o'clock in the morning and at 6 o'clock at night and hassling me and hassling me for-I gave her a false name, and they were asking me for a date of birth – and I was going 'I can't remember' – And I can't remember loads of folk that I've been out with, like because I said we split up when the boys were

> born and it was an absolute nightmare, and then I started to realise, 'oh my god, is this the way that it's all changed? 'shit' kinda thing,' so I don't think I did realise until that. And that was the beginning of this year. Scary. It was really scary, it was really horrible. It was really really horrible.

For Nicola, the introduction of civil partnership sparked an enquiry from the CSA into her personal circumstances, as she was claiming benefits as a single mother. From the perspective of legal consciousness, Nicola did not describe law as majestic, or as a game, or as a product of power, arbitrary and capricious. Rather, Nicola hardly mentions law at all; the only reference to law being that it was this unwelcome intrusion from the CSA that drew her attention to the changes in benefits law introduced at the same time as the Civil Partnership Act. Nicola does (implicitly) describe the CSA as a legal entity, in that it is obviously a public body, which must draw its authority from law, but the actions of the CSA are described by Nicola in terms of inappropriate behaviour – 'hassling' phone calls, making assumptions. She feels that the CSA's intrusion into her life could have been prevented if she had not been truthful about how she conceived her child: 'I wish I'd just said I had a one night stand' because then the CSA would not have been able to trace the father of the child, or claim that there was anyone else liable to pay child maintenance. Eventually, and in an attempt to get the CSA to stop 'hassling' her, Nicola told them that she had been in a relationship with a woman when she was treated by the Clinic, but that she and her partner had split up when the babies were born, due to the stress of the premature birth and the death of one of the children. Finally, Nicola turned to others for assistance, managing to finally close the story through using someone else to advocate on her behalf.

In many respects, Nicola's story is similar to those described as containing 'against the law' legal consciousness, because Nicola used some of the resistant strategies outlined by Ewick and Silbey (1998) as typical of 'against the law' legal consciousness. But she also turned to others for help, and asked someone to be an advocate for her. She turned to other, more powerful people to make her case to the CSA in order to convince them that they could not claim child maintenance payments from Nicola's (ex) partner. One of the most interesting parts of this story is where Nicola said 'I knew that they had no case, but they didn't know that they had no case.' Here, Nicola is claiming to have had greater knowledge of the legal situation than the CSA, and that she was able to utilise her knowledge of the situation to resolve the issue, bringing in aspects of a 'with the law' legal consciousness. There are also hints at 'before the law' legal consciousness in that Nicola did what she was told (initially) by the CSA, she told them that her child was conceived with donor sperm and she arranged for a letter confirming that this was the case. In this story then, we see evidence of all three 'types' of legal consciousness and can map the route through these conceptualisations of law within this one account. Nicola's initial actions would fit into the category of 'before the law'; when she was being 'hassled' by the CSA, her understanding of the place of law in her life was closer to an 'against the law' legal consciousness, and finally, when she asked for someone to be an advocate for her, her actions would fit more within a 'with the law' type of legal consciousness. But the categories of legal consciousness seem to do nothing more than place a label on a particular account of legal process at a particular point in Nicola's story.

Nicola's story raises a number of important issues to do with the ways in which she conceptualises the place of law in her everyday life; issues that legal consciousness alone cannot fully comprehend. Rather, this story also involves multiple examples of relations of power and resistance. In the first instance, Nicola conceptualises the power of the CSA to ask her to do things much in the way that Foucault described the 'old' form of juridical power, that which is held by the sovereign or government and is used against subordinates (Foucault, 1998). The CSA, as a governmental agency, had the power to ask Nicola to produce evidence of her donor insemination treatment, so she did so, acting as would be expected in the face of a request from a 'powerful' institution such as the CSA.

Where we see the shift to 'against the law' legal consciousness in this account, we also see a shift in ways of thinking about power and resistance. Rather than thinking of the CSA as powerful and herself as powerless, Nicola uses strategies of resistance to try to prevent the CSA from continuing to investigate her circumstances. She deceives them by claiming to be single, she invents a false name for the partner that she said left when the boys were born, and she claims not to either know where the person she was treated with lives or to remember her date of birth. These resistant strategies could be described as 'stabilising resistance' in that the effects they have on the power relation between Nicola and the CSA is one of stabilising or levelling out the power relationship between them. In a different reading of the situation, these resistant acts could also be described as fracturing the power relation between Nicola and the CSA. Without the necessary information to identify a person who is liable for child maintenance payments, the CSA's power to interfere in Nicola's life is broken – perhaps only momentarily, and perhaps only in relation to this one individual – but enough to make them (at least temporarily) powerless. The power relations between Nicola and the CSA reach an impasse – the CSA is unwilling to give up, and Nicola is unwilling to give it any more information. Finally, Nicola involved a third party to advocate on her behalf; she shifted her approach to this legal problem from 'against the law' to 'with the law', playing the game of law by introducing someone with the skill to resolve the issue. The end result is that the CSA no longer phones her several times a day, and her benefit payments have not changed.

But even though Nicola 'won' this battle with the state over child support payments, it is unlikely that this will be the last interaction or conflict that she has with the various social security agencies over her social security benefit payments. She hopes to have another child, possibly through a clinic, and if she does so while in a relationship, she is likely to have another interaction with the CSA – and it is impossible to tell whether she will tell the truth, and risk losing her benefits, deceive them by pretending to have had a one-night stand, or whether she will find another way of resisting their investigations. In any case, it will be much more difficult to argue that there is no one liable for child maintenance payments, as same-sex partners are now treated in the same way as different-sex partners for the purposes of child support.[12]

Nicola's story also therefore highlights another important point about power and resistance in everyday life – that of governmentality:

> It is the tactics of government which make possible to continual definition and redefinition of what is within the competence of the state and what is not, the public versus the private, and so on; thus the state can only be understood in its survival and its limits on the basis of the general tactics of governmentality.
>
> (Foucault, 1991a: 103)

Nicola's conflict with the CSA is an example of the effects of governmentality. Through the redefinition of familial relationships that were introduced into UK law through the Civil Partnership Act 2004, the government opened up the possibility of regulation of familial relationships that were not, previously, within the competence of the state. Cohabiting same-sex couples (whether or not they enter into a civil partnership) are assessed together for the purposes of social security benefits, bringing those who were outside the law within its scope, as part of the process of recognition. So the introduction of civil partnership can be described as a mode of governmentality. But problems remain with the colonisation of same-sex partners and their families by the state. This method of the governmentalisation of lesbian and gay families throws up problems, because in spite of the widening of the legal recognition of familial relationships the heteronormativity of the family remains important as a social norm. The power of the entrenched heteronormativity of the family means that even after extensive, favourable change for lesbians and gay men, relations of power still exist, and as a result, spaces for resistance remain.

Concluding remarks

In this chapter, I have outlined the multiplicity of perspectives that these participants hold on the place of law in their everyday lives in relation to the legal recognition of same-sex relationships and lesbian (and gay) parenting. The complexities and contradictions inherent both within and between these participants' views about relationship recognition and parenting highlight the difficulties in coming up with easy categories to describe the ways in which people conceptualise law. Participants often draw on discourses and understandings of law that involve all three of the 'types' of legal consciousness created by Ewick and Silbey (1998). Rather than categorising all 'marginalised' individuals as being situated 'against the law' in their 'legal consciousness', the discussion of the views both within individual accounts and between participants above highlights that individuals' understandings, perceptions, attitudes and views about law change depending on what they are talking about, their life experiences and other factors. Legal change impacts lesbians and gay men in different ways, depending on their personal circumstances, and people respond in different ways to the effects of law and power in their lives.

In the analysis above, I have drawn out some of these complexities and noted the areas in which participants seemed to have different views depending on their gender. Aside from the fact that none of the gay men I interviewed were parents, there were two areas in which gender seemed to be a salient factor in the experience of law in the everyday lives of these participants: the issue of appropriately gendered role models for children, and concerns about the potentially assimilationist and normalising effects of the legal recognition of same-sex relationships. Two of the male participants stated during their interviews that they could only speak as/for gay men: 'I speak obviously as a gay man and not a woman' (Michael); 'I cannot speak for lesbians because they are a whole other kettle of fish, so to speak' (Peter), but none of the women I interviewed felt that they could not speak about the situation for gay men. This, I think, is also an interesting gendered difference, because it suggests that while gay male culture (as the dominant non-heterosexual culture) seems fairly understandable and open to lesbians, lesbian culture seems somewhat elusive or incomprehensible to these gay male informants.

Throughout the analysis above, I have also drawn out attitudes to power and examples of resistance where these are evident in how participants talk about law, parenting and relationships. Drawing out the complexities of relationships of power and resistance helps to make legal consciousness analysis richer, as these concepts look beyond the expressions of how these participants view law in their everyday lives to the ways in which law works in their everyday lives, and the ways in which these lesbians and gay men continue to resist not only homophobia and heterosexism, but also the presence of law in their lives. A governmentality perspective has also been useful in exploring the effect of the creation of new regulatory frameworks around sexuality; the places where modes of governance, whether legal or societal, affect and impinge on lesbian and gay lives.

The views and attitudes of these interviewees about the introduction of legal recognition of same-sex relationships often mirrored the discourse around formal equality, the differences between civil partnership and marriage, and second-class citizenship discussed in Chapter 4. That similar discourse can be found in both of these chapters again highlights the entrenched nature of formal equality discourse in lesbian and gay struggles. The ways in which these participants described their experiences of thinking about, being and becoming parents also reflects and refracts the themes from published personal narratives discussed in Chapter 5. Again, the similarities in these very different data sources draw attention to persistence of problematic constructions of lesbian and gay parents as 'illegitimate'. In both parts of these interviews, approaches to power and resistance were again similar to the discourse discussed in Chapters 4 and 5. These interviewees' attitudes to both relationship recognition and parenting again brought out examples of stabilising and moderating resistance. That fracturing resistance is markedly less common in lesbian and gay legal consciousness is very interesting and this is a concern I will return to in the next chapter.

Notes

1 As with the rest of the book, I use the term 'lesbian and gay' throughout this chapter, as although some of these interviewees were reluctant to claim a specifically 'lesbian' or 'gay male' identity (see Table 6.1), the issues I am concerned with are those which form a part of the wider struggles for 'lesbian and gay' equality. An alternative (and possibly more inclusive) formulation of the people interviewed in this chapter could be 'non-heterosexual' people, but this term is problematic in a number of ways, not least in that it presents lesbian and gay sexuality as a negative identity category, rather than a positive one.

2 Civil partnership has been available in the UK since December 2005, although none of the ten interviewees had entered into a civil partnership. Four of the interviewees were living with their partner in Scotland, and would therefore be automatically covered by the provisions relating to financial provision on the breakdown of cohabiting relationships introduced by the Family Law (Scotland) Act 2006. Interestingly, none of these participants mentioned this legislation or noted that they had any specific rights and/or responsibilities as cohabitants.

3 Hospital visitation rights and 'next of kin' status were often cited as reasons for the introduction of civil partnership (e.g. Women and Equality Unit, 2003), but the legal regulation of this issue is very unclear – in English law there is no legal category of 'next of kin' and the rules surrounding who can visit who in hospital are based on Department of Health guidelines, rather than legislation.

4 It is important to note that this was an 'equalising' move, as different-sex cohabiting couples have been assessed together for the purposes of state benefits for many years. Problematically, however, this formal equality move does not take into consideration the effects of the continuing gender pay gap, which could mean that same-sex couples (especially lesbian couples) are more likely to be disadvantaged than heterosexual couples (see also Young & Boyd, 2006).

5 This, again, mirrors the discourse that civil partnership 'is not enough', discussed in Chapter 4.

6 At the time these interviews were conducted, s. 13(5) of the HFE Act 1990 stated: 'A woman shall not be provided with treatment services unless account has been taken of the welfare of any child who may be born as a result of the treatment (including the need of that child for a father), and of any other child who may be affected by the birth.' In 2008, the Human Fertilisation and Embryology Act amended this legislation to replace the 'need of that child for a father' with 'the need for supportive parenting', thus potentially compounding the issues related to accessing assisted conception services for single women.

7 See Kandaswamy (2008) for an insightful analysis of the race and class implications of similar discourse in the US context.
8 Importantly, societal assumptions that all children have two parents (a mother and a father) can also be exclusionary of and upsetting to children in single-parent families, who either do not have contact with their absent parent, or who have experienced the death of a parent.
9 Parental responsibility is the legal framework that covers 'all the rights, duties, powers, responsibilities and authority which by law a parent has in relation to the child and his property' – Children Act 1989 s. 3(1) in England and Wales. At the time of these interviews, the only persons who automatically had parental responsibility when a child was born were the child's legal (gestational) mother and, if she were married to a man, the husband of the birth mother. Other persons could obtain parental responsibility under the Children Act 1989, either through Parental Responsibility Agreements formed with the child's mother or by application to the court. The CPA did not change this legal framework, and the differences in the ways civil partners and husbands were treated was one of the few substantive differences between civil partnership and marriage in the UK. Since April 2009, the civil partner of a woman who gives birth following donor insemination or other forms of assisted conception will now be automatically considered a legal parent of that child, listed on the child's birth certificate and have automatic parental responsibility. Where a same-sex couple are treated at a licensed clinic, the non-birth mother will have legal status as a parent and automatic parental responsibility, even if the couple are not in a civil partnership, provided the relevant consent forms are signed (Children Act 1989, ss 2–4A; Human Fertilisation and Embryology Act 2008, ss 42–47; Stonewall, 2009).
10 Recent legal reforms, including the CPA 2004 and the HFEA 2008, have significantly changed the legal situation in the UK. For children born into a civil partnership between December 2005 and (approximately) December 2009, the civil partner of the birth mother was not considered a legal parent, and did not have automatic parental responsibility, but she was treated as a step-parent to the child, and the child was considered a 'child of the family.' A woman in this situation would be able to attain parental responsibility through a Parental Responsibility Agreement under the terms of the Children Act 1989 s. 4A. Step-parents can also adopt through the step-parent adoption process, which does not require the birth parent to adopt their own child. For children conceived after 6 April 2009 (likely to be born from January 2010) the situation would fall under the new HFEA framework set out in note 9 above.
11 She conceived her children through IVF, and gave birth to twins. The twins were premature and, sadly, one died shortly after birth.
12 Civil Partnership Act 2004, Schedule 24, Part 8.

Chapter 7

Imagining a different world

In this final substantive chapter, I move away from examining 'real-life' attitudes to and perceptions of law as it relates to lesbians and gay men, and shift my focus to visions for a different world. Whereas in the three previous chapters, my emphasis was on how lesbians and gay men experience law in their everyday lives, my concern in this chapter is to explore alternative visions of the place of law in the everyday lives of lesbians and gay men. To do this, I compare and contrast the approaches to the regulation of relationships and parenting in two texts: Marge Piercy's 1979 novel *Woman on the Edge of Time,* which is widely recognised as one of the most important examples of feminist utopian literature, and the 2000 film *Big Eden*, written and directed by Thomas Bezucha, winner of 14 audience choice awards at lesbian and gay film festivals in 2000 and 2001. These two texts are examples of very different types of utopia, both of which can provide significant insights into the place of law in the everyday lives of lesbians and gay men. I argue that looking to utopian fiction can bring to light different perspectives on legal consciousness and the place of power and resistance in the regulation of lesbian and gay relationships and families. I begin with an exploration of utopian studies and I consider whether and why these two very different texts can be described as utopian, followed by a discussion of my reasons for examining utopian space within a project on sexuality and legal consciousness. In the second section of this chapter, I provide more detailed analysis of the background stories and utopian vision in these two texts, before moving on to evaluate their different approaches to the issues of same-sex relationship recognition and lesbian and gay parenting, and the insights into relationships of power and resistance that are present within them. I argue that these utopian texts can provide frameworks for alternative ways of thinking about the place of sexuality within contemporary legal frameworks.

Utopia and legal consciousness

As discussed in detail in Chapter 2, legal consciousness studies have focused on the ways in which 'ordinary' people approach, experience and think about law[1] (see e.g. Cowan, 2004; Ewick & Silbey, 1998; Merry, 1990). Legal consciousness studies are, therefore, grounded within an empirical framework that has limited analysis to individuals' experiences of law as told to researchers in the context of the in-depth interview. In Chapter 2, I argued that the framework of legal consciousness can, and should, be expanded to include other texts, including online survey responses (see Chapter 4) and published personal narrative (see Chapter 5). In this chapter, I seek to include a third new form of text in my exploration of sexuality and legal consciousness: utopian fiction.[2] Utopia is, in essence, the creation of imaginary worlds; worlds where life is better than in our present day reality: attempts to create a place we would want to live if we could live anywhere. As such, taking an utopian studies approach to the question of the place of law in everyday lesbian and gay lives can help to move beyond the constraints of considering law as it *is* and to include conceptions of how, perhaps, law *should* be.

Utopian studies and utopianism

The founder of the utopian genre is widely held to be Sir Thomas More, with his 1516 text *Utopia*. The roots of the modern meaning of 'utopia' can be traced to More's *Utopia*, where he used the word as a pun on two words derived from ancient Greek – eutopia (good place) and outopia (no place), though utopianism itself has roots even further back (Levitas, 1990). The creation of 'utopia' from this good place/no place fusion has created an element of ambiguity in the meanings given to the term utopia in contemporary definitions. On the one hand, utopia is figured to mean a perfect place, an imagined world without the imperfections of the present. On the other hand, utopia is conceived of as impossible and unattainable – nothing more than fantasy. These simultaneous descriptions of utopia as both optimistic and impossible have created tensions in the way utopia has been used within philosophical and academic literature.

Alongside consideration of the aims of utopianism, some debate has coalesced around whether it is content, form or function that is crucial in identifying a text as utopian (Levitas, 1990). Lucy Sargisson has argued that relying on form or content as the marker of utopian texts 'can have the insidious functions of disciplinary or cultural imperialism' (Sargisson, 1996: 36). Utopia as function, however, is defined by the way that utopia depicts some sort of goal for the future. This focus on the function of utopia is interesting because it moves away from the characterisation of utopia as being a fantasy, whether possible or impossible, which is at the core of definitions of utopia cohering around content and form. Rather, where the defining feature of utopia is its function, it is the envisioning of a goal for the future that marks a text as utopian. Levitas argues that a definition of utopia in terms of function moves away from the common sense idea of utopia and therefore function is a limited way of thinking about utopia. Rather than focusing on conventional definitions of utopia, as characterised by form, content or function, Levitas (1990: 8) argued for a definition of utopia as 'the expression of the desire for a better way of being', thus expressly decrying the potentially problematic and totalising implications of utopianism (Johnson, 2002).

Indeed, a recent resurgence in utopian studies has been marked by a move away from considering the (im)possibility of totalising visions of utopian society. Rather, contemporary work in utopianism seeks to 'recover (or, more accurately, acknowledge the already existing) utopian impulse at the centre of critical scholarship' (Blomley, 2007: 60). A major part of this new utopian movement has explored changing understandings of hope (Bloch, 1986) and the role that utopianism can play in providing critical and transformative ways of hoping for a better future (Webb, 2008). But the utility of utopian articulations of different and better ways of living, is not solely in its expression *per se*, but rather as a method (Levitas, 2007). Utopia provides us with a way of thinking through alternative possibilities for supporting and sustaining a better world. As Levitas argues:

> Utopia ... entails refusal, the refusal to accept that what is given is enough ... the refusal to accept that living beyond the present is delusional, the refusal to take at face value current judgements of the good, or claims that there is no alternative.
>
> (Levitas, 2007: 294)

Through analysis of Piercy's (1987) novel and Bezucha's (2000) film, I seek to explore the possibilities that they provide for conceptualising lesbian and gay familial lives beyond the present and for challenging current judgements about the way we should approach the recognition and regulation of the family.

Utopian texts: Woman on the Edge of Time *and* Big Eden

Before I can turn to an analysis of what insights can be drawn from Piercy's *Woman on the Edge of Time* and Bezucha's *Big Eden*, it is important to understand why each of these texts can be described as 'utopian'. Marge Piercy's *Woman on the Edge of Time* is widely recognised as a depiction of a feminist utopia (see e.g. Lefanu, 1988; Levitas, 1990; Moylan, 1987). The content and form of this novel make it an explicitly utopian text; it contains a depiction of an imagined future in a society where power imbalances have been balanced, people live 'at one' with nature and the environment, and every member of society is treated and valued equally. *Big Eden*, by way of contrast, does not have the critical pedigree of Piercy's novel – it is a low-budget, limited release 'gay film', which although it received a number of awards from lesbian and gay film festivals, and favourable media reviews (e.g. Foreman, 2001; Hartl, 2001) has not had much attention within utopian literature. This film does, however, provide a useful contrast with Piercy's radical feminist utopia in

Woman on the Edge of Time because it is grounded in an (almost) plausible version of present day society. In essence, if Piercy's (1987) utopia is a radical feminist[3] utopia, then *Big Eden* could be described as a liberal gay utopia.

Big Eden is utopian because it fulfils any and all of the definitions of utopia identified by Levitas (1990), including content, form, function and desire. The content of *Big Eden* is clearly utopian, as it is a depiction of a near-perfect, rural idyll, society.[4] Indeed, as is common with utopian fiction, reviews of this film have included criticism of the 'perfection' depicted in both the community and the individual characters in *Big Eden*. For example, a review in the *New York Post* states: 'The film has been criticized for its unrealistically sunny depiction of the way Big Eden embraces its gay citizens' (Foreman, 2001). Normative evaluation of the impossibility or unrealistic nature of a perfect society is common in criticism of utopian texts (Moylan, 1987).

In relation to the form of *Big Eden*, if the marker of a utopian text is 'the fictional depiction of an alternative society in some detail' (Levitas, 1990: 5), or even if the form of utopia is characterised by 'its vision of a total, perfect, ordered, environment' (Davis, 1981: 38), then this film fulfils the definition of utopia as form. The film depicts the Big Eden community in detail, from cowboys sitting outside the general store, to cappuccino machines, computers and the place of religion in the community, all without even a hint of homophobia. Whether or not the community depicted in *Big Eden* is indeed a 'perfect' society is a matter for debate, but it is most certainly a detailed depiction of a society that does not currently exist and could be the perfect place for some. Barbara Goodwin and Keith Taylor (1982) argued that the function of utopia is 'constructive criticism of the present via an ideal alternative (future or present)' (Goodwin & Taylor, 1982: 25). In this respect, *Big Eden* can also be argued to contain elements of utopia. The depiction of a rural society without homophobia must, at least in part, be a criticism of the present omnipresence of heteronormativity, heterosexism and homophobia. By showing a place where liberal humanist egalitarianism takes precedence over the 'othering' of non-heterosexual sexuality, the everyday presence of heterosexism in contemporary society is brought into focus. *Big Eden* also satisfies Ruth Levitas' (1990) definition of utopia as 'the expression of the desire for a better way of being' (p. 8), as the stated aim of Thomas Bezucha (writer/director) in making *Big Eden* was 'very much an experiment in taking away the bigotry' (Bezucha, 2000: 'interviews'). So, both *Woman on the Edge of Time* and *Big Eden* describe fictional utopias – both 'other place' and 'no place'. Both of these texts can give the reader or viewer an insight into how society might work better, including an element of criticism of the way contemporary society works.

Utopia, legal consciousness and sexuality

Before I move on to examine the content of Piercy and Bezucha's utopian spaces and the insights these visions offer, it is important to situate this analysis more firmly within my exploration of sexuality and legal consciousness. What, then, is the place of these 'imagined worlds' or 'utopian visions' in this project, a critical exploration of the regulation of sexuality and legal consciousness in lesbian and gay lives? I have three main reasons for including analysis of fictional utopia in this book: first, that fictional utopian visions can be read as examples of legal consciousness; second, that lesbian, gay and feminist utopian vision operate as examples of resistance to dominant, heteronormative ways of living and being; and, third, that utopian fiction provides examples of alternative ways of conceptualising the place of law and rules in everyday life, and is a technique for describing how the writer thinks law *should* work. I will briefly explore each of these reasons before moving on to analyse the content of the utopian societies depicted in *Woman on the Edge of Time* and *Big Eden*.

As Ewick and Silbey (2003) have noted, stories are attempts to explain the way the world works, and I would argue that this is equally true of utopian fiction as it is for personal stories and autobiographical narratives. Fictional utopian stories can be read as examples of legal consciousness because of the critique of contemporary society that is an inherent part of the creation of utopian vision. In *Woman on the Edge of Time,* for example, there is a strong inherent critique of the way that contemporary systems of rule in the mid- to late twentieth century worked to oppress women and other minority groups (Moylan, 1987). In *Big Eden,* the focus of critique is the omnipresence of heterosexism and homophobia, particularly in rural space. If, as Silbey and Ewick (2003) argue, 'people invoke pieces of legality to fashion solutions to ordinary everyday life matters, to constitute and sometimes to refashion everyday life' (Silbey & Ewick, 2003: 504), then the creation of utopian fiction should also be conceived as a method of offering solutions to the problem areas of everyday life.

Feminist and lesbian/gay utopia fulfils a second function, in that these texts provide examples of different conceptions and relationships of power and resistance, as well as insights into the way in which egalitarian ways of living are depicted in these utopian spaces. As I will demonstrate later, the understandings of power and resistance in *Woman on the Edge of Time* and *Big Eden* are reminiscent of the theoretical approaches to power and resistance outlined in Chapter 3 and reflected in lesbians and gay men's experiences as discussed in Chapters 4–6. Here, however, the utopian context facilitates a slightly different approach to the interrogation of how relationships of power and resistance exist in society. Looking to utopian fiction allows a deeper exploration of how these key concepts in the regulation of sexuality might work differently in everyday life. In this chapter, therefore, I move away from Ewick and Silbey's (1998) tripartite schema of legal consciousness to focus directly on issues of power and resistance in the regulation of sexuality. The 'before the law' and 'with the law' aspects of legal consciousness seem less relevant when considering utopian fiction, as the focus of both of these texts is resistance to current ways of living. As such, I would position utopian fiction within Ewick and Silbey's (1998) 'against the law' schema, because the critique of contemporary society embedded in utopian fiction is necessarily situated 'up against' or in opposition to current forms of legal regulation and social and political mores.

Finally, the creation of a utopia – a no place/good place imagined world – is the expression of the author's idea of how society could be different. Through the ways in which law and regulation are represented in utopian fiction, these texts also include representations of how the author thinks that law should work in everyday life, how society should be organised and the place of law in an ideal or 'perfect' place. It is not my aim here to focus on the authors of these texts, as it is impossible to know whether the representation of law, legality and regulation contained in their fiction is a 'true' representation of their legal consciousness. Rather, my aim is to explore the possibilities that utopian texts offer for different understandings of the place of law in the everyday lives of lesbians and gay men, to find alternatives to the current drive towards more and more regulation of lesbian and gay lives and to think about alternative forms of regulation of sexuality in society.

Creating utopia: plot, background and community

Woman on the Edge of Time is a novel about a woman's (Connie) struggle against mind control experiments in a mental hospital, and the future world she visits through a psychic link with an inhabitant of that time. The utopian future that Connie visits is Mattapoisett, a village in Massachusetts, in the year 2137. Her guide in Mattapoisett is Luciente, with whom Connie has a psychic link, which allows them to time-travel. This time-travel plot device allows Piercy to describe life in Mattapoisett in great detail, while Luciente shows Connie around. There are a number of important aspects to the utopian future described in this novel, some of which I will examine in more depth later.[5] One of the most important differences between Mattapoisett and the present-day 'reality' depicted in the novel is that gender has been eradicated as an organising principle of the future society. Gender-specific pronouns (she/he) have been removed from language and replaced with 'person' or 'per'; reproduction takes place outside of the body in a machine called a 'brooder'; each child has three parents ('co-mothers' or 'coms'), usually including both males and females, who may or may not be in a sexual relationship with each other; and bisexuality and polyamory are both normative in Mattapoisett.

The 2000 film *Big Eden* is a very different sort of utopia from that depicted in *Woman on the Edge of Time*, in that it is set in the present day, in a small town in Montana. The film is a romantic comedy, following the experiences of, and a developing love triangle between, Henry Hart, Dean Stewart and Pike Dexter. *Big Eden* does not look to the future, as in *Woman on the Edge of*

Time; rather, it is a depiction of a community without homophobia that 'exists' as a fictitious part of the present. Whereas *Woman on the Edge of Time* is very much a feminist utopia, *Big Eden* is more grounded in a liberal-humanist conception of an ideal world. It is a place without discrimination on the basis of sexual orientation, rather than a place where sexuality is no longer an organising principle in society. There are a number of important points to be made about the society represented in *Big Eden*, aside from the depiction of a place without homophobia: gender is still very much in existence in *Big Eden*;[6] organised religion (Christianity) is a large part of community life; the couple pair is the normative organising unit within this community and monogamous heterosexuality is very much still the norm within the community of *Big Eden*.

Piercy's *Woman on the Edge of Time* and Bezucha's *Big Eden* are, therefore, grounded in very different ways of visualising an idealised notion of life. It is important to note that these texts also stem from two very different eras and political situations – Piercy's (1987) novel is, in many respects, reflective of the ideals of second-wave feminisms from the 1970s and 1980s, and Bezucha's (2000) film seems to be firmly rooted in twenty-first-century liberal attitudes to lesbian and gay equality. There are, however, striking similarities between these two very different texts. The most interesting similarity to note is that the utopian communities depicted in both Piercy's *Woman on the Edge of Time* and Bezucha's *Big Eden* are set against a rural background. In *Woman on the Edge of Time,* when Connie first visited Mattapoisett, she saw:

> A river, little no account buildings, strange structures like long-legged birds with sails that turned in the wind, a few large terracotta and yellow buildings and one blue dome ... No skyscrapers, no spaceports, no traffic jam in the sky.
>
> (Piercy, 1987: 68)

Rather than seeing this 'rural idyll' immediately as a good place to live, Connie then goes on to compare life in Mattapoisett with the life of poverty lived by her family in rural Texas:

> "Goats! Jesús y María, this place is like my Tío Manuel's in Texas. A bunch of wetback refugees! Goats, chickens running around, a lot of huts scavenged out of real houses and white folks' garbage. All that lacks is a couple of old cars up on blocks in the yard! What happened – that big war with atomic bombs they were always predicting?"
>
> (Piercy, 1987: 69–70)[7]

For Connie, then, the rural way of life of the people of Mattapoisett is seen initially as a backward and retrograde step, one that is conceptualised through a comparison with the ways of life of the poorest people in the US in the twentieth century. Through this device of comparing the utopian future to the difficult life of Mexican migrants in twentieth-century Texas, Piercy highlights the disjunction between popular science fiction projections of a high-tech, high-speed technologically advanced future and the vision she has for a better place.

Big Eden is also predominantly set in a rural environment – the wide open spaces of Montana. The film opens in the glossy arts world of New York, where the main protagonist, artist Henry Hart, is setting up for a gallery opening. He is called home to Big Eden, a small town in Montana, when his grandfather (Sam Hart) has a stroke. Henry misses his 'big opening' and travels back home to Big Eden to look after his grandfather. As Big Eden is a film, the rural idyll is depicted through visual imagery rather than description. Aside from the expansive landscapes of the Montana National Park (where the movie was filmed), the community of Big Eden is also shown as an idyllic or utopian space, with the local men whiling away the hours sitting outside the local general store, with no imperative to work.[8]

That these utopian tales are both set in rural space is interesting, as this seems to be at odds with the ways that most academic literature around sexuality and space presents lesbian and gay space. David Bell and Jon Binnie (2001), in their analysis of the ways in which sexuality intersects with citizenship, argued that 'the city is the prime site both for the materialization of sexual identity, community and politics, and for conflicts and struggles around sexual identity, community and politics' (p. 83). This locating of non-normative sexual identity within urban space can be traced to a number of studies of gay male lifestyles, one important example of which is Henning Bech's (1997) *When Men Meet*, in which he argues that the city is the 'home' of the homosexual:

> The city is the social world proper of the homosexual, his life space; it is no use objecting that lots of homosexuals have lived in the country. Insofar as they wish to be homosexual, the vast majority must get out into 'the city' one way or another, into the open mass of strangers.
>
> (Bech, 1997: 98)

Bech (1997) argues that the city serves this function as the home of homosexuality (by which he predominantly means gay men) because of the ways in which urban space creates a 'special blend of closeness and distance, crowd and flickering, surface and gaze, freedom and danger ... anonymity and the absence of immediate social control' (p. 141). For Bech (1997) then, the city is the space for homosexuality because it creates the ideal conditions in which people can experience same-sex attraction, using the anonymity of the city as a cover for surreptitious, non-normative and illicit sexual behaviours.

I would argue that both *Woman on the Edge of Time* and *Big Eden* show the ways that this situating of lesbian and gay sexuality within the confines of an anonymous cityscape is dependent on the continued oppression of same-sex sexual practices and the reification of heterosexuality. In *Woman on the Edge of Time*, same-sex relationships are common, and bisexuality is normative in Mattapoisett's rural community. In *Big Eden*, the story revolves around the ways that the community pulls together to ensure that Henry and Pike can be together, as well as supporting the relationship between Henry and Dean. The revaluing of same-sex sexuality within these utopian communities demonstrates that the need for anonymity in same-sex sexual encounters is dependent on the particular construction of sexuality that places heterosexuality as the norm and all other forms of sexual identity as not only other, but inferior. These utopian texts depict fictional 'other' places; places where sexuality is less of an organising principle of society, but they still show that the city is not the only relevant space for lesbians and gay men.

Bell and Valentine (1995a) also discussed rural lesbian and gay lives, and provided three categories of rural lesbian and gay life: those who use the countryside as a recreational space; those who live(d) in lesbian/gay communes; and those who grew up in rural locations and experienced the oppression of rural life and the pull of the city. They argue that 'as an imaginative resource, the rural can be a place of fantasy and utopia, a place for living an idyllic "gay" life ... [but] for many with same-sex feelings ... the countryside offers nothing but isolation and loathing' (Bell & Valentine, 1995a: 120). Both Piercy's (1987) Mattapoisett and Bezucha's (2000) *Big Eden* do, to an extent, fit with this analysis – because they are both fictional spaces, they can be put in the category of the rural 'gay imagination' and criticised as both unrealistic fantasy and unrealisable utopia. Where sexuality is removed from the city, however, and placed in a rural setting, these fantastical utopian rural locations allow for sexuality and space to be thought of in more complex ways: what happens when non-heterosexual sexuality does not have to be surreptitious, anonymous or secret? How is lesbian, gay or bisexual sexuality manifest when removed from the specifically queer space of the urban 'gay village'? How can non-heterosexual identities really flourish in rural space without assimilation into the heterosexual norm? Or is the fantasy of rural queer lives simply an expression of dissatisfaction with the consumer culture of modern living, an attempt to show a different way of life? These are complex questions, and ones that cannot fully be addressed in this book.

Interestingly, in each of these texts, the rural idyll is positioned in opposition to an urban dystopia. In *Big Eden*, the dystopian imagery is quite light – a simple comparison between a life of rural beauty and strong community in Big Eden with a lonely life revolving around work, making money, a 'great apartment' and few friends in New York. Henry is made to choose between his life in the city and his life in *Big Eden*. An example of the way this choice is positioned in the film is between Henry and Grace, a good friend of the family:

GRACE: So, just like that?
HENRY: I never intended to stay.
GRACE: Well you sure fooled me.
HENRY: I live in New York.
GRACE: Right.
HENRY: Y'know I'm like a whole person there – you wouldn't even recognize me. I've got er ... a really nice apartment – I mean a really, really nice apartment, I make a lot of money and I have friends there, good friends, they have restaurants there –
GRACE: – that's it? You wanna go to a restaurant?
HENRY: I've gotta go back.
GRACE: Henry – just hang on a minute (pause) Listen, you know what they say when you get lost in the woods? If you stay put, stay in one place and don't wander they'll find you. And I was just hoping you'd let yourself be found this time. I was hoping you'd let us find you. But you keep wandering, and we can't.

Here, Grace tries to convince Henry that he would be better staying in Big Eden – that he can 'find himself' and lead a happier life in this small town than he can in the anonymity of city life. Rather than Henry's decision to move back to the city being described as a choice, Grace tries to convince Henry that his desire to go away is because he is 'lost in the woods' and 'wandering'. This excerpt shows quite clearly the ways that Bezucha positions Big Eden as a utopian place with the city as Henry's dystopian alternative, by contrasting the community life of Big Eden with the isolation of city life, revolving around material possessions.

In *Woman on the Edge of Time,* Connie only visits the possible dystopian future once (see Piercy, 1987: 287–301). Piercy's dystopian vision of the future, is described as a society where women are routinely sold to men either as one-night stands or on longer term contracts, as this is the only way to ensure their survival. This urban future is controlled and run by 'the multis' – multinational corporations. The rich and powerful live for up to 200 years, buying the organs of the poor, whose life expectancy is somewhere in the region of 40 years. Everyone lives in high-rise tower blocks, which are a physical metaphor for the highly regulated, extremely hierarchical structure of this society. The rich are figuratively and literally on top: they live highest up, some on space platforms, above the thick smog of pollution. This dystopian future is, again, held up as a choice – just one possible future among many. Moylan (1987) argues that this dystopian vision acts as a catalyst for Connie's resistance to the mind control experiments she experiences in her present reality; paving the way for the future of Mattapoisett and ecological and social harmony.

Both of these utopian texts position the rural utopia and the urban dystopia as a choice for the main protagonist. In *Big Eden*, this choice is a seemingly simple one, but for Henry the possibilities of being gay and out in a small town in Montana seem like impossibilities, with the draw of the city figuring strongly in his decision-making as is common for lesbians and gay men who grow up in rural environments (Bell & Valentine, 1995b). In *Woman on the Edge of Time,* however, the choice confronting Connie is not whether to choose to live herself in either an urban or rural future; rather, it is whether to give in to those who hold the power to control her or to resist that control, and help to pave the way to Mattapoisett in the future.

In *Woman on the Edge of Time,* then, space, location and community are used as devices to show that utopia is a conscious choice for people. The underlying message seems to be that individuals need not accept the status quo, that contemporary dominant power systems are not invincible, and through activism the contemporary ideology of multinational power systems can be challenged, a message based firmly in left wing, feminist, anti-racist politics. *Big Eden* also uses choice as a device to show that a better way of life is possible. Rather than drawing on themes like activism and resistance as revolution, Bezucha (2000) explores the individual, everyday choices that people make in relation to their own lives. So in both of these texts, the dystopia of the city is a choice, not a certainty, which depends on the outcome of challenges to dominant ways of thinking – whether that be of the current capitalist economic and political system (as in *Woman on the Edge of Time*) or the myth of urban space as the only suitable space for lesbian and gay sexuality (as in *Big Eden*).

Utopian families?

In both *Woman on the Edge of Time* and *Big Eden,* the issue of the recognition of same-sex relationships is placed firmly outside the legal sphere.[9] Rather than being concerned with legal issues such as same-sex marriage, the recognition of relationships in both of these fictional utopias is limited to consideration of the social recognition afforded to same-sex relationships. While the specific legal context of relationship recognition is not, therefore, tackled by either *Woman on the Edge of Time* or *Big Eden,* both texts deal in some way with the important social considerations surrounding the legal recognition of same-sex relationships. *Woman on the Edge of Time* and *Big Eden* differ quite substantially in their depiction of relationships. *Big Eden* is a film in the romantic comedy genre, and the developing relationships between Henry and Pike, and between Henry and his (straight) school friend Dean are central themes in the plot. The need to be in a coupled relationship seems to be a central organising principle of Big Eden's community. For example, when Henry arrives back in Big Eden, Mrs Thayer (Big Eden's resident busybody) throws a party to introduce him to the 'ladies in town'. Interestingly, one of the devices that Bezucha (2000) uses to show the lack of homophobia in Big Eden is through a repetition of the party with all male guests after Mrs Thayer discovers that Henry is gay:

[OUTSIDE CHURCH]

MRS THAYER: If it's not too inconvenient for you I'd like you to drop by the house this afternoon.

HENRY: Oh I-

MRS THAYER: Oh no no it's no trouble-

MAN: Mrs Thayer, Jack and I are heading over to pick up Bob and Spencer; they're bringing the deserts-

MRS THAYER: Good, good-

MAN: (to Henry) Hi (to Mrs Thayer) [and then] uh Todd and Mitchell are heading up from Polson, and they're bringing sandwiches. (walks off)

MRS THAYER: Y'know Henry it is my pleasure to introduce friends.

[Henry stands with his mouth gaping open. Scene cuts to Mrs Thayer's house, full of men, one group are standing around the piano singing cowboy songs, while others sit around chatting]

MRS THAYER: Hello Dave! (to Henry) Oh! That over there is Earl Stevens, General Council, all the way up from Missouri. See – I got lawyers for you!

These 'party scenes' are important, as they show that although the residents of Big Eden are not 'homophobic' (in that Henry gets a party of women and a party of men), they do highlight that the community sees the fact that Henry is not in a relationship to be problematic. The repetition of the party scene (one straight, one gay) also shows a commitment to sameness of treatment, and a conceptualisation of equality as formal equality – like should be treated alike.

The issue of relationships is predominantly dealt with in *Big Eden* through the characters of Henry and Dean. In this conversation between Henry and Dean during the thanksgiving dinner, Dean tries to explain to Henry what he means to him:

DEAN: Henry, I need to feel close

HENRY: Close to what?

DEAN: Close to you.

HENRY: Can't you pick on someone else?

DEAN: I'm not-we used to be best friends man, and I don't even know how to be with you anymore. You act like this is so easy for you, just cutting me out, don't you care? Is it this easy for you?

HENRY: Dean! Focus! I have waited 20 years and you 'can't' I've spent the past 6 months here hoping that I was wrong, but I'm not, I'm right. I'm right.

DEAN: Selfish. No-no it's all about you isn't it? Man, I would do anything in the world for you, anything, anything that I could. You think this has been easy for me? Do you know how hard I have tried, how much I wish I could? And just because I'm not something you dreamed up I should be for you, you'd cut me off. You're full of shit. Going on and on about how you've waited, you've wasted all these years. You may be in love, but I can tell you it's not with me … You are all hung up on some bullshit and you're punishing me because you're too damn scared to get on with it. Well screw you Henry Hart, I do know what love is. You are my family. And I'm sorry. I'm sorry that's not good enough for you.

HENRY: Dean, wait.

This scene is the turning point in the film in Henry's relationship with Dean. They do continue to be close, and later in the film Dean seems to be jealous of Henry's developing relationship with Pike, but their friendship is undoubtedly very changed from that moment on. An interesting point to note about the relationship between Henry and Dean, however, is where Henry refers to Dean saying that he 'can't'. This is a reference back to an earlier scene where they kissed, but Dean stopped, saying 'I can't, I can't.' This seems to highlight that in *Big Eden* sexuality is clear, essential and pre-defined – there is no room for bisexuality, fluidity or change in sexual orientation.

In *Woman on the Edge of Time,* on the other hand, Piercy (1987) tries to move away from the couple and the nuclear family unit, with Mattapoisett being a place where bisexuality is normative, every adult has their own living space, and people have a number of different relationships. People's relationships in Mattapoisett are not judged on the basis of whether they are sexual or not; rather, all friendships are valued and respected – the three main types of relationship described in *Woman on the Edge of Time* are 'hand friends', 'sweet friends' and 'pillow friends'. Hand friends are non-sexual close friendships, sweet friends are longstanding relationships that may or may not be sexual relationships, and pillow friends are sexual relationships. Luciente explains all this to Connie on her first visit to Mattapoisett:

> 'We're sweet friends. Some of us use the term 'core' for those we're closest to. Others think that distinction is bad. We debate. Myself, I use core, cause I think it means something real. Bee, Jackrabbit, Otter are my core-'
>
> 'Another lover!'
>
> 'No, Otter's a hand friend, not a pillow friend. We've been close since we were sixteen. Politically we are very close … '
>
> (Piercy, 1987: 72)

So, in Mattapoisett, rather than people living as family units, they each have a number of 'core' relationships, which all have similar status, and there is no division into nuclear family units. There is no mention in *Woman on the Edge of Time* of any legal institutions surrounding relationships, and certainly nothing similar to marriage. Close friendships and sexual relationships are respected in the same ways. This lack of differentiation between conjugal and non-conjugal relationships is, arguably, reflected in present-day legal recognition of same-sex relationships in the UK. As Nicola Barker (2006) has argued, civil partnership could be a radical alternative to marriage as there is no requirement for a conjugal relationship in the Civil Partnership Act 2004.[10] Unlike current legislation in the UK, however, same-sex relationships are valued in the same way as different-sex relationships in Mattapoisett, and this is positioned by Piercy as a non-contentious issue.

Relationship life is not all perfect in Mattapoisett, however, and there are a number of very interesting devices used in the text to show the flaws and points of friction which can appear in this way of organising society. The first way that the difficulties inherent in this way of life are shown is when Luciente is describing a former lover, Diana:

> In truth, the most intense mating of my life was a woman named Diana – the fire that annealed me, as Jackrabbit says in a poem. But it was a binding, you know, we obsessed. Not good for growing. We clipped each other. But I love Diana still and sometimes we come together ... Mostly I've liked males.
>
> (Piercy, 1987: 64)

So, in Mattapoisett, an overly close relationship between two people is seen as a bad thing, something which prevents each person in that relationship from growing as an independent individual. A second problem with the polyamorous lifestyle of Mattapoisett is highlighted through an exploration of jealousy and conflict between members of a person's 'core'. This comes up in the context of a strained relationship between Luciente and another of Jackrabbit's lovers, Bolivar, which culminates in a 'worming':

> 'Luciente and Bolivar have not been communing. Meshing badly. Sparks and bumps. Tonight we try to comprehend that hostility and see if we can diffuse it.'
>
> 'Aren't people allowed to dislike each other?'
>
> 'Not good when they're in the same core. Jackrabbit is close to both. Such bumping strains per. They compete for Jackrabbit's attent. They are picky toward each other's ways. We have critted them for it before, but matters lift only briefly. When they crit each other it does not hold up under scrutiny as honest – but self-serving.'
>
> (Piercy, 1987: 207)

The 'worming' is a community event, where the two people who have not been getting on and the rest of the community all sit down and try to talk through the problems they have had. This 'worming' is one of the few examples of a 'legal' framework in Mattapoisett; it is a requirement placed on Luciente and Bolivar by the wider community that they resolve their conflict. The format of the 'worming' is reminiscent of alternatives to formal legal process such as family mediation, arbitration and other forms of alternative dispute resolution, as the focus is on airing grievances and compromise. There are sanctions attached to the worming process however:

> 'Suppose after a worming they still can't stand each other?'
> 'Jackrabbit may choose to see neither for some time. Both may be sent into temporary wandering. We may impose invisibility. We resort to that after bad quarrelling.'
>
> (Piercy, 1987: 207)

So 'worming' is a form of alternative dispute resolution of tensions between individuals that can result in 'punishment' of those individuals.

An interesting point to make about these explorations of friction in the ways that relationships are managed in Mattapoisett is that the two 'problem' relationships hinge around same-sex relationships: the relationship between Luciente and Diana and Luciente's jealousy of the relationship between Jackrabbit and Bolivar. It is not that same-sex relationships are given any lower value than different-sex relationships in Mattapoisett, only that it is through these relationships that Piercy (1987) explores the tensions that could be present in a bisexual polyamorous lifestyle. Connie points out that a reason for Luciente being jealous of Jackrabbit and Bolivar's relationship could be related to this being a same-sex relationship:

> 'Something puzzles me. It seems like everybody is careful not to say what seems real obvious to me – that Jackrabbit and Bolivar have ... well, they're both men. It's homosexual. Like that might bother a woman more.' 'But why?' Parra looked at her as if she were really crazy. 'All coupling, all befriending goes on between biological males, biological females, or both. That's not a useful set of categories. We tend to divvy up people by what they're good at and bad at, strengths and weaknesses, gifts and failings.'
>
> (Piercy, 1987: 214)

This is interesting as it highlights a potential problem within the genderless society of Mattapoisett. Even where same-sex relationships and different-sex relationships are given the same value in society, it can be difficult to get over the biological differences between males and females. In *Woman on the Edge of Time* it is the outsider (who sees gender in a way that the inhabitants of Mattapoisett do not, and who places importance on the differences between women and men) who is shown by Piercy (1987) to understand that jealousy can arise from the fear that one's lover can get from another something that they cannot get from oneself. While this is not necessarily a problem within *Woman on the Edge of Time*, it is a noteworthy literary device that forces the reader to examine why same-sex and different-sex relationships are valued and treated differently in contemporary society.

As with the ways that same- and different-sex relationships are treated in *Big Eden* the equal value placed on same- and different-sex relationships in *Woman on the Edge of Time* can be described as a manifestation of formal equality – to be equal means to be treated alike, even if there are characteristics which distinguish one person from another. *Woman on the Edge of Time* and *Big Eden*, therefore, both deal with issues surrounding the value placed on same-sex and different-sex relationships, and this is manifested through a commitment in both texts to formal equality and equal value in the social recognition of same- and different-sex relationships. In many respects these representations of same-sex relationships and the social (if not legal) recognition of them mirror contemporary discourse around the legal recognition of lesbian and gay relationships.

Whereas the ways that relationships are represented in these two utopian texts seems to mirror current debates and arguments about the social and legal recognition of same-sex relationships, the ways that Piercy and Bezucha deal with the issue of parenting is more complex. Both the fictional utopias depicted in *Woman on the Edge of Time* and *Big Eden* include examples of parent/child relationships, but it is Piercy's (1987) novel that highlights a remarkably different way of organising this part of society. Parenting in *Big Eden*, while in some respects depicting non-normative ways of parenting (e.g. Dean is a single father) is very much positioned within the nuclear family.

One scene in *Big Eden* that encapsulates the way that parent/child family relationships are dealt with in this film is in a scene between Henry and his Grandfather, Sam:

HENRY: Ok, I'll bite. What?

SAM: [sigh] that's just it son, what? (pause) I want to know what your plans are. What are your intentions?

HENRY: My 'intentions'?

SAM: Mmm. People starting to count on you. Helping Grace, teaching at the school, those boys Henry – taken more than a shine to you.

HENRY: Well I-you were-

SAM: Don't use me for an excuse. What do you plan to become to these people?

HENRY: I-

SAM: Y'know I expect I'll be seeing your grandma before long, and your mama and your daddy. And I'm going to have to be able to tell them 'I did my job.' I made sure you had a home, with people there who loved you, but I'm gonna need to know if that's here or in New York.

> And I don't think you know. So I'm gonna need you to decide. I won't be able to look your grandma in the eye if I haven't done my job.

This scene continues with Sam trying to get Henry to come out to him, asking 'Why won't you tell me who you are?' and 'Did I teach you shame?' This is an important scene for a number of reasons, first because it shows that Sam knows that Henry is gay, but also because of the ways that familial and parental roles and relationships are conceptualised by Bezucha in this film. In *Big Eden,* Henry was raised by his grandparents and, in this scene, Sam is trying to find out Henry's 'intentions' to discover whether Henry will be living in Big Eden or in New York. Perhaps what is most interesting about this conversation is that Sam refers to his 'job' as a parent to be to make sure that Henry had a home and people who love him. That Henry must choose between rural Big Eden and urban New York reflects the essentialist approach to sexuality discussed above – just as Dean can only be either straight *or* gay, Henry can live in Big Eden *or* New York – there is no space in this society for fluidity and flux. There is, however, space for more people than a child's biological family to care for and love them, which brings back in the conceptualisation of community discussed above. In the excerpt above, Sam refers to 'those boys', by whom he means Dean's children. The relationship between Henry and Dean's children is largely unspoken in the film, but it is clear that they become close, and that Henry does get along well with them. At one point, when Henry is going to move back to New York, the boys are obviously upset about the prospect of not seeing him. This alludes to a strong relationship, but obvious representations of parenting in the film are limited to those involving Dean and Anna Rudolph, who is the other single parent in Big Eden, and the person with whom Dean eventually pairs off.

In *Woman on the Edge of Time*, on the other hand, the way that parenting is done in Mattapoisett is described in much detail, as it is a fundamental point of difference between contemporary society and the ecological and social harmony of this futuristic vision. On Connie's second visit to Mattapoisett, she is shown the way that children are raised there. Her first stop is the 'brooder, where our genetic material is stored. Where the embryos grow' (Piercy, 1987: 101). In Piercy's utopian society, all babies are grown and born in this way – the reason for this and the finer details are explained by Luciente:

> It was part of women's long revolution. When we were breaking up all the old hierarchies. Finally there was that one thing we had to give up to, the only power we ever had, in return for no more power for anyone. The original production: the power to give birth. Cause as long as we were biologically enchained, we'd never be equal. And males would never be humanized to be loving and tender. So we all became mothers. Every child has three. To break nuclear bonding.
>
> (Piercy, 1987: 105)

Thus in Piercy's (1987) utopia, the only way to ensure gender equality and to remove imbalances of power in society, was for women to relinquish the power to give birth. In certain respects, this can be described as an essentialist argument, wherein the root cause of women's inequality and oppression is wholly and completely in the body, and linked to reproductive ability. In Mattapoisett, not only are embryos grown outside the body, but parenting is something which is done in groups of three.[11] As a rule the co-mothers (or coms) are not lovers, in an attempt to ensure that children do not get caught up in lovers' arguments. Childrearing in Mattapoisett is very much a community endeavour, biological females and males can both breast-feed and young children live together in the children's house,[12] until they are old enough to have their own space, rather than with their comothers.

In Mattapoisett, children 'come of age' at around 13 years, through an experience known as 'naming' (Piercy, 1987: 114). The young person is taken to a spot in the wilderness, where they stay on their own for a week and think about what they would like to do. They also choose the name that they would like to be known as in adulthood. When the young person returns from their week in the wilderness, they become a full member of the community, and their mothers are not allowed to speak to them for three months (in case they forget that their child has become a youth); rather, they choose three 'aunts' who act as their advisors in their young adult life. Once they return from their 'naming', the young person is officially a 'youth' and an equal member of the community. They can decide what and where they want to study, what they want to do, and have their own space.

So, in *Woman on the Edge of Time,* young people are as much a part of the community as adults. They are 'set free' to make their own decisions in life and to participate fully in the community of Mattapoisett. In many respects, this is one of the most radical aspects of Piercy's (1987) utopia, because it highlights (through a stark contrast with contemporary society) the respect each person has for and is granted by the other members of the community, and the lack of hierarchical organising principles in Piercy's utopia. All people in Mattapoisett, irrespective of their age, are full members of the society, and each person's input is valued in the same way. Indeed, one of the strongest features of Piercy's utopia is the ways that people are differentiated on the basis of their skills and qualities, rather than their gender, age or sexual orientation.

In summary, lesbian and gay parenting and relationships are represented in these two utopian texts as socially accepted, and even normative. In certain respects, the ways that Piercy (1987) and Bezucha (2000) approach relationships are very similar, even though superficially they seem quite different. In both *Woman on the Edge of Time* and *Big Eden,* there is recognition that people have more than one affective relationship and can have close emotional ties with more than one person. In *Woman on the Edge of Time*, this is explored through the normative status of polyamory in Mattapoisett society and the ways that sexual and non-sexual friendships are equally valued. In *Big Eden*, similar themes are explored through Henry's relationships with Dean and Pike. The ways that these texts deal with lesbian and gay parenting are, however, very different, with parenting in *Woman on the Edge of Time* offering a radical feminist solution to the gendered power relations arising from childbirth and childcare.

What then, do these two texts say about law, legal consciousness and the regulation of lesbian and gay relationships and parenting? The primary question that is raised by these texts in relation to legal consciousness is which (if either) of them would be more in accord with lesbians' and gay men's perceptions of how relationships and parenting should be recognised and regulated. It is, of course, impossible to predict how any, and certainly not all, lesbians and gay men would react to either of these texts. In posing this question, therefore, I am not so much concerned with specific individuals, but rather which of these utopias sits more easily alongside the ways that lesbians and gay men, as highlighted in previous chapters, have conceptualised law and regulation. At first glance, it would appear that the liberal, formal equality, vision offered by *Big Eden* would be much more appealing than the radical re-organisation of society presented in *Woman on the Edge of Time*. Given the discursive focus on formal equality in debates around same-sex marriage,[13] the non-discriminatory and egalitarian ethos of *Big Eden* seems to capture the aspirations of lesbians and gay men. Yet while *Big Eden* does seem to offer a vision of a 'good place' for lesbians and gay men, I would argue that this utopian vision remains very much a heteronormative and gendered society.

As I argued in Chapters 5 and 6, there are gendered differences in the ways in which lesbians and gay men experience and conceptualise the place of law in everyday life, so this gendered society may not be as appealing to lesbians as it may be to gay men. *Woman on the Edge of Time*, on the other hand, considers gender and sexuality together, and offers a utopian society in which gender has ceased to be an organising principle in society. This could, therefore, be a more attractive utopian possibility for lesbians and feminists. The resistance to increased regulation and 'fixing' of same-sex relationships, which was raised by some of the participants in Chapter 6 would seem to support this claim. The radical parenting ideas contained in *Woman on the Edge of Time,* however, seem not to be reflected in any of the personal stories and narratives in either Chapters 5 or 6. It is possible, then, that whereas more radical approaches to relationship recognition may find support, the radical approach to parenting outlined above seems to be in direct conflict with current ideas around who is and should be described as a mother or father. In summary then, I would argue that both of these utopian texts have insights to offer in considering how sexuality could be regulated in society, but that the more radical approaches to parenting reflect current views about the regulation of the family less well than the ways that these texts represent same-sex relationships.

Equality, power and resistance in Utopia

The differences between the ways in which Piercy (1987) and Bezucha (2000) deal with relationships and parenting highlight the different conceptions of equality used by these writers, as well as the way(s) that they conceptualise the relationship between power and resistance and equality. The utopia in Piercy's (1987) novel has its roots in a full-scale re-imagination of the way people live in Western society, albeit with some 'real-life' resonances. Both the utopian society of Mattapoisett and the inherent critique of contemporary society in *Woman on the Edge of Time* are grounded in a radical feminist perspective on equality, including a critique of the liberal capitalist underpinnings of contemporary society. *Big Eden,* however, is depicted by Bezucha (2000) as a place that could actually exist within the present-day capitalist system. Rather than being based in a critique of systemic problems which cause inequality, this film is a depiction of a liberal egalitarian utopia – a place where differences in sexuality and sexual identity are respected and same- and different-sex relationships are given the same status in society. Although these two texts are undoubtedly very different in their approaches to imagining an equal society, there are a number of similarities in the ways these two utopian communities function.

There are a number of different ways of conceptualising theoretical approaches to 'equality'. The society depicted in *Big Eden* relies heavily on the concept of equality of recognition and speaks to the idea that if non-normative sexual identities were not misrecognised, then all of the inequalities experienced by lesbians and gay men would be eradicated (Fraser, 1997). The limitations of the egalitarian society as depicted in *Big Eden* can also be explained through the critique of this form of equality – especially Judith Butler's (1998) discussion of the ways that equality of recognition supports the heteronormativity of the capitalist system, the continuation of gendered divisions of labour, and the ways that heteronormativity works to support economic inequalities. For example, the emphasis on 'coming out' and declaring a non-heterosexual identity in *Big Eden* is indicative of a continued emphasis on (and differential valuing of) sexual orientation and sexual identity within this supposedly utopian community. An interesting example of this is a scene in the film between Pike Dexter and Jim (one of the cowboys who spends his life at Pike's store) where Jim is questioning what Pike's new found interest in cooking fancy food means:

JIM: Say uh Pike (pause) if you don't mind my asking-

PIKE: I wish you wouldn't.

JIM: Seems we've uh known each other a long time Pike. I don't mean to pry, I don't but uh well, I never suspected that you-I mean did you ever think you might – well uh well what does all this mean, Pike?

PIKE: I don't know what it means Jim.

JIM: (pause) Well – this looks like a mighty fine dinner.
PIKE: Thanks Jim.

In this scene, Jim tries to find out if Pike is gay (or at least attracted to Henry), without actually asking the question – which is similar to the way that both Sam and Mrs Thayer approach Henry's sexuality in the extracts reproduced above. What is most important about this way of dealing with sexuality in *Big Eden* is that it requires some form of disclosure of non-normative sexual identity (a lack of denial of same-sex attraction can be read as a form of coming out), drawing attention to the non-normative status of homosexuality within the wider Big Eden community. The difficulties inherent in this liberal recognition-based egalitarian utopia do not, however, detract from the status of *Big Eden* as a utopian text. The utopian society created by Bezucha (2000) is not an unpleasant place – indeed the film is very much a 'feel good' depiction of a community working together without substantive differences in the level of respect or value placed on non-heterosexual members of the community.

The ways that 'discrimination' is depicted in both *Woman on the Edge of Time* and *Big Eden* is another important facet of these utopian visions. While both these fictional utopias are concerned with the depiction of a society where discrimination is not an everyday part of life, it is *Big Eden* that perhaps has more to say specifically around discrimination on the basis of sexual orientation than *Woman on the Edge of Time*. In *Woman on the Edge of Time*, issues of discrimination are predominantly depicted through discussions of gender, race and age, with sexuality as an unimportant feature of this society. In *Big Eden*, however, Bezucha's (2000) vision was an attempt to depict a utopian space with no discrimination on the basis of sexual orientation. While it can be claimed that he succeeded in a number of different ways, I would argue that the depiction of Big Eden as a society with no discrimination in relation to sexuality also fails.

The successful devices that Bezucha (2000) uses to depict a non-homophobic society are ones such as those discussed above – the bachelor parties and the attempts by members of the community to get Henry to stay in Big Eden. The problem, however, lies in the way that *Big Eden* continues to be a depiction of a heteronormative society, which exists outside of capitalism, labour relations and outside the regulatory functions of law and the state. So while Henry, Pike and the two (minor) lesbian characters are supported in their relationships by the rest of the community of Big Eden, heterosexuality continues to be the assumed and normative sexual orientation of everyone in Big Eden. There is, for example, a certain degree of emphasis placed on coming out – in particular Henry seems to feel an obligation to come out to his grandfather (which he never actually does). There is also a moment in the film shortly after Mrs Thayer's first party for Henry, where she and three other women bring cookies and refreshments to Henry's house, which he refuses. This conversation takes place when the women get back in their car:

MRS THAYER: Oh, I just knew it!
WOMAN 1: What a shame!
WOMAN 2: You know what they say-
WOMAN 3: All the good-looking ones!
MRS THAYER: Y'know that Rachel Sawyers said no-no she didn't think so she didn't think he was. I said yes, absolutely. Mmmmm ... she thinks she knows everything. Why doesn't he say something already?

In this scene, the women somehow deduce that Henry is not heterosexual from the way he reacted to their cookie delivery, and then laugh and joke that 'all the good-looking ones' are gay. Although this conversation is depicted in a friendly way, and without malice, it does draw attention to the heteronormativity of the community in Big Eden. If sexuality were not a salient factor in differentiating between people in Big Eden, then this conversation would not have taken place. In *Woman on the Edge of Time*, sexuality has ceased to be a salient factor in the community (as there are no differentiations made on the basis of gender); in *Big Eden*, sexuality is obviously still an important part of the lives of people in this community.

There are a number of points that can be made about the reasons why the depiction of a society without discrimination in *Woman on the Edge of Time* seems to be more effective than that described in *Big Eden*. First, whereas *Big Eden* is firmly situated within an idealised version of the present, *Woman on the Edge of Time* is a utopian society in which, from Piercy's perspective, the problems with contemporary society have been addressed. This is important because whereas Piercy's utopian vision includes ways of addressing inequalities through the removal of gender, race, religion, age and economic status as salient factors in society, Bezucha's film, while attempting to show an utopian rural space for a gay man does not tackle the ways that sexual orientation intersects with other 'identities' in the creation and perpetuation of disadvantage.

The vision of equality depicted in *Woman on the Edge of Time* is based on a fundamentally different conception of what 'equality' means. In Mattapoisett, Piercy (1987) has created a place where every member of the community has equal power (Cooper, 2004), equality of recognition (Fraser, 1997), equality of resources (Dworkin, 2002) and equality of opportunities (Rawls, 1971). Whereas *Big Eden* could be described as an exercise in formal equality within a liberal egalitarian framework, *Woman on the Edge of Time* is a more radical conceptualisation of an egalitarian society, firmly rooted in radical feminist politics. Through the creation of the utopian society in Mattapoisett, Piercy (1987) highlights that such a complete, substantive version of equality is not possible within the current economic and political climate, and may not be possible without a radical change in the ways that human beings reproduce.

The main focus of equality in *Woman on the Edge of Time* is in the area of gender equality – at its heart, Piercy's novel is an exercise in showing how the world might be different if there were no structural inequalities between women and men, and if gender ceased to be relevant in society. Perhaps the most important device used in *Woman on the Edge of Time* to demonstrate gender equality is the removal of gendered pronouns from the language of Mattapoisett, and the consequent blurring of the dichotomous boundaries of gendered division. It is important to note that gender is not completely absent from *Woman on the Edge of Time* – the reader experiences Mattapoisett through the eyes of Connie, the main protagonist, and so when this narrator describes people and scenes in the utopian future it is Connie's version of the future that the reader sees. Often this leads to a gendering of the characters in Mattapoisett through Connie's interpretation of the people she meets. Indeed, when Connie first encounters Luciente, near the beginning of the novel, she assumes that Luciente is male:

> Pressed reluctantly, nervously against Luciente, she felt the coarse fabric of his shirt and ... breasts! She jumped back.
> 'You're a woman! No, one of those sex-change operations.'
> 'If you hop around, we'll never get it right ... Of course I'm female.' Luciente looked a little disgusted.
> She stared at Luciente. Now she could begin to see him/her as a woman.
> (Piercy, 1987: 67)

Throughout the novel, when Connie encounters new people in Mattapoisett, she genders them, although sometimes she finds this difficult, as often there are not obvious differences between females and males in Mattapoisett. This is an important part of the utopian project in *Woman on the Edge of Time*, because it allows the future society to be understandable by the reader, while at the same time the reader learns to disregard the gender of the characters. As discussed above, part of Piercy's (1987) vision in *Woman on the Edge of Time* concerns the removal of reproduction from the body, to remove the biological differentiation between women and men; the power of women to give birth was relinquished so that power relations were removed completely. Through this removal of birth and the genetic and biological connection between parents and children, Piercy (1987) argues that not only gendered power relations are dismantled, but also those related to race and ethnicity. So, in *Woman on the Edge of Time* we are shown Piercy's (1987) vision of how society would be without relationships of power and resistance.

Another side of the depiction of a society without relations of power and resistance in *Woman on the Edge of Time* is the ways that Piercy (1987) deals with the questions of government and law and order. In Piercy's utopia, there is no central government; rather, people are 'chosen by lot' to serve on the 'planning council' for a year (Piercy, 1987: 151). After a period of being involved in such decision-making, people then go on to do some menial labour to remind them that holding power is not something that individuals do, that government is a collective enterprise. In relation to crime and punishment, if a person commits a violent crime, they must atone, either by doing menial labour or by wandering, and have a tattoo on their hand. If a person commits a violent crime for a second time:

> Second time someone uses violence, we give up. We don't want to watch each other or to imprison each other. We aren't willing to live with people who chose to use violence. We execute them.
>
> (Piercy, 1987: 209)

Thus, while the community depicted in *Woman on the Edge of Time* seems enlightened in a number of ways, the removal of state apparatus of control and the lack of governmental forms of disciplinary power (e.g. criminal justice systems, courts, prisons, etc.) gives rise to somewhat extreme measures in relation to the punishment of violent crime. This, I would argue is, in part, because relationships of power and resistance are an essential part of all communities. Rather than being indicative of a society where there is no power and resistance, *Woman on the Edge of Time* seems to be a depiction of a place were power is held by the community – community values (non-violence, co-operation) are ascendant, to the point where deviation from (or resistance to) these values is punishable by death. So, the removal of disciplinary mechanisms of power emanating from the state seems to result in a closing off of possibilities for resistance. This is reminiscent of Foucault's (1980) conceptualisation of disciplinary power, discussed in Chapter 3, and that it is through disciplinary power that resistance is made possible. Where there is disciplinary power, there is resistance; where there are no disciplinary forms of power (for example when power is exclusively held by the sovereign, or in the exercise of juridical power) the space for resistance is closed down.

A second area in Mattapoisett where relationships of power and resistance are brought into focus is with the discussion of the ongoing war between the people of Piercy's utopian society and the people who live on space platforms, a society which is reminiscent of the dystopian vision Connie visits (Piercy, 1987: 287–301). There is an ongoing power struggle between these two factions, which is positioned as the main focus of power and resistance in Piercy's utopia. By creating an external power struggle, and one which is easily recognisable as such, Piercy draws attention away from the internal relationships of power and resistance within the Mattapoisett community and diverts the focus to power and resistance as war – the most extreme form of struggle.

This exploration of power and resistance is a key theme within *Woman on the Edge of Time*, and on a number of occasions Luciente and other people in Mattapoisett talk to Connie about the ways that change and revolution happen:

> 'What good can I do? Who could have less power? I'm a prisoner. A patient. I can't even carry a book of matches or keep my own money. You picked the wrong saviour this time!'
> 'The powerful don't make revolutions,' Sojourner said with a broad yellow grin, 'Oh, revolution!' She grimaced. 'Honchos marching around in imitation uniforms. Big talk and bad-mouthing everybody else. Noise in the streets and nothing changes.'
> 'No, Connie! It's the people who worked out the labor-and-land intensive farming we do. It's all the people who changed how people bought food, raised children, went to school!'
>
> (Piercy, 1987: 198)

This quote recalls the three types of resistance I outlined in Chapter 3, stabilising, moderating and fracturing resistance. Stabilising resistance, the constant counterbalance to power, is highlighted through the idea that it is ordinary people who change minor things in life, like how to farm or where to buy food. Examples of moderating resistance (those resistant acts that are public, and aimed at challenging the status quo) are also present in this part of *Woman on the Edge of Time*. Connie's perspective on 'revolutions' – all big talk and no change – is challenged by the inhabitants of Mattapoisett, who highlight that changing things like how children are raised and schooled make a substantive difference to society. The focus on stabilising and moderating forms of resistance is, again, reminiscent of the attitudes of lesbians and gay men discussed in Chapters 4–6. Stabilising and moderating forms of resistance, whether these be expressed through small, everyday resistant practices, or large-scale re-imagining of how people could live, are ascendant in lesbian and gay struggles.

Unlike in previous chapters, fracturing resistance (resistance which causes a break in the flow of power) is also present in *Woman on the Edge of Time*. This form of resistance is, however, conflated with 'revolution' and 'war'. We are, for example, told that Connie realises she is 'at war', leading her to commit an act of violence that kills four of the six members of the team of scientists who are responsible for the mind control experiments. This act of violence shuts down the mind control experiments and paves the way for a peaceful future. When Connie talks of her reservations about carrying out this act of violence to Luciente, she is reminded that 'power *is* violence. When did it get destroyed peacefully? We all fight when we're back to the wall' (Piercy, 1987: 367). So, through the critical positioning of utopian and dystopian space and community in *Woman on the Edge of Time*, relationships of power and resistance are brought sharply into focus. For Piercy, activism is the key to a utopian future – the creation of a better society for the future depends on small as well as large acts of resistance by those who otherwise would be conceptualised (either by themselves or others) as powerless.

In contrast, *Big Eden* does not really deal with relationships of power and resistance explicitly, but rather these concepts are relegated to the background of the society. If there is one aspect of *Big Eden* that draws on relationships of power and resistance, it is the way the urban lifestyle Henry leads in New York is positioned in contrast to the rural idyll of Big Eden. Whereas in Big Eden, the values that are most important are those of community, family and co-operation, the value system that is depicted in city life is opulent and concerned primarily with money, success and individualism. That Henry chooses to stay in Big Eden rather than to return to the city is an act of resistance; resistance to the pull of the city for gay men and resistance to the loneliness and isolation of individualistic city life.

In many respects then, the concepts of power and resistance are depicted in very different ways in *Big Eden* and *Woman on the Edge of Time*. There are some similarities, with the focus on rural lives, community and co-operation being positioned in both texts as the cornerstone of utopian society and the individualistic, money-oriented and discriminatory competing urban dystopia being positioned as the (negative) source of power, and that which must be resisted. A close reading of the ways that relationship recognition and parenting are depicted in *Woman on the Edge of Time* and *Big Eden*, alongside consideration of Piercy (1987) and Bezucha (2000)'s differing conceptualisations of equality, power and resistance, brings the ways that these utopian visions depict the place of law in everyday life sharply into focus.

The ways that the concepts of equality, power and resistance are represented in these texts help to elucidate the ways that law *ought* to work in the everyday lives of lesbians and gay men. As discussed above, *Big Eden* seems to be grounded in understandings of formal equality, whereas *Woman on the Edge of Time* takes a far more nuanced and substantive approach to equality. As such, the vision for society depicted in *Big Eden* may be more attractive or palatable in the current political and economic climate than that represented in *Woman on the Edge of Time*. There are a number of possible explanations for why this may be the case, including the assumed futility of revolution, the difficulties of challenging 'powerful' state institutions, and the seeming impossibility of such a peaceful, co-operative society. Through the way that understandings of the operation of equality, power and resistance work in these utopian societies are represented, it is clear that these utopian texts offer inspiration for changing the way that relationships and parenting are regulated in society. Instead of accepting that marriage is the way that the state regulates relationships, or that people should live in nuclear family units, or that parenting necessarily needs to be linked to genetic ties, both of these utopian societies place their emphasis on community, friendship and explicitly valuing all relationships.

Concluding remarks

My focus throughout this book has been to interrogate how lesbians and gay men experience the impact and effects of recent 'positive' legal developments on their everyday lives. This final substantive chapter has allowed me to approach this question from a slightly different angle. My aim in this chapter was to offer some tentative answers to the following questions: if we step outside the current legal and social debates about the recognition and regulation of lesbian and gay relationships and parenting, what other perspectives can be brought to bear on sexuality and legal consciousness? How could and should law impact differently on the everyday lives of lesbians and gay men?

As the above discussion makes clear, utopian literature provides insights into the place of law in everyday life and offers frameworks for alternative ways of thinking about the regulation of sexuality within contemporary legal frameworks. Examining fictional utopia illuminates not only on how the authors of these texts approach relationships of power and resistance and ways of conceptualising equality, but also brings into focus a critique of contemporary society. In both *Big Eden* and *Woman on the Edge of Time,* there is a strong critique of the ways that current legal frameworks deal with inequalities, whether related to gender or sexuality. An examination of fictional utopias also gives insights into different ways of being, ways of living without discrimination. It is these alternative ways of living that hold the key to the place of fictional utopian writing within a study of legal consciousness.

Fictional utopian texts are, in themselves, examples of 'legal consciousness'. Such texts highlight the ways that the author thinks about the place of law in everyday life, as well as making the author's argument about how law *should* work in everyday life, or how the world could be organised differently. As the above analysis of *Woman on the Edge of Time* and *Big Eden* shows, lesbian/gay and feminist utopian spaces can be read as examples of resistance to normative ways of being in contemporary society and as a critique of the individualistic underpinnings of capitalist economic systems. These two texts use different methods to highlight problems in contemporary society: *Big Eden* stresses the heteronormativity of contemporary society; *Woman on the Edge of Time* draws attention to much more complex manifestations of power within contemporary society – sexism, heterosexism, racism and imperialism. The creation of utopian space, then, is itself an act of resistance, which acts as a mirror and critique of contemporary society.

Perhaps the most startling thing that my analysis of these two utopian text brings to this book is, from a legal consciousness perspective, the overwhelming lack of (official) law and regulation of people's everyday and familial lives in both Piercy's (1987) and Bezucha's (2000) utopian societies. The lack of obvious legal systems and structures in Big Eden and Mattapoisett highlight that 'utopian legal consciousness' is marked by a desire to live outside of formal legal regulation. This lack of law is, at first glance, in stark contrast to calls for more legal recognition and regulation of lesbian and gay relationships, such as those discussed in Chapter 4, or the problematic effects of parenting outside the law discussed in Chapter 5. These fictional utopian societies reflect complex and contradictory attitudes to the place of law in everyday life, and call to mind the distrust of legal regulation expressed by participants in Chapter 6.

Utopian texts not only draw out critiques of contemporary society, but also provide possibilities. The impact of utopian vision – what utopia is capable of – is the underlying message in both *Woman on the Edge of Time* and *Big Eden*. In *Woman on the Edge of Time*, Connie is empowered by the utopian future to fight for it – to do what she can to break down the control of the oppressed by those with power. In *Big Eden*, the focus is the simple choice between the lonely life of the city and the rural community ideal, a version of how life could be without homophobia. So, looking to utopia within this study of sexuality and legal consciousness offers a window into alternative ways of being; alternative conceptualisations of relationships of power and resistance, and different approaches to the place of law in everyday life.

Notes

1 As with the rest of this book, 'law' in this chapter is construed in a pluralist sense.
2 Like the published personal narratives explored in Chapter 5, this analysis of fictional texts draws more on textual analysis methods from the humanities than the social scientific methodologies relied on in Chapters 4 and 6.
3 And, as such, perhaps more easily identifiable with lesbian lives and lesbian feminism.
4 *Big Eden* is set in a small community in rural Montana. By describing *Big Eden* as a 'near perfect' society, I do not wish to infer that I personally believe that it would be the perfect place to live, rather that it was intentionally created as a 'utopian' space.
5 I specifically explore the aspects of Piercy's (1987) utopia that relate to lesbian and gay relationships and parenting and the regulation of these areas of life. There are, of course, other aspects of Piercy's utopian vision that I do not have space to cover in this book. For example, one very interesting aspect of *Woman on the Edge of Time* that is outside the scope of my analysis here is the ways that Piercy deals with work/life balance, the value placed on different types of labour and the decisions about what does and does not get done by machines. For example, much of the mundane, everyday work in Mattapoisett (like washing dishes, or factory assembly lines) is automated. This does raise questions about the gendered nature of such work, particularly in light of the technological automation of reproduction in Piercy's utopia, an issue that I will return to later.
6 An interesting facet of this, and one that is in direct contrast with the organisation of labour in *Woman on the Edge of Time*, is that it seems to be the women in this community who do the vast majority of the work, while the men sit around on the porch of the general store.
7 It is important to note the racism inherent in the use of the term 'wetback' here.
8 The lack of imperative to work for most members of the community in Big Eden raises interesting questions about how this community survives economically, and how any society can exist outside of the relations of labour and capital. As with the

ways in which working lives are represented in *Woman on the Edge of Time* (see note 5 above), this is a very interesting aspect of the utopian society depicted in *Big Eden*, but, unfortunately, one that falls outside the scope of this book and which I do not have the space to consider in detail in this analysis.

9 Which is, of course, in stark contrast to much contemporary Western lesbian and gay activism and academic scholarship, where the legal recognition of same-sex relationships seems to be a primary goal.

10 There is no requirement for consummation (as there is in heterosexual marriage) and adultery is not a ground for dissolution of a civil partnership. These differences are, however, more likely to stem from a reluctance on the part of the legislature to define what counts as 'sex' in the context of lesbian/gay relationships, rather than as a radical alternative to marriage (see further: Barker, 2006; Stychin, 2006).

11 Interestingly, in a recent Canadian case (*AA v BB* 2007 ONCA 2), three parents (the biological mother, her same-sex partner, and their sperm donor) were recorded on the birth certificate of a child, in the first case of its kind, so perhaps Piercy's (1987) utopian vision of shared parenting which does not rely solely on biological ties is becoming closer to a reality, at least in some jurisdictions.

12 Which was the model used in the early days of kibbutzism, although this is no longer generally practised, in part because of psychological research into child development which focuses on attachment theories (Fox, 1977; Scharf, 2001).

13 By this I mean both within academic literature and between 'ordinary' lesbians and gay men.

Chapter 8

Afterword

> You will be assimilated ... Resistance is futile.
>
> (*Star Trek*: Voyager)

The traditional Borg greeting, that 'resistance is futile' will be familiar not just to 'Trekkies' but much more generally, as this phrase has come to encapsulate the hegemonic approach to 'resistance' in contemporary society. A generic Google search on the phrase 'resistance is futile' provides links to nearly 800,000 web pages; a Google Scholar search, over 100,000. While it may be interesting to debate why this phrase has been 'assimilated' into popular culture in the two decades since its first use in *Star Trek: The Next Generation*,[1] such an analysis is outside the remit of this book. More relevant here is to consider these themes of assimilation and resistance in relation to the lesbian and gay equality struggles that have been my focus throughout this book. A recurring theme in the academic literature on same-sex marriage has been the tension between whether arguing for inclusion in a heteronormative institution will either transform the nature of marriage (see e.g. Harding, 2007; Hunter, 1992; Peel & Harding, 2004) or simply assimilate lesbians and gay men into heteronormative ways of living (see e.g. Barker, 2008; Clarke, 2003; Polikoff, 1993). Similarly, lesbian and gay parents have to contend with the spectre of the heteronormative family, particularly when it comes to providing evidence of appropriately gendered role models for their children (Clarke & Kitzinger, 2005), or dealing with heteronormative representations of the ideal family (Gavigan, 1995).

The different texts that have informed the empirical analysis presented in this book highlight that, even following the recent shifts in the positive legal recognition and regulation of lesbian and gay family lives, the issues of assimilation, transformation and resistance remain key to understanding lesbian and gay equality struggles. It has been my aim to explore, situate and interrogate the experience of these legal and social developments in the everyday lives of lesbians and gay men. I have demonstrated that the regulation of sexuality through the legal recognition of same-sex relationships and families is not without tensions, and that achieving legal and social equality for lesbian and gay families requires more than straightforward inclusion in heteronormative legal institutions. Attaining formal legal equality is and must be a mainstay of lesbian and gay equality struggles, but it cannot and does not represent the end of the road for lesbian and gay social movements.

Throughout this book, I have been telling stories about law; I have told stories about how lesbians and gay men think about relationship recognition, stories about experiences of being and becoming a parent, stories about power and stories about resistance, stories about equality and stories about legal consciousness. In this final chapter, I want to tell a slightly different tale of law: my own stories of law, legal consciousness, relationship recognition, parenting and resistance. As with all research, I bring my own identity and experiences to this project – my sexuality, my relationship status, my experience, my future hopes and plans. My aim here, therefore, is to reflect on my own 'legal consciousness', to examine how I, the researcher, have been influenced by the stories I have recounted, and to interrogate my own attitudes to, perceptions and understandings of law and the recent legal developments in the regulation of lesbian and gay lives.

Legal storytelling

Think back to 1997. Where were you? What were you doing then? How did law intersect with your everyday life? I was 18 years old, and law was omnipresent in my everyday life, even back then. I did a lot of new things in 1997: I completed my first year of an undergraduate law degree at the University of Edinburgh. I went to a gay club for the first time. I exercised my democratic right as a citizen to vote. I stayed up all night to watch New Labour's landslide victory in the UK general election. I moved in with my first serious girlfriend. I wondered if relationships like mine would ever be mentioned positively in the family law textbooks I read. I struggled to understand why anyone would consider lesbian and gay families 'pretend', or why there was a difference in the 'age of consent' for gay male sex. When meeting new people (and I met a lot of new people that year) I played the 'don't use names or gender pronouns' game when talking about my partner, or what I did at the weekend, until I knew whether the person I was speaking to was going to accept my sexuality. I decided not to follow a career in legal practice, because at the time it seemed too difficult to be a woman, let alone to be out as a lesbian, in that field. I voted 'Yes/Yes' in the referendum on creating a Scottish Parliament. I watched in awe as human rights were 'brought home' by the Human Rights Bill. I was afraid when homophobic abuse was shouted at my girlfriend and I in the street.

Now, as we move into the second decade of the twenty-first century, much has changed. Family law textbooks now all need some coverage of same-sex relationships, because now such relationships are recognised and regulated by official law. My partner and I were married in Canada in 2006. Our relationship is recognised in Canada as a marriage, in the UK as a civil partnership,[2] and may or may not be recognised at all in other countries around the world, depending on their domestic laws governing the recognition of overseas registered same-sex relationships.[3] In some jurisdictions, my sexuality and relationship status would still mark me as a criminal. I am privileged; I can choose not to visit those countries where lesbians and gay men are still victimised, criminalised and subjected to imprisonment, corporal or even capital punishment.

Fundamentally, I find the multiplicity of forms of recognition and regulation that 'law' subjects my relationship to fascinating. My partner and I chose to marry in Canada (when civil partnership was available to us in the UK) for a number of different reasons, some of which have direct relevance to this project. It gratifies me that my relationship is recognised and regulated by law, but is concurrently unrecognised and unregulated; the strange legal position that I (alongside many other lesbians and gay men) find myself in exposes, for me, the contingency and fluidity of law. But at the same time, being positioned in a place of legal uncertainty is unsettling. After all, throughout my initial legal education, I was conditioned to think of law as rational, ordered, certain and objective. Legal education often seeks to tell the 'before the law' story of law. Although I have remained (in spite of a doctrinal, blackletter legal education) critical of legal systems and structures I do, on some level, and at some times, hold a 'before the law' legal consciousness.

Perhaps the most salient example of when I have found myself believing in the formally ordered, rational and objective law of Ewick and Silbey's (1998) 'before the law' schema was when I was the 'victim' of crime. A while back, I experienced an attempted break-in while at home. It was frightening. I phoned the police, they apprehended a suspect. I was called in to the police station to identify the would-be burglar; I picked him out from a video line-up. The suspect was charged. I was summonsed as a witness. Before trial the accused pleaded guilty, so I did not have to give evidence; I did not have to 'go to court'. I was relieved not to have to give evidence, but pleased that 'justice' had been served. In many respects, however, this story has little relevance to my everyday life: it was a 'one-off' incident, I was not harmed or injured (although I was perhaps a little shaken up), and it was the result of a random act, unrelated to any aspect of my identity.

The stories we tell of law, like all stories, depend on the time, space and location of the story. They depend on who is asking the questions, what they are asking questions about, and how we perceive the questions being asked of us. I also have stories of law that could be described as examples of 'with the law' legal consciousness. One example is that I quite enjoy writing complaint letters. An older relative suffers from dementia and, at times, we have had to battle with social services and his local NHS primary care trust to access services or for NHS continuing care funding for his placement in a nursing home.

As a person with the necessary skills to read legal documents such as judgments, legislation and government policy statements, regulations, guidelines and briefing documents, I am able to synthesise all of this information and present a convincing argument. We fought the system and won. It was a victory. We know that in a few months' time his care will be subject to review; we know we may need to 'fight' the 'system' again. We expect to win again; as middle-class, educated, white professionals, we can expect to win. We have the necessary skills to play the game of law. So I hold a 'with the law' legal consciousness. But again, although this is perhaps more a part of my everyday life, because it is ongoing, than my 'before the law' example above, this 'with the law' form of legal consciousness is not the best way to describe my attitudes to, perceptions and understandings of law. What is perhaps most interesting about these two stories of law is that they are the sorts of story I may have recounted if I were a participant in a 'legal consciousness' study. These are the kinds of stories that formed the basis of Ewick and Silbey's (1998) influential text on legal consciousness.

I do not have a story from my life that would fit with the 'against the law' variety of legal consciousness described by Ewick and Silbey (1998). My experience of law is not about 'pilfering, violence or threats of violence, tricks, institutional disruptions, foot dragging, humor, storytelling and gossip' (Ewick & Silbey, 2003: 1336). Even so, I think my legal consciousness does include resistance, but it is resistance that is different from the 'up against it' forms described above. Many of the stories I have discussed and analysed in this book have included what I have called stabilising and moderating forms of resistance; resistance that seeks to challenge the everyday assumptions about family, relationships and sexuality. As such, it is this form of resistance, of being 'against the law' that I suffuse my everyday experience of law, whether official or not.

I bought a new car recently. After a lengthy period of discussion, and two test-drives (where both I and my partner drove the model I was purchasing), we progressed to the financial side of the purchase. I was taking advantage of a finance deal to buy the car. The salesperson was filling in the finance form and asked, as they so often do, 'are you married or single?' I said, 'in a civil partnership'. My response flummoxed her for a moment. She paused, then had to clarify: 'so is that like "single"?' I responded with 'no, it's like "married"'. This conversation has stayed with me, not because it is desperately unusual, but because it was the first time I'd had that particular conversation. It was not the last!

It seems now that every time I have a spoken interaction with an insurance company, bank, or other service provider who, for whatever reason, needs to know my 'relationship status', I play out another version of the same conversation. It becomes a little dull at times. Often, as this portion of the interaction plays out, there's a small, almost imperceptible, 'double-take'; a pause where the person providing the service realises that I've just disclosed my (homo)sexuality to them. Sometimes it feels uncomfortable, inserting sexuality into these mundane interactions. Although it's important to remember that sexuality is always already there, it's just that it's heterosexuality that is normative, expected, and mundane (Peel, 2001). Sometimes the 'outing' changes the dynamic of the interaction completely; other times any change is barely perceptible, but usually, I find, there is something: an indefinable, intangible shift in tone or timbre. These sorts of interaction seem to me to represent a change in the place of law in the everyday lives of lesbians and gay men. They have become another manifestation of the complex interplay between recognition and regulation, between transformation and assimilation. But just as these conversations provide opportunities for stabilising and moderating resistance, they also can be crushingly assimilationist. Depending on how the question is asked, or the options given, I can simply claim to be 'married', I can hide behind the assumption of heterosexuality. After all, under the official law of several jurisdictions across the world, I *am* married. It seems trite, therefore, not to realise that it must take more than the mere existence of civil partnerships to transform the heteronormativity of 'the family'. That 'family' is 'heterosexual' seems so deeply ingrained in British culture, that challenging heteronormativity will undoubtedly require much more active, moderating, resistance than the simple registration of civil partnerships by upwards of 35,000 same-sex couples.[4]

A strong theme that has emerged throughout this book has been that achieving formal legal equality for lesbians and gay men is a key motivation behind calls for legal recognition of same-sex relationships and families. But there are tensions inherent in asking for formal equality – most specifically the complex interplay of heteronormativity, assimilation and transformation. What is important, and a key argument that I have made in this book, is that by looking to the mundane interactions that constitute everyday life, the complex interplay of assimilation and transformation in the recognition and regulation of lesbian and gay families becomes increasingly apparent. Every time I fail to correct the gender pronoun offered by a stranger in an official interaction, I miss one opportunity for resistance, I take a step towards assimilation. I try not to do that very often. Every time I proudly 'out' myself by giving my relationship status as 'in a civil partnership', I seize my moment of (stabilising) resistance to heteronormativity.

Assuming all goes to plan, I will become a parent soon: not a mother or a father, but a *parent*.[5] So, I will not be a *wife* and *mother*, but a *civil partner* and *parent*. I will inhabit two new forms of legal status, both created specifically for people in same-sex relationships, both designed to recognise non-heterosexual familial bonds. Is this assimilation or transformation? Surely it must involve elements of both. I explored the challenges of understanding nomenclature in Chapter 4, with survey respondents expressing the opinion that creating new terms like these perpetuates discrimination and stigma. It is probable that, at least some of the time, this is true. The perspectives I have offered in this book suggest that while positive legal change for lesbians and gay men is an imperative step in the quest for sexual equality, once this happens, there are inevitably more (and new) challenges to face. I have no doubt that my future, mundane, everyday experiences as a parent will provide me new opportunities for resistance: resistance to the heteronormativity of the family, resistance to other familial norms, perhaps even resistance to official law. I am, therefore, very much like the survey respondents, interview participants and authors of published personal narratives whose legal consciousness I explored in Chapters 4–6 of this book. Their stories demonstrate that the place of law in the everyday lives of lesbians and gay men is far from mundane. That the everyday recognition and regulation afforded by law in society is key to being fully included in society; to being granted full citizenship by the state; to recognising the different ways non-heterosexual lives are lived; to having personal life choices both understood and appropriately regulated. As lesbians and gay men move from being 'outsiders' to 'insiders', perhaps there is now more scope for the development of more critical distance from the problems and limitations of formal equality.

The utopian fiction analysed in Chapter 7 highlights alternative ways of living, different ways of approaching the regulation of family life, where law is not the focus of familial regulation. Perhaps the primary insight that the inclusion of perspectives from utopian fiction has brought to this consideration of legal consciousness and sexuality is that maybe the only way to achieve equality for lesbians and gay men is to move away from official law, to radically de-centre law in the regulation of family life. I find it hard to choose between the utopian possibilities offered by Piercy (1987) and Bezucha (2000); both have their own distinct appeal. In many respects, the future of social and ecological harmony imagined by Piercy (1987) in *Woman on the Edge of Time* is, instinctively, more appealing to me than the 'formal equality' perspective offered in Bezucha's (2000) *Big Eden*. And yet a future like that lived in Mattapoisett seems more unrealistic and further away from reality than ever before. *Big Eden,* in contrast, seems achievable, realistic and possible, and perhaps, as a result, is less alluring.

The stories that have been the focus of this book have shown, therefore, that even with the tectonic shift in the ways that lesbian and gay lives are recognised and regulated in law, there is still a long way to go. In many respects, lesbian and gay relationship recognition is about more than the practical and pragmatic legal rules that determine who can inherit without paying tax, or who is legally defined as 'next of kin'. It is also about recognising the different ways that lesbians and gay men form families, the different kinship structures that exist in lesbian and gay communities (Weeks et al., 2001; Weston, 1991), and myriad ways in which lesbians and gay men become parents. The legal recognition of same-sex relationships and families has to be accompanied by nuanced understandings of the differences between lesbian and gay lives and (hetero)normative ways of living. If not, then while lesbians and gay men may achieve something approximating formal equality, or even equality of recognition, there is no real chance of gaining equality of power (Cooper, 2004) or equality of condition (Baker et al., 2004). Without radical changes in the ways that all familial and relational lives are recognised and regulated, lesbians and gay men will continue to be positioned 'up against' heteronormative society.

Conclusions

Throughout this book, I have analysed the impacts and effects of recent legal developments in the recognition of lesbian and gay families on those whose lives have been affected by them. In order to comprehend the effects of the introduction of civil partnership and the changes in the regulation of lesbian and gay parenting, I used the toolbox of legal consciousness studies in conjunction with insights from Foucauldian and feminist scholarship. In so doing, I have highlighted that even in the wake of positive legal change, it is vitally important to be attentive to the plural forms regulation takes, as well as the complex interactions of power and resistance in everyday life.

In the empirical chapters of this book, I demonstrated that although legal consciousness studies is a helpful framework when considering the place of law in the everyday lives of lesbians and gay men, Ewick and Silbey's (1998) three schemas of legal consciousness ('before the law', 'with the law' and 'against the law') are not sufficient to explain lesbians and gay men's attitudes to law and legal change. I have shown that there is evidence of 'before the law' and 'with the law' legal consciousness in lesbians and gay men's accounts of law, but that the 'against the law' schema requires more nuanced understandings of power and resistance to be useful in understanding the impact and effects of legal change on the everyday lives of lesbians and gay men. 'Before the law' legal consciousness is manifest (predominantly) in support for formal equality and legal recognition, and where lesbians and gay men draw on understandings of the power of law to create social change. 'With the law' legal consciousness can be seen through the equal rights, human rights and citizenship discourse that infuse lesbian and gay claims for legal equality. The types of resistance that infuse discourse from lesbians and gay men about the place of law in everyday life, however, require that the 'against the law' schema is revisited to include finer distinctions in the way that resistance is conceptualised.

In order to complicate and refine the 'against the law' category of legal consciousness, I argued that power and resistance are important concepts in understanding the place of law in the everyday lives of lesbians and gay men. I proposed that because law works to both recognise and regulate lesbian and gay lives, lesbians and gay men experience law and legal change as both empowering and oppressive. In the texts analysed in this book, the power of law appears as a positive force when concerned with recognition, such as the introduction of civil partnership, or the recognition of same-sex co-parents as legal parents. Legal recognition is understood to increase visibility and allow for positive social affirmation of lesbian and gay families. The power of law becomes a negative force, however, when law is concerned with regulation. Increased legal regulation, such as accompanied the introduction of civil partnership and changes to adoption laws, involves assimilation of lesbian and gay lives into heteronormative frameworks and therefore can reduce the radical possibilities of living outside of heteronormativity. This legal regulation has the potential to discipline lesbians and gay men into conforming to heteronormative ways of being.

These understandings of law as both a positive and negative source of power are linked to understandings of resistance that are present in lesbian and gay accounts of how law and legal change impacts on their lives. Throughout the empirical chapters I sought to demonstrate that lesbians and gay men use strategies of resistance to render the negative power of law benign. In Chapter 3, I argued for a tripartite conceptualisation of resistance (stabilising, moderating and fracturing resistance) that exposes everyday, micro-resistant practices. Throughout the empirically grounded chapters, I explored everyday examples of resistance in lesbians' and gay men's stories of law. I found that stories of 'stabilising' and 'moderating' resistance were common, and infused many accounts of law in everyday life. Fracturing resistance, on the other hand, appears to be rare and less relevant to lesbian and gay lives. In part this must be because claims for substantive recognition of familial and relational lives, through same-sex marriage and/or recognition of the realities of lesbian and gay parenting, are claims which official law has the power to grant.

Throughout this book I have posited that the appropriate way to conceptualise equality in lesbian and gay struggles should be through a nuanced and expansive approach to equality, such as those offered by equality of power (Cooper, 2004), or equality of condition (Baker et al., 2004). In contrast to these nuanced and complex approaches to equality, however, it has been clear throughout my analysis that the way that equality is conceptualised in the material I have analysed is predominantly simple, formal equality. The lesbians and gay men whose stories I have explored understand equality as achieving the same forms of legal recognition and regulation as other groups.

Utilising a legal consciousness perspective has allowed me to interrogate the entrenched nature of formal equality in lesbians and gay men's understanding of law. The everyday focus of legal consciousness highlights the experience of power relations and exposes resistant practices. Ewick and Silbey's (1998) three schemas of legal consciousness have been useful in understanding the place of equality in the everyday lives of lesbians and gay men and in lesbian and gay struggles. The 'before the law' schema is typified in lesbian and gay equality struggles by a desire for recognition and a belief that through equal recognition in law will come equal respect in society. The 'with the law' schema has been useful in understanding the equality-seeking activism that was alluded to in each of the empirical chapters of this book. Claims of 'equal rights', 'human rights' and 'citizenship' are typical examples of 'with the law' legal consciousness in lesbian and gay struggles.

The 'against the law' type of legal consciousness has, again, highlighted the most interesting discourse from the survey respondents, interview participants, and authors of utopian fiction or personal narratives. 'Against the law' legal consciousness has been typified by resistance. Again, however, it is important to note that the form of resistance I am referring to here is different from the types of resistance that Ewick and Silbey had in mind when they created their tripartite typology of legal consciousness. Rather than attempts to avoid law, the lesbians and gay men whose stories underpin this book resist the assimilationist, normalising and regulatory functions of law. They want lesbians and gay men to have equality, but to continue to have all of the options that they have had before in how to live their lives. They resist the idea that the governmentalisation and regulation of lesbian and gay lives is a necessary part of achieving equality; they find ways to resist the disciplinary power of law. As will be clear from the substantive chapters, lesbian and gay resistance to heteronormativity, by and large, draws on what I have termed 'stabilising' and 'moderating' resistance: living in non-heteronormative ways, seeking legal equality through public activism. But what of my third category of resistance: fracturing resistance? Is it possible to 'break' heteronormativity through resistance?

Perhaps the 'answer' to the question of whether it is possible to fracture heteronormativity has to come from a field other than official law. Lesbian and gay struggles for legal equality can only go so far – formal equality is, in many respects, the outer limit. By making this claim, I realise that I lay myself open to accusation of being overly pessimistic in positing that legal struggles can go no further than formal equality, or that heteronormativity cannot be challenged through legal means, but my intention here is not to provide a negative view. Achieving formally equal rights for lesbians and gay men is a major legal achievement, and one for which there is still much work to be done. There is no doubt that while anyone, as a result of their sexuality, who wants to marry cannot, or has no legal relationship to the child(ren) they parent, then the struggle must go on. Rather, it seems to me that dismantling heteronormativity has much less to do with law and legal struggle than it has to do with how we live our everyday lives. The key to dismantling heteronormative (legal and social) approaches to the family is to show how our everyday lives do not conform to normative ideals of the nuclear family; to highlight the multiple affective relationships that we all have; and to challenge the very authority of law and the state to regulate sexuality.

I have, throughout this book, argued that everyday life provides fertile ground for considering the impact, effects and possibilities of lesbian and gay struggles for legal equality. By exploring the ways in which lesbians and gay men express their understandings of the place of law in their everyday lives, I have highlighted both the need for and limitations of formal equality in lesbian and gay struggles. In Britain today, the social and legal backdrop to lesbian and gay lives has shifted almost to the point where it is unrecognisable. As Jeffrey Weeks (2007: 3) has argued 'attitudes have surely changed in fundamental ways. We are living now, clearly, in a different world'. This different world requires different strategies of resistance, different approaches to equality and, perhaps most fundamentally, different ways of understanding the place of law in society.

In this book, I have demonstrated that by exploring the everyday strategies of resistance that people use, we can glean a more nuanced way of understanding the experience of legal change, power, resistance and governmentality. As Foucault said, when discussing resistance to 'the indefinite governmentality of the state':

> There must be a moment when, breaking all the bonds of obedience, the population will really have the right, not in juridical terms, but in terms of essential and fundamental rights, to break any bonds of obedience it has with the state and, rising up against it, to say: my law, the law of my own requirements, the law of my very nature as population, the law of my basic needs must replace the rules of obedience.
>
> (Foucault, 2009: 356)

My exploration of legal consciousness in lesbian and gay lives, demonstrates that we have not yet reached that moment when resistance can fracture either heteronormativity or formal legal structures. But we do know that the Borg are wrong: resistance is far from futile. Resistance, in all its forms, is necessary, everyday and often mundane. The perspectives, stories and narratives I have explored in this book show that in researching the everyday, including everyday resistance to law, we can get closer to understanding not only how people experience the regulation of sexuality, whether through official law, governmentality or society, but also how strategies of resistance create new modes of living before, with and up against the law.

Notes

1 *Star Trek: The Next Generation* 'The Best of Both Worlds', written by Michael Piller, Directed by Cliff Bole. First aired in June 1990 (part 1) and September 1990 (part 2).

2 *Wilkinson* v *Kitzinger* [2006] EWHC 2022; Civil Partnership Act 2004 s. 212.

3 It is important to remember that under the rules of private international law, heterosexual marriage, provided it was legal under the jurisdiction in which it was formed, is recognised the world over (*Berthiaume* v *Dastous* [1930] A.C. 79).

4 According to data published by the Office of National Statistics, by December 2008, 33,956 same-sex couples had registered a civil partnership in the UK (www.statistics.gov.uk). Interestingly, the government's Regulatory Impact Assessment for

the Civil Partnership Act 2004 estimated that on a 'high take up scenario' it would take until 2035 for this number of civil partnerships to be formed (DTI, 2004). These statistics also do not include any same-sex couples who register their relationships overseas.

5 Following the Human Fertilisation and Embryology Act 2008, with consequential amendments of the Children Act 1989 and other relevant legislation, the civil partner of a woman who gives birth to a child (conceived after 6 April 2009) will be considered a legal parent of that child.

Bibliography

Abbot, Deborah and Farmer, Ellen (eds) (1995) *From Wedded Wife to Lesbian Life: Stories of Transformation,* Freedom, CA: Crossing Press.

Abrams, Kathryn (1991) 'Hearing the Call of Stories', *California Law Review,* 79(4): 971–1052.

Abu-Lughod, Lila (1990) 'The Romance of Resistance: Tracing Transformations of Power Through Bedouin Women', *American Ethnologist,* 17(1): 41–55.

Aizley, Harlyn (ed.) (2006) *Confessions of the Other Mother: Nonbiological Lesbian Moms Tell All!* Boston, MA: Beacon Press.

Allen, Mike and Burrell, Nancy (1996) 'Comparing the Impact of Homosexual and Heterosexual Parents on Children: Meta-analysis of Existing Research', *Journal of Homosexuality,* 32(2): 19–35.

Arnup, Katherine (1999) 'Out in this World: The Social and Legal Context of Lesbian and Gay Families', *Journal of Gay & Lesbian Social Services,* 10(1): 1–26.

Arnup, Katherine and Boyd, Susan (1995) 'Familial disputes? Sperm donors, lesbian mothers and legal parenthood', in D. Herman and C. Stychin (eds) *Legal Inversions: Lesbians, Gay Men and the Politics of Law* (pp. 77–101), Philadelphia, PA: Temple University Press.

Auchmuty, Rosemary (2004) 'Same-sex Marriage Revived: Feminist Critique and Legal Strategy', *Feminism & Psychology,* 14(1): 101–26.

Aviram, Hadar (2008) 'Make Love, Not Law: Perceptions of the Marriage Equality Struggle Among Polyamorous Activists', *Journal of Bisexuality,* 7(3/4): 261–86.

Baker, John, Kathleen Lynch, Sara Cantillon & Judy Walsh (2004) *Equality: From Theory to Action*, Basingstoke: Palgrave Macmillan.

Ball, Milner S. (1989) 'Stories of Origin and Constitutional Possibilities', *Michigan Law Review,* 87: 2280–319.

Barker, Nicola (2006) 'Sex and the Civil Partnership Act: The Future of (Non) Conjugality?', *Feminist Legal Studies,* 14(2): 241–59.

——(2008) *Not the Marrying Kind?*, unpublished PhD thesis, Keele University.

Barret, Robert and Robinson, Bryan (2000) *Gay Fathers: Encouraging the Hearts of Gay Dads and Their Families*, San Francisco, CA: Jossey-Bass.

BBC News (2005) 'Timeline: French riots' BBC News website 14 November 2005. Available at http://news.bbc.co.uk/1/hi/world/europe/4413964.stm (accessed 13 January 2010).

Bech, Henning (1997) *When Men Meet: Homosexuality and Modernity*, Cambridge: Polity Press.

Bedford, Kate (2005) 'Loving to Straighten Out Development: Sexuality and "Ethnodevelopment" in the World Bank's Equadorian Lending', *Feminist Legal Studies,* 13: 295–322.

Bell, David and Binnie, Jon (2001) *The Sexual Citizen: Queer Politics and Beyond*, Cambridge: Polity Press.

Bell, David and Valentine, Gill (1995a) 'Queer Country: Rural Lesbian and Gay Lives', *Journal of Rural Studies,* 11(2): 113–22.

Bell, David and Valentine, Gill (eds) (1995b) *Mapping Desire: Geographies of Sexualities*, London: Routledge.

Bell, Derrick A. (1987) *And We Are Not Saved: The Elusive Quest for Racial Justice*, New York: Basic Books.

Bell, Vikki (1993) *Interrogating Incest: Feminism, Foucault and the Law*, London: Routledge.

Berlant, Lauren and Warner, Michael (2000) 'Sex in public', in Lauren Berland (ed.) *Intimacy* (pp. 311–30) Chicago, IL: University of Chicago Press.

Bezucha, Thomas (2000) *Big Eden*, Chaiken Films.

Bloch, Ernst (1986) *The Principle of Hope*, 3 vols, Cambridge, MA: MIT Press.

Blomley, Nicholas (2007) 'Critical Geography: Anger and Hope', *Progress in Human Geography,* 31(1): 53–56.

Boyd, Susan B. (2006) '"Robbed of their families"? Fathers' rights discourses in Canadian parenting law reform processes', in S. Sheldon and R. Collier (eds) *Fathers' Rights Activism and Law Reform in Comparative Perspective* (pp. 27–51) Oxford: Hart.

——(2007) 'Gendering Legal Parenthood: Bio-genetic Ties, Intentionality and Responsibility', *Windsor Yearbook of Access to Justice,* 25: 55–85.

Boyd, Susan B. and Young, Claire F.L. (2003) '"From Same-Sex to No Sex?": Trends Towards Recognition of (Same-Sex) Relationships in Canada', *Seattle Journal for Social Justice,* 1(3): 757–94.

Braun, Virginia and Clarke, Victoria (2006) 'Using Thematic Analysis in Psychology', *Qualitative Research in Psychology,* 3(2): 77–101.

Brown, Wendy (1995) *States of Injury: Power and Freedom in Late Modernity*, Princeton, NJ: Princeton University Press.

Bumiller, Kristin (1988) *The Civil Rights Society*, Baltimore and London: Johns Hopkins University Press.

——(1991) 'Fallen Angels: The Representation of Violence Against Women in Legal Culture', in M.A. Fineman and N.S. Thomadsen (eds) *At the Boundaries of Law: Feminism and Legal Theory* (pp. 95–113) London: Routledge.

Burchell, Graham, Gordon, Colin and Miller, Peter (eds) (1991) *The Foucault Effect: Studies in Governmentality*, Chicago, IL: University of Chicago Press.

Butler, Judith (1990) *Gender Trouble*, London: Routledge.

——(1998) 'Merely Cultural', *New Left Review,* I/227: 33–44.

——(2002) 'Is Kinship Always Already Heterosexual?', *Differences: A Journal of Feminist Cultural Studies,* 8(3): 369–90.

——(2004) 'Bodies and Power Revisited', in Dianna Taylor and Karen Vintges (eds) *Feminism and the Final Foucault* (pp. 183–94) Chicago, IL: University of Illinois Press.

Calhoun, Cheshire (2000) *Feminism, The Family and the Politics of the Closet*, Oxford: Oxford University Press.

Carrabine, Eamonn (2004) *Power, Discourse and Resistance: A Genealogy of the Strangeways Prison Riot*, Aldershot: Ashgate.

Carter, David (2004) *Stonewall: The Riots that Sparked the Gay Revolution*, New York: St. Martin's Press.

Chambers, Samuel A. (2007) '"An Incalculable Effect": Subversions of Heteronormativity', *Political Studies*, 55: 656–79.

Chan, Raymond W., Brooks, Risa C., Raboy, Barbara & Patterson, Charlotte, J. (1998) 'Division of Labor among Lesbian and Heterosexual Parents: Associations with Children's Adjustment', *Journal of Family Psychology*, 12(3): 402–19.

Chrisp, Jill (2001) 'The Four Letter Word – Sons: Lesbian Mothers and Adolescent Sons', *Journal of Lesbian Studies*, 5: 195–209.

Clarke, Victoria (2002) 'Sameness and Difference in Research on Lesbian Parenting', *Journal of Community & Applied Social Psychology*, 12: 210–22.

——(2003) 'Lesbian and Gay Marriage: Transformation or Normalisation?', *Feminism & Psychology*, 13(4): 519–29.

——(2005) 'Feminist Perspectives on Lesbian Parenting: A Review of the Literature 1972–2002', *Psychology of Women Section Review*, 7(2): 11–23.

——(2006) '"Gay Men, Gay Men and More Gay Men": Traditional, Liberal and Critical Perspectives on Male Role Models in Lesbian Families', *Lesbian & Gay Psychology Review*, 7(1): 19–35.

Clarke, Victoria, (2007) 'Romance, Rights, Recognition, Responsibilities and Radicalism: Same-Sex Couples' Views on Civil Partnership and Marriage', in V. Clarke and E. Peel (eds) *Out in Psychology: LGBTQ Perspectives* (pp. 173–93) Chichester: Wiley.

Clarke, Victoria, Burgoyne, Carol & Burns, Maree (2006) 'Just a Piece of Paper? A Qualitative Exploration of Same-sex Couples' Multiple Conceptions of Civil Partnership and Marriage', *Lesbian & Gay Psychology Review*, 7(2).

Clarke, Victoria and Kitzinger, Celia (2005) 'We're Not Living on Planet Lesbian: Constructions of Male Role Models in Lesbian Families', *Sexualities*, 8(2): 137–52.

Conley, John and O'Barr, William (1990) *Rules versus Relationships: The Ethnography of Legal Discourse*, Chicago, IL: University of Chicago Press.

Connolly, Catherine (2002) 'The Voice of the Petitioner: The Experiences of Gay and Lesbian Parents in Successful Second-parent Adoption Proceedings', *Law & Society Review*, 36(2): 325–46.

Connor, Steve (2007) 'The Prospect of All-female Conception', *The Independent*, published 13 April 2007. Available at http://news.independent.co.uk/sci_tech/article2444462.ece (accessed 14 January 2010).

Coolidge, David Oregon (1998) 'Playing the *Loving* Card: Same-sex Marriage and the Politics of Analogy', *BYU Journal of Public Law*, 12(2): 201–38.

Coombs, Mary (2001) 'Transgenderism and Sexual Orientation: More Than a Marriage of Convenience?', in M. Bernstein and R. Reimann (eds) *Queer Families, Queer Politics: Challenging Culture and the State*, New York: Columbia University Press.

Cooper, Davina (1995a) 'Local Government Legal Consciousness in the Shadow of Juridification', *Journal of Law and Society*, 22(4): 506–26.

——(1995b) *Power in Struggle: Feminism, Sexuality and the State*, Buckingham: Open University Press.

——(2004) *Challenging Diversity: Rethinking Equality and the Value of Difference*, Cambridge: Cambridge University Press.

Cooper, Davina and Herman, Didi (1991) 'Getting "The Family Right": Legislating Heterosexuality in Britain, 1986–91', *Canadian Journal of Family Law*, 10: 41–78.

Cossman, Brenda (2002a) 'Family Feuds: Neo-Liberal and Neo-Conservative Visions of the Reprivatization Project', in Brenda Cossman and Judy Fudge (eds) *Privatization, Law and the Challenge to Feminism* (pp. 169–217) Toronto: University of Toronto Press.

——(2002b) 'Sexing Citizenship, Privatizing Sex', *Citizenship Studies*, 6(4): 483–506.

Cott, Nancy (1977) *The Bonds of Womanhood: "Woman's Sphere" in New England, 1780–1835*, New Haven, CT: Yale University Press.

Cowan, Dave (2004) 'Legal Consciousness: Some Observations', *Modern Law Review*, 67(6): 928–58.

Cowan, Dave and McDermont, Morag (2006) *Regulating Social Housing: Governing Decline*, Abingdon: Routledge Cavendish.

Cox, Barbara J. (2000) 'But Why Not Marriage: An Essay on Vermont's Civil Unions Law, Same-sex Marriage, and Separate but (Un)equal', *Vermont Law Review*, 25: 113–47.

Davies, Margaret (2005) 'The Ethos of Pluralism', *Sydney Law Review*, 27: 87–112.

Davis, J.C. (1981) *Utopia and the Ideal Society*, Cambridge: Cambridge University Press.

Dean, Mitchell (1999) *Governmentality: Power and Rule in Modern Society*, London: Sage.

Department of Trade and Industry (DTI) (2004) *Final Regulatory Impact Assessment: Civil Partnership Act 2004*, London: DTI, online. Available at www.berr.gov.uk/files/file23829.pdf (accessed 15 January 2010).

Department for Work and Pensions (DWP) (2005) *Getting It Right*. Available at www.dwp.gov.uk/lifeevent/workage/getitright.pdf (accessed 10 October 2006).

Douglas, Gillian (1993) 'Assisted Reproduction and the Welfare of the Child', *Current Legal Problems*, 46: 53–74.

Duberman, Martin (1993) *Stonewall*, New York: Penguin.

Duggan, Lisa (2003) *The Twilight of Equality? Neoliberalism, Cultural Politics and the Attack on Democracy*, Boston, MA: Beacon Press.

Dunne, Gillian A. (2000) 'Opting Into Motherhood: Lesbians Blurring the Boundaries and Transforming the Meaning of Parenthood and Kinship', *Gender & Society*, 14(1): 11–35.

Dworkin, Ronald (2002) *Sovereign Virtue: The Theory and Practice of Equality*, Cambridge, MA: Harvard University Press.

Engel, David (1984) 'The Oven Birds Song: Insiders, Outsiders and Personal Injuries in and American Community', *Law & Society Review*, 18(4): 551–82.

——(1993) 'Law in the Domains of Everyday Life: The Construction of Community and Difference,' in A. Sarat and T.R. Kearns (eds) *Law in Everyday Life* (pp. 123–70) Ann Arbor, MI: University of Michigan Press.

——(1998) 'How Does Law Matter in the Constitution of Legal Consciousness?', in B. Garth and A. Sarat (eds) *How Does Law Matter?* (pp. 109–44) Evanston, IL: Northwestern University Press.

Eskridge, William N. (1994) 'Gaylegal Narratives', *Stanford Law Review*, 46: 607–40.

——(1996) *The Case for Same Sex Marriage*, New York: Free Press.

——(2002) *Equality Practice: Civil Unions and the Future of Gay Rights*, New York: Routledge.

Estrich, Susan (1986) 'Rape', *Yale Law Journal,* 95: 1087–184.

Ettelbrick, Paula (1992) 'Since When is Marriage a Path to Liberation?', in Suzanne Sherman (ed.) *Lesbian and Gay Marriage* (pp. 20–26) Philadelphia, PA: Temple University Press.

Ewick, Patricia and Silbey, Susan S. (1992) 'Conformity, Contestation and Resistance: An Account of Legal Consciousness', *New England Law Review,* 26: 731–49.

——(1998) *The Common Place of Law: Stories from Everyday Life*, Chicago and London: Chicago University Press.

——(2003) 'Narrating Social Structure: Stories of Resistance to Legal Authority', *American Journal of Sociology,* 108(6): 1328–72.

Fajer, Marc A. (1992) 'Can Two Real Men Eat Quiche Together? Storytelling, Gender-role Stereotypes, and Legal Protection for Lesbians and Gay Men', *University of Miami Law Review,* 46: 511–651.

Fineman, Martha A. (1995) *The Neutered Mother, the Sexual Family and other Twentieth-Century Tragedies*, New York: Routledge.

——(2004) *The Autonomy Myth: A Theory of Dependency*, New York: The New Press.

Fish, Julie (1999) 'Sampling Lesbians: How to Get 1000 Lesbians to Complete a Questionnaire', *Feminism & Pscyhology,* 9(2): 229–38.

Flaks, David K., Ficher, Ilda, Masterpasqua, Frank & Joseph, Gregory (1995) 'Lesbians Choosing Motherhood: A Comparative Study of Lesbian and Heterosexual Parents and Their Children', *Developmental Psychology,* 31(1): 105–14.

Fleurry-Steiner, Ben and Nielsen, Laura Beth (eds) (2006) *The New Civil Rights Research: A Constitutive Approach*, Aldershot: Ashgate.

Foreman, Jonathan (2001) 'Big Eden': A Garden of Comic Delights', *New York Post* Friday 13 July 2001. Available at www.bigeden.com/graphics/NYPOST_0713.pdf (accessed 12 January 2010).

Foucault, Michel (1979) *Discipline and Punish: The Birth of the Prison.* London: Peregrine.

——(1980) *Power/Knowledge: Selected Interviews and Other Writings Michael Foucault*, edited by Colin Gordon. New York: Pantheon.

——(1991a) 'Governmentality', in G. Burchell, C. Gordon and P. Miller (eds) *The Foucault Effect: Studies in Governmentality* (pp. 87–104) Chicago, IL: University of Chicago Press.

——(1991b) 'Nietzsche, Genealogy, History', in P. Rabinow (ed.) *The Foucault Reader: An Introduction to Foucault's Thought* (pp. 76–100) London: Penguin.

——(1998) *The Will to Knowledge: The History of Sexuality*, Volume 1, London: Penguin.

——(2002a) 'The Subject and Power', in James D. Faubion (ed.) *Power: Essential Works of Foucault 1954–1984, volume 3* (pp. 326–48) London: Penguin Books. [Reprinted from Hubert Dreyfus and Paul Rabinow (eds) (1982) *Michel Foucault: Beyond Structuralism and Hermeneutics*].

——(2002b) *Power: Essential works of Foucault 1954–1984, volume 3*, ed. J.D. Faubion; trans: Robert Hurley and others, London: Penguin Books.

——(2009) *Security, Territory, Population: Lectures at the College de France 1977–1978*, edited by Michel Senellart and Francois Ewald, New York: Picador.

Fox, Nathan A. (1977) 'Attachment of Kibbutz Infants to Mother and Metapelet', *Child Development,* 48: 1228–39.

Fraser, Nancy (1981) 'Foucault on Modern Power: Empirical Insights and Normative Confusions', *Praxis International,* 3: 272–87.

——(1985) 'Michel Foucault: A "Young Conservative?"', *Ethics,* 96(1): 165–84.

——(1997) *Justice Interruptus: Critical Reflections of the "Postsocialist" Condition,* New York: Routledge.

——(2003) 'From Discipline to Flexibilization? Rereading Foucault in the Shadow of Globalisation', *Constellations,* 10(2): 160–71.

Garcia-Villegas, Mauricio (2003) 'Symbolic Power without Violence? Critical Comments on Legal Consciousness Studies', *International Journal for the Semiotics of Law,* 16: 363–93.

Gavigan, Shelley M. (1995) 'A Parent(ly) Knot: Can Heather Have Two Mommies' in D. Herman and C.F. Stychin (eds) *Legal Inversions: Lesbians, Gay Men and the Politics of Law* (pp. 102–17) Philadelphia, PA: Temple University Press.

Genn, Hazel (1999) *Paths to Justice: What People Do and Think about Going to Law,* Oxford: Hart.

Gies, Lieve (2003) 'Explaining the Absence of the Media in Stories of Law and Legal Consciousness', *Entertainment Law,* 2(1): 19–54.

Goldberg-Hiller, Jonathan (2002) *The Limits to Union: Same-Sex Marriage and the Politics of Civil Rights,* Ann Arbor, MI: University of Michigan Press.

Golombok, Susan and Tasker, Fiona (1994) 'Children in Lesbian and Gay Families: Theories and Evidence', *Annual Review of Sex Research,* 5: 73–100.

Goodwin, Barbara and Taylor, Keith (1982) *The Politics of Utopia,* London: Hutchinson.

Gordon, Colin (1991) 'Governmental Rationality: An Introduction', in G. Burchell, C. Gordon and P. Miller (eds) *The Foucault Effect: Studies in Governmentality* (pp. 1–52) Chicago, IL: University of Chicago Press.

Griffiths, John (1986) 'What is Legal Pluralism?', *Journal of Legal Pluralism & Unofficial Law,* 24: 1–56.

Halley, Janey (1998) 'Gay Rights and Identity Imitation: Issues in the Ethics of Representation', in David, Kairys (ed.) *The Politics of Law* (pp. 115–46) Philadelphia, PA: Temple University Press.

Harding, Rosie (2005) 'Psychology, Human Rights and Law: The Case of Planned Lesbian Families', *Lesbian & Gay Psychology Review,* 6(1): 23–34.

——(2006) '"Dogs are 'Registered', People Shouldn't Be": Legal Consciousness and Lesbian and Gay Rights', *Social & Legal Studies,* 15(4): 511–33.

——(2007) 'Sir Mark Potter and the Protection of the Traditional Family: Why Same-sex Marriage is (Still) a Feminist Issue', *Feminist Legal Studies,* 15(2): 223–34.

——(2008) 'Recognising (and Resisting) Regulation: Attitudes to the Introduction of Civil Partnership', *Sexualities,* 11(6): 741–62.

Harding, Rosie and Peel, Elizabeth (2006) 'We Do? International Perspectives on Equality, Legality and Same Sex Relationships', *Lesbian & Gay Psychology Review,* 7(2): 123–40.

——(2007) 'Surveying Sexualities: Internet Research with Non-heterosexuals', *Feminism & Psychology,* 17(2): 277–85.

Harris, Anita, Carney, Sarah & Fine, Michelle (2001) 'Counter Work: Introduction to "Under the Covers: Theorising the Politics of Counter Stories"', *International Journal of Critical Psychology,* 4(1): 6–18.

Hart, H.L.A. (1958) 'Positivism and the Separation of Law and Morals', *Harvard Law Review,* 71: 593–629.

Hartl, John (2001) "Eden": A Gay Film of Unbiased Charm' *The Seattle Times*, Friday 8 June 2001. Available at www.bigeden.com/graphics/seattle_times_0601.pdf (accessed 12 January 2010).

Hartsock, Nancy (1990) 'Foucault on Power: A Theory for Women?', in Linda Nicholson (ed.) *Feminism/Postmodernism* (pp. 157–75) New York: Routledge.

——(1996) 'Postmodernism and Political Change: Issues for Feminist Theory', in Susan Hekman (ed.) *Feminist Interpretations of Michel Foucault* (pp. 39–58) University Park, PA: Pennsylvania State University Press.

Heath, Susan (1997) 'On Being a Lesbian in the Backlash', in A. Oakley, and J. Mitchell (eds) *Who's Afraid of Feminism: Seeing Through the Backlash* (pp. 99–110) New York: The New Press.

Herek, Gregory M. and Berrill, Kevin (1992) 'Documenting the Victimization of Lesbians and Gay Men: Methodological issues', in G. Herek and K. Berrill (eds) *Hate Crime: Confronting Violence Against Lesbians and Gay Men* (pp. 270–86) Thousand Oaks, CA: Sage.

Herman, Didi (1994) *Rights of Passage: Struggles for Lesbian & Gay Legal Equality*, Toronto: University of Toronto Press.

——(1997) "'Then I Saw a New Heaven and a New Earth': Thoughts on the Christian Rights and the Problem of "Backlash"' in L.G. Roman and L. Eyre (eds) *Dangerous Territories: Struggles for Difference and Equality in Education* (pp. 63–74) London: Routledge.

——(2005) "I'm Gay": Declarations, Desire, and Coming Out on Prime-Time Television', *Sexualities*, 8(1): 7–29.

Hertogh, Marc (2004) 'A "European" Conception of Legal Consciousness: Rediscovering Eugen Ehrlich', *Journal of Law and Society*, 31(4): 457–81.

——(2009) 'What's in a Handshake? Legal Equality and Legal Consciousness in the Netherlands', *Social & Legal Studies*, 18(2): 221–39.

Hicks, Stephen (2005) 'Queer Genealogies: Tales of Conformity and Rebellion amongst Lesbian and Gay Foster Carers and Adopters', *Qualitative Social Work*, 4(3): 293–308.

Hicks, Stephen and McDermott, Janet (1999) *Lesbian and Gay Fostering and Adoption: Extraordinary Yet Ordinary*, London: Jessica Kingsley.

Hirsch, Susan F. (1993) 'Subjects in Spite of Themselves: Legal Consciousness among Working-Class New Englanders', *Law & Social Inquiry*, 17(4): 839–57.

Hull, Kathleen E. (2003) 'The Cultural Power of Law and the Cultural Enactment of Legality: The Case of Same-sex Marriage', *Law & Social Inquiry*, 28(2): 629–56.

——(2006) *Same-Sex Marriage: The Cultural Politics of Love and Law*, Cambridge: Cambridge University Press.

Hunter, Nan D. (1991) 'Marriage, Law and Gender: A Feminist Inquiry', *Law & Sexuality*, 1: 9–30.

Jackson, Emily (2002) 'Conception and the Irrelevance of the Welfare Principle', *Modern Law Review*, 65(2): 176–203.

Jagose, Annamarie (1994) *Lesbian Utopics*, London: Routledge.

Jeffrey-Poulter, Stephen (1991) *Peers, Queers, and Commons: The Struggle for Gay Law Reform From 1980 to the Present*, London: Routledge.

Jeffreys, Sheila (2004) 'The Need to Abolish Marriage', *Feminism & Psychology*, 14(2): 327–31.

Jivani, Alkarim (1997) *It's Not Unusual: A History of Lesbian and Gay Britain in the Twentieth Century*, London: Michael O'Mara Books.

Johnson, Greg (2002) 'The Situated Self and Utopian Thinking', *Hypatia,* 17(3): 20–44.

Jolly, Margaret (2001) 'Coming Out of the Coming Out Story: Writing Queer Lives', *Sexualities,* 4(4): 474–96.

Josephson, Jyl (2005) 'Citizenship, Same-Sex Marriage, and Feminist Critiques of Marriage', *Perspectives on Politics,* 3(2): 269–84.

Kandaswamy, Priya (2008) 'State Austerity and the Racial Politics of Same-Sex Marriage in the US', *Sexualities,* 11(6): 706–25.

Kelly, Fiona (2004) "Nuclear Norms or Fluid Families? Incorporating Lesbian and Gay Parents and their Children into Canadian Family Law", *Canadian Journal of Family Law,* 21: 133–80.

Kitzinger, Celia and Wilkinson, Sue (2004a) 'The Re-branding of Marriage: Why We got Married Instead of Registering a Civil Partnership', *Feminism & Psychology,* 14 (1): 127–50.

——(2004b) 'Social Advocacy for Equal Marriage: The Politics of "Rights" and the Psychology of "Mental Health"', *Analyses of Social Issues and Public Policy,* 4(1): 173–94.

Kleinhans, Martha-Marie and Macdonald, Roderick (1997) 'What is a *Critical* Legal Pluralism?', *Canadian Journal of Law & Society,* 12: 25–46.

Klesse, Christian (2006) 'Heteronormativity, Non-monogamy and the Marriage Debate in the Bisexual Movement', *Lesbian & Gay Psychology Review,* 7(2): 162–73.

——(2007) '"How to be a Happy Homosexual?!": Non-monogamy and Governmentality in Relationship Manuals for Gay Men in the 1980s and 1990s', *The Sociological Review,* 55(3): 571–91.

Koppelman, Andrew (1988) 'The Miscegenation Analogy: Sodomy Law as Sex Discrimination', *Yale Law Journal,* 98: 145–85.

Langdridge, Darren and Blyth, Eric (2001) 'Regulation of Assisted Conception Services in Europe: Implications of the New Reproductive Technologies for "the Family"', *Journal of Social Welfare and Family Law,* 23(1): 45–64.

Lannutti, Pamela J. (2005) 'For Better or Worse: Exploring the Meanings of Same-sex Marriage within the Lesbian, Gay, Bisexual and Transgendered Community', *Journal of Social & Personal Relationships,* 22(1): 5–18.

Lefanu, Sarah (1988) *In the Chinks of the World Machine: Feminism & Science Fiction,* London: The Women's Press.

Lessard, Hester (2004) 'Mothers, Fathers and Naming: Reflections on the Law Equality Framework and *Troicuk v British Columbia*', *Canadian Journal of Women and the Law,* 16(1): 165–211.

Levine, Kay and Mellema, Virginia (2001) 'Strategising the Street: How Law Matters in the Lives of Women in the Street-Level Drug Economy', *Law and Social Inquiry,* 26: 169–205.

Levitas, Ruth (1990) *The Concept of Utopia*, London: Philip Allan.

——(2007) 'Looking for the Blue: The Necessity of Utopia', *Journal of Political Ideologies*, 12(3): 289–306.

Lewin, Ellen (1999) *Recognising Ourselves: Lesbian and Gay Ceremonies of Commitment*, New York: Columbia University Press.

Liddle, Kathleen and Liddle, Becky J. (2004) 'In the Meantime: Same-sex Ceremonies in the Absence of Legal Recognition', *Feminism & Psychology,* 14(1): 52–57.

Litowitz, Douglas (2000) 'The Social Construction of Law: Explanations and Implications', in A. Sarat and P. Ewick (eds) *Studies in Law, Politics and Society* (pp. 215–42) Amsterdam and London: JAI.

Lopez, Gerald P. (1984) 'Lay Lawyering', *UCLA Law Review,* 32: 1–60.

Lorentzen, Jeanne M. (2008) '"I Know My Own Body": Power and Resistance in Women's Experiences of Medical Interactions', *Body & Society,* 14(3): 49–79.

Macaulay, Stewart (1987) 'Images of Law in Everyday Life: The Lessons of School, Entertainment, and Spectator Sports', *Law & Society Review,* 21(2): 185–218.

Macleod, Catriona and Durrheim, Kevin (2002) 'Foucauldian Feminism: The Implications of Governmentality', *Journal for the Theory of Social Behaviour,* 32(1): 42–60.

Mahoney, Martha R. (1991) 'Legal Images of Battered Women: Redefining the Issue of Separation', *Michigan Law Review,* 90(1): 1–94.

Maines, David R. (1993) 'Narrative's Moment and Sociology's Phenomena: Toward a Narrative Sociology', *Sociological Quarterly,* 34(1): 17–38.

Mallon, Gerald P. (2004) *Gay Men Choosing Parenthood,* New York: Columbia University Press.

Malone, Kareen and Cleary, Rose (2002) '(De)Sexing the Family: Theorizing the Social Science of Lesbian Families', *Feminist Theory,* 3(3): 271–93.

Manji, Ambreena S. (1999) 'Imagining Women's "Legal World": Towards a Feminist Theory of Legal Pluralism in Africa', *Social & Legal Studies,* 8(4): 435–55.

Marshall, Anna-Maria (2003) 'Injustice Frames, Legality, and the Everyday Construction of Sexual Harassment', *Law & Social Inquiry,* 28(3): 659–89.

McGoldrick, Dominic (2001) 'The United Kingdom's Human Rights Act 1998 in Theory and Practice', *International Comparative Law Quarterly,* 50: 901–53.

McLaren, Margaret A. (2004) 'Foucault and Feminism: Power, Resistance, Freedom', in Dianna Taylor and Karen Vintges (eds) *Feminism and the Final Foucault* (pp. 214–34) Chicago, IL: University of Illinois Press.

McNay, Lois (1992) *Foucault and Feminism,* Cambridge: Polity Press.

Melissaris, Emmanuel (2004) 'The More the Merrier? A New Take on Legal Pluralism', *Social & Legal Studies,* 13(1): 52–79.

Merry, Sally Engle (1988) 'Legal Pluralism', *Law & Society Review,* 22(5): 869–96.

——(1990) *Getting Justice and Getting Even: Legal Consciousness among Working-class Americans,* Chicago, IL: University of Chicago Press.

Mezey, Naomi (2001) 'Out of the Ordinary: Law, Power, Culture, and the Commonplace', *Law and Social Inquiry,* 26: 145–68.

Millbank, Jenni (2008) 'The Limits of Functional Family: Lesbian Mother Litigation in the Era of the Eternal Biological Family', *International Journal of Law, Policy and the Family,* 22: 149–77.

Millns, Susan (2002) 'Reproducing Inequalities: Assisted Conception and the Challenge of Legal Pluralism', *Journal of Social Welfare and Family Law,* 24(1): 19–36.

Monk, Daniel (1998) 'Beyond Section 28: Law, Governance and Sex Education', in L. Moran, D. Monk and S. Beresford (eds) *Legal Queeries* (pp. 96–112) London: Cassell.

Moore, Sally Falk (1986) 'Legal Systems of the World', in Leon Lipson and Stanton Wheeler (eds) *Law and the Social Sciences* (pp. 11–62) New York: Russell Sage Foundation.

Moylan, Tom (1987) *Demand the Impossible: Science Fiction and the Utopian Imagination,* London: Methuen.

Munt, Sally R., Bassett, Elizabeth H. and O'Riordan, Kate (2002) 'Virtually Belonging: Risk, Connectivity and Coming Out On-line', *International Journal of Sexuality and Gender Studies*, 7(2/3): 125–37.

Murphy, Julien S. (2001) 'Should Lesbians Count as Infertile Couples? Antilesbian Discrimination in Assisted Reproduction', in M. Bernstein and R. Reeimann (eds) *Queer Families, Queer Politics: Challenging Culture and the State* (pp. 182–200) New York: Columbia University Press.

Nicol, Nancy and Smith, Miriam (2008) 'Legal Struggles and Political Resistance: Same-sex Marriage in the US and Canada', *Sexualities*, 11(6): 667–87.

Nielsen, Laura Beth (2000) 'Situating Legal Consciousness: Experience and Attitudes of Ordinary Citizens about Law and Street Harassment', *Law and Society Review*, 34: 1055–90.

——(2004) *Licence to Harass: Law, Hierarchy, and Offensive Public Speech*, Princeton, NJ: Princeton University Press.

Nygren, Rolf (2003) 'Interpreting Legitimacy', *Journal of Family History*, 28(1): 149–60.

Oakley, Anne and Mitchell, Juliet (1997) *Who's Afraid of Feminism: Seeing Through the Backlash*, New York: The New Press.

Okin, Susan Moller (1989) *Justice, Gender and the Family*, New York: Basic Books.

Orbuch, Terri L. (1997) 'People's Accounts Count: The Sociology of Accounts', *Annual Review of Sociology*, 23: 455–78.

Pasquino, Pasquale (1993) 'Political-Theory of War and Peace–Foucault and the History of Modern Political Theory', *Economy and Society*, 22(1): 77–88.

Pateman, Carole (1988) *The Sexual Contract*, Stanford, CA: Stanford University Press.

Patterson, Charlotte J. (1992) 'Children of Lesbian and Gay Parents', *Child Development*, 63: 1025–42.

——(1994) 'Children of the Lesbian Baby Boom: Behavioral Adjustment, Self-concepts, and Sex Role Identity', in Beverley Greene and Gregory M. Herek (eds) *Lesbian and Gay Psychology: Theory, Research and Clinical Applications* (pp. 156–75) Thousand Oaks, CA: Sage.

——(1995) 'Families of the Lesbian Baby Boom: Parents' Division of Labor and Children's Adjustment', *Developmental Psychology*, 31(1): 115–23.

Peel, Elizabeth (2001) 'Mundane Heterosexism: Understanding Incidents of the Everyday', *Women's Studies International Forum*, 24(5): 541–54.

Peel, Elizabeth and Harding, Rosie (2004) 'Divorcing Romance, Rights and Radicalism: Beyond Pro and Anti in the Lesbian and Gay Marriage Debate', *Feminism & Psychology*, 14(4): 588–99.

Phelan, Shane (1993) '(Be)Coming Out: Lesbian Identity and Politics', *Signs*, 18(4): 765–90.

Piercy, Marge (1987) *Woman on the Edge of Time*, London: The Women's Press.

Plummer, Ken (1995) *Telling Sexual Stories: Power, Change and Social Worlds*, London: Routledge.

Polikoff, Nancy D. (1993) 'We Will Get What We Ask for: Why Legalizing Gay Marriage Will Not "Dismantle the Legal Structure of Gender in Every Marriage"', *Virginia Law Review*, 79(7): 1535–50.

——(2000a) 'Recognizing Partners but Not Parents/Recognizing Parents but Not Partners: Gay and Lesbian Family Law in Europe and the United States', *New York Law School Journal of Human Rights*, 17: 711–51.

——(2000b) 'Why Lesbians and Gay Men Should Read Martha Fineman', *Journal of Gender, Social Policy and Law,* 8: 167–76.

——(2003) 'Ending Marriage as We Know It', *Hofstra Law Review,* 32: 201–32.

Pollack, Sandra and Vaughn, Jeanne (eds) (1987) *Politics of the Heart: A Lesbian Parenting Anthology*, Ithaca, NY: Firebrand.

Pound, Roscoe (1910) 'Law in Books and Law in Action', *American Law Review,* 44: 12–36.

Rauch, Jonathan (2004) *Gay Marriage: Why it is Good for Gays, Good for Straights and Good for America*, New York: Times Books.

Rawls, John (1971) *A Theory of Justice*, Oxford: Oxford University Press.

Reece, Helen (1996) 'Subverting the Stigmatization Argument', *Journal of Law and Society,* 23(4): 485–505.

Rich, Adrienne (1980) 'Compulsory Heterosexuality and Lesbian Existence', *Signs: Journal of Women in Culture and Society,* 5(4): 631–60.

Richman, Kimberly D. (2006) 'LGBT Family Rights, Legal Consciousness, and the Dilemma of Difference', in B. Fleurry-Steiner and L.B. Nielsen (eds) *The New Civil Rights Research: A Constitutive Approach* (pp. 77–99) Aldershot: Ashgate.

Riggs, Damien (2004) 'On Whose Terms? Psychology and the Legitimisation of Lesbian and Gay Parents', *Gay and Lesbian Issues in Psychology Newsletter,* 3(1): 3–9.

Roberts, Simon (1998) 'Against Legal Pluralism: Some Reflections on the Contemporary Enlargement of the Legal Domain', *Journal of Legal Pluralism & Unofficial Law,* 42: 95–106.

Robinson, Bambi E.S. (1997) 'Birds do It. Bees do It. So Why Not Single Women and Lesbians?', *Bioethics,* 11(3): 217–27.

Robson, Ruthann (1994) 'Third Parties and the Third Sex: Child Custody and Lesbian Legal Theory', *Connecticut Law Review,* 26: 1377–414.

——(1997) 'Beginning from (My) Experience: The Paradoxes of Lesbian/Queer Narrativities', *Hastings Law Journal,* 48: 1387–428.

Roof, Judith (1996) *Come As You Are: Sexuality & Narrative*, New York: Columbia University Press.

Rose, Nikolas (1999) *Powers of Freedom: Reframing Political Thought*, Cambridge: Cambridge University Press.

Saffron, Lisa (1994) *Challenging Conceptions: Planning a Family by Self-insemination*, London: Cassell.

Santos, Boaventura de Sousa (1995) *Towards a New Common Sense: Law, Science and Politics in Paradigmatic Transition*, London: Routledge.

Sarat, Austin (1977) 'Studying American Legal Culture: An Assessment of Survey Evidence', *Law and Society Review,* 10(3): 339–75.

——(1985) 'Legal Effectiveness and Social Studies of Law', *Legal Studies Forum,* 9(1): 23–32.

——(1990) ' … The Law is All Over: Power, Resistance and the Legal Consciousness of the Welfare Poor', *Yale Journal of Law and the Humanities,* 2: 343–79.

Sarat, Austin and Kearns, Thomas R. (1993a) 'Beyond the Great Divide: Forms of Legal Scholarship and Everyday Life', in A. Sarat and T. Kearns (eds) *Law in Everyday Life* (pp. 21–61) Ann Arbor, MI: University of Michigan Press.

——(eds) (1993b) *Law in Everyday Life*, Ann Arbor, MI: University of Michigan Press.

Sargisson, Lucy (1996) *Contemporary Feminist Utopianism*, London: Routledge.

Sawicki, Jana (1991) *Disciplining Foucault: Feminism, Power and the Body*, London: Routledge.

——(2004) "Foucault's Pleasures: Desexualising Queer Politics", in Dianna Taylor and Karen Vintges (eds) *Feminism and the Final Foucault* (pp. 163–82) Chicago, IL: University of Illinois Press.

Scharf, Miri (2001) 'A Natural Experiment in Childrearing Ecologies and Adolescents Attachment and Separation Representations', *Child Development*, 72(1): 236–51.

Sheldon, Sally and Collier, Richard (eds) (2006) *Fathers' Rights Activism and Law Reform in Comparative Perspective*, Oxford: Hart.

Shipman, Beccy and Smart, Carol (2007) '"It's Made a Huge Difference": Recognition, Rights and the Personal Significance of Civil Partnership', *Sociological Research Online*, 12(1): January ISSN 1360–7804. Available at www.socresonline.org.uk/12/1/shipman.html (accessed 31 March 2010).

Silbey, Susan S. (2005) 'After Legal Consciousness', *Annual Review of Law and Social Science*, 1: 323–68.

Silbey, Susan and Ewick, Patricia (2000) 'The Rule of Law – Sacred and Profane', *Society*, 37(6): 49–56.

——(2003) 'The Double Life of Reason and Law', *University of Miami Law Review*, 57: 497–512.

Smart, Carol (1989) *Feminism and the Power of Law*, London: Routledge.

——(2007) *Personal Life: New Directions in Sociological Thinking*, Cambridge: Polity Press.

Smart, Carol and Neale, Bren (1999) *Family Fragments?* Cambridge: Polity Press.

Smith, Miriam (1999) *Lesbian and Gay Rights in Canada: Social Movements and Equality-Seeking, 1971–1995*, Toronto: University of Toronto Press.

Stonewall (2003) *Civil Partnership: Legal Recognition for Same Sex Couples*, London: Stonewall. Available at www.stonewall.org.uk/documents/Pre_White_Paper_briefing_June_2003.doc (accessed 10 February 2007).

——(2009) *Pregnant Pause: A Guide for Lesbians on How to Get Pregnant*, London: Stonewall. Available at www.stonewall.org.uk/documents/pregnant_pause_with_cover_2.pdf (accessed 27 January 2010).

Strah, David and Margolis, Susanna (2003) *Gay Dads: A Celebration of Fatherhood*, New York: Tarcher/Putnam.

Strasser, Mark (1997) *Legally Wed: Same Sex Marriage and the Constitution*, Ithaca, NY: Cornell University Press.

Stychin, Carl (2001) 'Civil Solidarity or Fragmented Identities? The Politics of Sexuality and Citizenship in France', *Social & Legal Studies*, 10(3): 347–75.

——(2003) *Governing Sexuality: The Changing Politics of Citizenship and Law Reform*, Oxford: Hart.

——(2006) 'Not (Quite) a Horse and Carriage: The Civil Partnership Act 2004', *Feminist Legal Studies*, 14(1): 79–86.

Sullivan, Andrew (1996) *Virtually Normal: An Argument about Homosexuality*, London: Picador.

——(1997) *Same-Sex Marriage: Pro and Con: A Reader*, New York: Vintage.

Sullivan, Maureen (2004) *The Family of Woman: Lesbian Mothers, Their Children, and the Undoing of Gender*, Berkley, CA: University of California Press.

Tamanaha, Brian Z. (1993) 'The Folly of the "Social Scientific" Concept of Legal Pluralism', *Journal of Law and Society,* 20: 192–217.

——(2000) 'A Non-Essentialist Version of Legal Pluralism', *Journal of Law and Society,* 27(2): 296–321.

Tasker, Fiona and Golombok, Susan (1991) 'Children Raised by Lesbian Mothers: The Empirical Evidence', *Family Law,* 184–87.

——(1997) *Growing Up in a Lesbian Family: Effects on Child Development,* New York: The Guilford Press.

——(1998) 'The Role of Co-Mothers in Planned Lesbian-led Families', *Journal of Lesbian Studies,* 2(4): 49–68.

Taylor, Dianna and Vintges, Karen (eds) (2004) *Feminism and the Final Foucault,* Chicago, IL: University of Illinois Press.

Teubner, Gunther (1992) 'The Two Faces of Janus: Rethinking Legal Pluralism', *Cardozo Law Review,* 13: 1443–62.

Thomson, Michael (2001) 'eXistenZ: Bio-ports/Boundaries/Bodies', *Legal Studies,* 21: 325–43.

Twining, William (2000) *Globalisation & Legal Theory,* London: Butterworths.

Valentine, Gill (1996) '(Re)Negotiating the 'Heterosexual Street': Lesbian Productions of Space', in N. Duncan (ed.) *BodySpace* (pp. 145–54) London: Routledge.

von Benda-Beckmann, Franz (2002) 'Who's Afraid of Legal Pluralism?', *Journal of Legal Pluralism & Unofficial Law,* 47: 37–82.

Waaldijk, Kees (2001) 'Small Change: How the Road to Same-Sex Marriage Got Paved in the Netherlands', in R. Wintemute and M. Andenaes (eds) *Legal Recognition of Same-sex Partnerships: A Study of National, European and International Law* (pp. 437–646) Oxford: Hart.

Wardle, Lynn D., Strasser, Mark, Duncan, William C. and Coolidge, David O. (2003) *Marriage and Same-Sex Unions: A Debate,* Westport, CT: Praeger.

Warner, Michael (1993) *Fear of a Queer Planet,* Minneapolis, MN: University of Minnesota Press.

Webb, Darren (2008) 'Exploring the Relationship between Hope and Utopia: Towards a Conceptual Framework', *Politics,* 28(3): 197–206.

Weeks, Jeffrey (2007) *The World We Have Won: The Remaking of Erotic and Intimate Life,* Abingdon: Routledge.

Weeks, Jeffrey, Heaphy, Brian and Donovan, Catherine (2001) *Same Sex Intimacies: Families of Choice and Other Life Experiments,* London: Routledge.

Weston, Kath (1991) *Families We Choose: Lesbians, Gays, Kinship,* New York: Columbia University Press.

Whittle, Stephen (2002) *Respect and Equality: Transsexual and Transgender Rights,* London: Cavendish.

Williams, Patricia J. (1992) *The Alchemy of Race and Rights,* Cambridge, MA: Harvard University Press.

Wintemute, Robert (2001) 'Introduction', in R. Wintemute and M. Andenaes (eds) *Legal Recognition of Same-sex Partnerships: A Study of National, European and International Law* (pp. 55–74) Oxford: Hart.

Wolfson, Evan (2005) 'Marriage Equality and Some Lessons for the Scary Work of Winning', *Law & Sexuality,* 14: 135–47.

Women and Equality Unit (2003) *Civil Partnerships: A Framework for the Legal Recognition of Same-sex Couples,* London: Department of Trade and Industry.

Wong, Simone (2004) 'Property Regimes for Home Sharers: The Civil Partnership Bill and Some Antipodean Models', *Journal of Social Welfare and Family Law*, 26(4): 361–75.

Woodman, Gordon R. (1998) 'Ideological Combat and Social Observation: Recent Debate about Legal Pluralism', *Journal of Legal Pluralism & Unofficial Law*, 42: 21–59.

Young, Claire F.L. and Boyd, Susan B.(2006) 'Losing the Feminist Voice? Debates on the Legal Recognition of Same Sex Partnership in Canada', *Feminist Legal Studies*, 14: 213–40.

Index

For Product Safety Concerns and Information please contact our EU representative GPSR@taylorandfrancis.com
Taylor & Francis Verlag GmbH, Kaufingerstraße 24, 80331 München, Germany

www.ingramcontent.com/pod-product-compliance
Ingram Content Group UK Ltd.
Pitfield, Milton Keynes, MK11 3LW, UK
UKHW011011180926
475701UK00004B/670
9780415521147